D1598878

THE ENDURING CIVIL WAR

CONFLICTING WORLDS

New Dimensions of the American Civil War

T. Michael Parrish, Series Editor

THE ENDURING CIVIL WAR

REFLECTIONS ON THE GREAT AMERICAN CRISIS

GARY W. GALLAGHER

LOUISIANA STATE UNIVERSITY PRESS

BATON ROUGE

Published by Louisiana State University Press
www.lsupress.org

Manufactured in the United States of America
First printing

Designer: Barbara Neely Bourgoyne
Typeface: Whitman
Printer and binder: Sheridan Books

Jacket image: *The Grand Review* (1881), by James E. Taylor, courtesy of the Ohio History Center.

The appendix contains the publication history of all the essays reproduced in this book.

LIBRARY OF CONGRESS CATALOGING-IN-PUBLICATION DATA
Names: Gallagher, Gary W., author.
Title: The enduring Civil War : reflections on the great American crisis / Gary W. Gallagher.
Description: Baton Rouge : Louisiana State University Press, 2020. | Includes index.
Identifiers: LCCN 2019055078 (print) | LCCN 2019055079 (ebook) | ISBN 978-0-8071-7348-0 (cloth) | ISBN 978-0-8071-7406-7 (pdf) | ISBN 978-0-8071-7407-4 (epub)
Subjects: LCSH: United States—History—Civil War, 1861–1865. | United States—History—Civil War, 1861–1865—Historiography.
Classification: LCC E468 .G3487 2021 (print) | LCC E468 (ebook) | DDC 973.7—dc23
LC record available at https://lccn.loc.gov/2019055078
LC ebook record available at https://lccn.loc.gov/2019055079

Once again, for Joan

CONTENTS

PART III. CONTROVERSIES   99

PART IV. HISTORIANS AND BOOKS   137

Contents

ILLUSTRATIONS

ACKNOWLEDGMENTS

The number of people who contributed in some way to the ideas and arguments represented in these seventy-one essays is far too large to acknowledge. I do want to mention those who specifically helped with the book. Joan Waugh convinced me to gather the essays in a collection and offered her usual sound counsel at every stage of the work. Dana Shoaf cheerfully granted permission to reprint the essays from *Civil War Times*, as did Terry Johnston for those from the *Civil War Monitor*. Beyond this venture, I have enjoyed working with Dana and Terry as editors over many years. Mike Parrish, a much-valued friend and colleague for more than forty years, encouraged me to send the manuscript to LSU Press, and Rand Dotson, editor in chief at the press, provided welcome assistance at every stage of the process. Cecily N. Zander generously pointed me toward a number of very useful sources relating to the Civil War and the West. I completed the book while serving as the Rogers Distinguished Fellow in Nineteenth-Century American History at the Henry E. Huntington Library in San Marino, California. I am most grateful to Steve Rogers, as well as to Steve Hindle, the W. M. Keck Foundation Director of Research at the Huntington, for the opportunity to spend an academic year in what I consider ideal surroundings. I also benefited from the very helpful criticism of the other long-term fellows at the Huntington. Chris Heisey, whose photographs are well known in the world of Civil War photography, kindly allowed me to use his image of the Longstreet statue at Gettysburg. I offer my warmest thanks to all of these people, whose efforts in my behalf underscore the cooperative nature of book-length endeavors.

THE ENDURING CIVIL WAR

INTRODUCTION

This book grew out of an invitation in the summer of 2008 to contribute brief essays to *Civil War Times*. Dana Shoaf, recently named editor, promised me the freedom to choose my own topics but said I would have to abide by a limit of one thousand words. The idea immediately appealed to me. I knew that *Civil War Times* had been established in 1962 and reached the largest popular audience in the field. In fact, it had been part of my life since I subscribed, in 1965, as a fourteen-year-old in Colorado captivated by the Civil War. The magazine published my first article, on Abraham Lincoln and black colonization, in 1980, and I subsequently contributed several more pieces. Many prominent historians had written for the magazine—including academics such as Bell I. Wiley, Mary Elizabeth Massey, and T. Harry Williams, as well as authors whose books reached a large popular audience, such as Bruce Catton, Glenn Tucker, and Stephen W. Sears. I accepted Dana's invitation, and the first essay appeared in April 2009. More than seventy others have followed.[1]

Walt Whitman comes to mind as I look back on the experience of writing six short essays annually. In *Specimen Days*, the poet famously predicted, "The real war will never get into the books." By that, Whitman meant the real story of the common soldiers, the "actual soldier of 1862–'65, North and South," as he explained. "The seething hell and the black infernal background of countless minor scenes and interiors, . . ." he suggested, "will never be written—perhaps must not and should not be." Indeed, the conflict's "interior history will not only never be written—its practicality, minutiae of deeds and passions, will never be even suggested."[2] Whitman's observations inspire writers who search for a novel way to enter a crowded and popular field and strive to illuminate what they consider neglected or ignored elements of the war.

I approached writing the essays convinced that a great deal of the real war *has* gotten into the books. Gifted historians have produced a corpus of scholarship on the Civil War era that, together with the mass of testimony bequeathed by participants ranging from Abraham Lincoln to men in the ranks, from Freedmen's Bureau workers to nurses and countless others, provides readers with bountiful options. For many decades, historians primarily dealt with causation, high politics, and conventional military operations—three topics essential to a basic familiarity with the whole subject. Over the past half century, however, the literature has become much richer and more expansive. We know far more than previously about Whitman's common soldiers, about women in the United States and the Confederacy, about African Americans and the process of emancipation, about white unionists and other dissenters in the Confederacy, about guerrilla operations, about the conflict in a global context, and, increasingly, about the American West as part of the war's overall mosaic. Scholars also have accorded considerable attention to the so-called dark side of the conflict—to its brutality, atrocities, cowardice, vicious activity by irregular bands, and physical and psychological wounds that left some veterans profoundly damaged.[3]

As the field of Civil War–era history has become increasingly complex, there has been an understandable tendency to place a new subject as close as possible to the center of the entire story and to question many long-accepted analytical frameworks. The traditional juxtapositions of North and South, slaveholders and nonslaveholders, United States and Confederacy have come into question, as has the four-year time frame that typically delineates the subject in the popular imagination. Many scholars insist that the war must be brought together with post-Appomattox events, including Reconstruction, with the West and Native Americans, and with world history to create a "long Civil War" far more inclusive and geographically varied than the one dominated by events that transpired east of the Mississippi River, and especially in Virginia, from 1861 to 1865.[4]

From the beginning, I wanted my essays for *Civil War Times* to expose tensions among parts of the recent literature that cover peripheral or secondary dimensions of the conflict and what I would call four foundational elements of the "real war" (to continue with Whitman's phrasing, if not his narrow meaning regarding common soldiers). Some new writings, however useful and praiseworthy, obscure realities that stand out clearly in the evidence and should be as apparent to us as they were to the wartime generation: The real war erupted over slavery-related political issues between North and South and retained that internal focus. Conventional armies decided its outcome, fielding millions of citizen-soldiers who waged some of the most famous and costly campaigns in American history. It ended in the early summer of 1865, having settled the issue of secession's constitutionality and destroyed the institution of slavery but leaving the question of equal rights for freedpeople unresolved. The twelve years of Reconstruction functioned as a long coda to the war itself, again centered on a clear central issue—how ten former Confederate states would return to the reconstituted Union (Tennessee was exempted from most of Reconstruction) and how that process would affect African American political rights and economic circumstances. Anyone who grasps these four things has made a very good start toward gaining a general understanding of the real war.

Writing the essays allowed me to place our contemporary understanding of the Civil War, both academic and popular, in conversation with testimony from people in the United States and the Confederacy who experienced and described it. Put another way, I could investigate how mid-nineteenth-century perceptions align with, or deviate from, some of those we now hold regarding the origins, conduct, and aftermath of the war. I hasten to make clear that our perspective and access to a plethora of sources can reveal patterns and produce insights not apparent to the wartime generation. Still, the essays presented a chance to discuss how a predilection for reading the past through the prism of our own experience often slights central themes that emerge clearly from the historical record. Too often, in my view, some of the new work also makes atypical experiences seem normative.

I readily concede that there is nothing novel about bringing contemporary political, cultural, and intellectual baggage to bear on historical analysis. The urge to find a fresh and usable past always has been and remains compelling and irresistible. Earlier generations of Civil War scholars certainly manifested this tendency—whether the "blundering generation" or "needless war" schools that drew on reactions to World War I, the "consensus school" that flowered in the wake of World War II, or the "ignore the military side of the Civil War altogether" social history approach of the post-Vietnam era. In all these instances, scholarship often revealed almost as much about the time in which it appeared as about the events and personalities it explored.[5]

Above all, the essays afforded an opportunity to bridge the gap between the academic and popular worlds of Civil War interest. I believe historians should find ways to share the insights of current scholarship with an interested lay audience. Nonprofessional readers gravitate toward the war's celebrated battles and generals, something those who lived through the conflict would understand. Abraham Lincoln spoke to this point in his second inaugural address, affirming that "The progress of our arms, upon which all else chiefly depends, is as well known to the public as to myself, and it is, I trust, reasonably satisfactory and encouraging to all." *Harper's Weekly*, the leading illustrated newspaper in the loyal states, similarly reinforced the centrality of military affairs by devoting approximately 80 percent of its front pages between April 1861 and April 1865 to battles, officers, and other martial subjects. Academic historians, now as in the past, much prefer to write about nonmilitary aspects of the conflict. I see no inherent tension between pursuing conventional military topics and appreciating the political, social, and memorial contexts of battles and campaigns. Indeed, any approach that fails to highlight the myriad ways in which the military and nonmilitary spheres intersected and affected one another promotes a deeply flawed understanding of the whole war.[6]

Yet my experiences over more than forty years have underscored the obvious degree to which the popular and academic worlds remain largely insulated from one another. Lay readers typically avoid jargon-filled academic studies that appeal to a limited professional audience, while academics often deplore the kind of military narratives and biographies that achieve commercial success and garner reviews in major newspapers and other outlets. Attitudes toward interpreting battlefields illuminate divisions in the field. As someone engaged in historic preservation at Civil War sites since the late 1980s, I have spoken with an array of people about whether such places deserve protection. In the 1990s, I applauded a cooperative effort by the Organization of American Historians and the National Park Service to assess interpretive emphases at battlefields. I served, between 1996 and 2000, on three-scholar teams that looked at Antietam National Battlefield, Richmond National Battlefield Park, and Kennesaw Mountain National Battlefield Park. Shortly after the last of the OAH/NPS projects, I joined Gabor S. Boritt, Eric Foner, Thavolia Glymph, James M. McPherson, and Nina Silber on the advisory board for a new visitor center and museum at Gettysburg National Military Park. That multiyear endeavor culminated in 2008 and highlighted the difficulty, when professional historians engage with NPS personnel and museum specialists, of agreeing about the type of exhibits best suited to serve the park's annual throng of visitors. For example, how should military action on July 1–3, 1863, be balanced by larger political framing? And should tourists be shown how memory of the battle has played out over the years?[7]

These activities left no doubt that Civil War buffs—a dismissive term in academic circles—typically visit battlefields to follow the movements of troops and ponder questions about leadership in the crucible of combat. At Gettysburg, for example, they congregate in large numbers at Little Round Top to see where Joshua Lawrence Chamberlain and the Twentieth Maine deployed on July 2, 1863, or at "the angle" on Cemetery Ridge, where fragments of George E. Pickett's brigades struck units in Winfield Scott Hancock's Second Corps the next day. Such activities confirm the value of examining terrain to appreciate tactical ebb and flow and also can serve as a bridge that somehow links our world to that of the Civil War generation. But most scholars would argue that, rather than immersing themselves in on-the-ground details, visitors to Gettysburg should focus on the political forces that sundered the Union and brought two armies of citizen-soldiers to Adams County in the summer of 1863, on how military events there and elsewhere affected issues such as emancipation and the rhythms of civilian life, and on how Americans later developed disparate memories of the battle. Some skeptical academics, and they are not uncommon, doubt the value of preserving battlefields at all, seeing them as sites that glorify war and cater to a militaristic streak in American society.[8]

My effort to address controversial relationships between scholarly and popular concerns yielded essays for *Civil War Times* that cluster in several categories. As a longtime bibliophile drawn to books as both researching tools and collectible objects, I enjoy writing about notable titles and authors. Some essays feature essential published primary accounts, both Union and Confederate, military and civilian, famous and lesser known. Others assess historians who, though their names have receded with the passage of time, produced works that remain pertinent in terms of analysis or information. I also relish revisiting conventional interpretations of events and personalities, many of them almost universally accepted among nonspecialists. A number of essays thus challenge, among other things, commonly held notions about Gettysburg and Vicksburg as decisive turning points, Ulysses S. Grant as a general who profligately wasted Union manpower, the Gettysburg Address as a watershed that turned the war from a fight for Union into one for Union and emancipation, and Robert E. Lee as an old-fashioned general ill-suited to waging a modern mid-nineteenth-century war.

As I noted, recent scholarly trends invite similar scrutiny. For brief essays alerting a nonacademic readership to the evolving nature of the field, possible topics came quickly to mind. Has a fascination with famous armies and generals obscured the importance of guerrilla operations? Did the conflict end in 1865 or continue through Reconstruction and beyond? How did the West—especially the area beyond the 100th meridian—figure in Union and Confederate planning and allocation of resources? Did emancipation join Union as an equivalent or even more important war aim for the mass of loyal soldiers and civilians in the United States? Should clashes between Indians and the U.S. Army and territorial units be considered part of the Civil War or elements of a much longer historical drama that unfolded between the late eighteenth century and the last third of the nineteenth century? Has the Eastern Theater unfairly dominated the literature on the war? And has the "dark side" of the war been slighted?

Cultural manifestations of the war's continuing resonance figure in another group of essays. Hollywood's influence, always important, remains significant in shaping popular perceptions through films such as Steven Spielberg's *Lincoln* and Timur Bekmambetov's *Abraham Lincoln: Vampire Hunter*, both released in 2012. Ken Burns's documentary *The Civil War*, initially aired in 1990 and digitally restored for its twenty-fifth anniversary in 2015, still reaches viewers during PBS fund-raising efforts and on Netflix. Clashes over Confederate symbols periodically capture national headlines—to a striking degree after nine congregants died in a shooting at the Emanuel African Methodist Episcopal Church in Charleston, South Carolina, on June 17, 2015, and violence attending a Unite the Right rally in Charlottesville, Virginia, on August 12, 2017, claimed another life.

Some debates about the war have unfolded primarily on blogs and social media and only secondarily in print, perhaps most obviously the give-and-take about whether thousands of black men "served" in the Confederate army. The issue of black Confederates reminds us of just how far from scholarship's conclusions, and historical facts, some popular notions can stray. No reputable historian believes that more than an infinitesimal number of black men shouldered arms in the Confederacy, yet claims of fifty thousand or more, based on a profoundly misinformed use of "evidence," appear regularly.[9]

The tension between history and memory forms a leitmotif throughout the essays. All my classes and public presentations combine attention to both history and historical memory. I stress the importance of what actually happened, while also showing that successive generations remember historical events and personalities in starkly different ways. Popular memory often trumps reality, I emphasize, because people almost always act on what they perceive to be the truth, however far that perception might stray from historical reality.

Many essays touch on the shifting cultural and literary importance of four memory traditions created by the wartime generation. Two of the four sprang from the winning side. The Union Cause celebrated, above all else, the saving of the republic created by the founding generation, while the Emancipation Cause pronounced the end of slavery the war's greatest achievement. Former Confederates offered their version of the war's origins and history in what came to be called the Lost Cause. Finally, the Reconciliation Cause united some Americans, North and South, in lauding the valor of white troops on both sides, muting the question of who was right and who was wrong and cheering a united nation positioned, by 1900, to take its place among the world's leading powers. An ability to detect the presence or absence of the four traditions assists any effort to chart the changing relationship between different groups of Americans and the Civil War. Films provide a rich target to identify memory traditions. The impact of *The Birth of a Nation* (1915) and *Gone with the Wind* (1939) in advancing the Lost Cause, or of *Glory* (1989) and *Lincoln* in reminding filmgoers of the Emancipation Cause, cannot be overemphasized.[10]

Part of my motivation in accepting Dana Shoaf's invitation to write for *Civil War Times*, beyond what I already have mentioned, lay in using the essays to sharpen my thinking about questions and issues I have dealt with in several books. Careful readers will find evidence of this process in *The Confederate War* (1997), *Causes Won, Lost, and Forgotten: How Hollywood and Popular Art Shape What We Know about the Civil War* (2008), *The Union War* (2011), *Becoming Confederates: Paths to a New National Loyalty* (2013), and *The American War: A History of the Civil War Era* (2015; revised edition 2019). I hoped the essays would elicit considerable reaction from readers of *Civil War Times* and thus allow me to hone some of my arguments. That in fact happened. Dana published a sample of positive and negative responses in the magazine and shared others with me. Both lay readers and scholars weighed in.

My essay about Shelby Foote prompted divergent reactions. "I don't think I ever read such a mess before in my life," read one letter to the editor, which added, "I don't know who Gallagher is, nor do I care." The same essay inspired a positive reaction from another reader: "I think it's great when academic historians step back from their own work long enough to address the 'peanut gallery' of critics who take issue with professional approaches to history." Two essays dealing with the war in the far western territories triggered a heated exchange among scholars and others (to which I did not contribute), which began on Twitter and migrated to other social media. E-mails and letters sent directly to me by readers, many of them quite stridently approving or disapproving of what I had written, further indicated that many of the essays had touched sensitive nerves.[11]

Writing the essays allowed me to share my enthusiasm for studying the war with an audience I knew held similar interests. It supplemented other opportunities to examine the subject—with thousands of undergraduate students at Penn State University and the University of Virginia, more than 1,500 middle and high school teachers from across the country in summer seminars, thousands of adults who have attended conferences and lectures over the years, and people who watched a video course on the Civil War I offered for The Teaching Company (now called The Great Courses).

My lifelong interest in the Civil War era stems from its profusion of dramatic events, compelling personalities, unlikely political and social twists and turns, and engrossing military action. As a society and a people, Americans of the period grappled with elemental questions that continue to demand attention today. Would the Union forged by the Revolutionary generation be scuttled because part of the electorate did not like the outcome of the presidential election of 1860? Would the institution of slavery, which had mocked the soaring language of the nation's founding documents, be eliminated? Would the relative power of the central government and the states and localities be reoriented in a fundamental way? Would conflicts over reconstructing the Union undercut efforts to establish genuine social and political equality for black people? And by far most important within an international context, would the nation emerge intact and become an economic and military powerhouse? Confederate victory in the war, something surely possible, though few Americans appreciate that fact now, would have altered the trajectory of twentieth-century world history.

In my essays, as in other venues, I argue that only by coming to terms with the Civil War, as well as with how people have remembered and used it in politics and popular culture, can anyone understand the broader arc of United States history. The war functioned as both an end and a beginning. It resolved huge issues left unresolved by the generation that won independence and wrote the Constitution, providing closure for long-term wrangling about slavery and the permanence of the Union. United States victory in turn set the stage for economic and territorial expansion. Postwar Reconstruction, however, failed to prevent political and social strife relating to race, to the relationship between the central government and the states and localities, and to meanings of U.S. citizenship.

Ongoing controversies over the Confederate memorial landscape constitute just one element in the Civil War's long-standing power to affect the nation and its citizens. Sadly, some school administrators, both public and private, support avoiding the Civil War because discussions about slavery, massive bloodshed, and controversial memorial landscapes can cause discomfort among students and their parents. But a free society should confront its past, warts and all. The many sharp edges and troubling dimensions of the Civil War must be set against uplifting and empowering elements that helped create a better version of the founders' republic.[12]

Joan Waugh, my coauthor for *The American War* and collaborator in innumerable ways on other Civil War–related endeavors, first suggested that my essays might work as a book. Our ensuing conversations led me to consider how, taken as a group, the essays reflect my belief that narrative, chronology, and biography are essential to forging a true understanding of the past. These are unfashionable tools in some academic quarters today, where many people dismiss chronological frameworks as too simplistic or even contrived, too prone to favor narrative over analysis, and too likely to bring individual personalities into play. But I have seen the confusion among my students and the general public that too often results from purely thematic or theoretical approaches to history—most notably those devoid of human beings. Far too many students, even very bright ones, arrive at college with a hopeless muddle of information about American history and no real sense of how eras, movements, and events fit together. They need to learn that chronology not only matters but also provides an essential point of departure toward the goal of historical literacy. The bombardment of Fort Sumter followed the secession of the lower South, which had occurred as a result of Abraham Lincoln's election. These episodes did not happen in that order by chance—each proceeded from the earlier one. A large number of students over many years expressed appreciation for my attention to chronology, often adding that it helped them see, for the first time, how and why events unfolded and connected with one another.

The essays, usually obliquely, also get at the relationship between political ideology and historical analysis. I will mention students again on this point. Most undergraduates enroll in classes to learn something about a subject, and they typically resent being held hostage to harangues regarding contemporary politics. I find this very encouraging. All historians have political views, but we should strive to check them at the classroom door. For example, my voting choices have nothing to do with how I explain why men from New Hampshire or Wisconsin or Iowa, who faced absolutely no threat to their property and families from Confederate military forces, voluntarily donned blue uniforms and risked their lives to save the Union. If students could not account for such enlistments by the end of my class on the Civil War, I would have failed miserably. Injecting my own political views into the process would only get in the way. At the close of almost every semester, a few students remarked they had not been able to tell whether I am a Democrat or a Republican. "Now that the semester is over," they asked, "will you tell us?" I always said no—because my politics had nothing to do with the class or my relationship with the students.

Political ideology and passion too often dictate how historians and the public deal with certain elements of the past—and even how they determine what parts of the past ought be studied. It often encourages a simplistic division of dead historical actors into "good" and "bad" people who should be treated accordingly. Nothing is easier than feeling superior to long-dead individuals, almost none of whom satisfy our current ideas regarding race and other issues. But the past is never simple. In fact, my forty years of studying the Civil War has yielded one unequivocal truth; namely, however complicated I imagined some episode or character, further research unmasked far greater complexity. Vexing shades of gray, rather than stark tones of black and white, usually await anyone who ventures honestly into the thickets of historical investigation. Letting ideology fuel an interpretation recalls Lost Cause writers who used selective evidence, airbrushed slavery and other negative elements of the southern rebellion, and came up with a shiny version of the Confederacy.

Ideology can lead to pretending slavery-related issues were not central to the coming of the war, or, conversely, to suggesting that the Union war effort had little or no meaning beyond its eventual embrace of emancipation.[13]

My essays in *Civil War Times* often angered readers who deplored what they considered my transgressions against their ideological preferences. Neo-Confederates scorned my placing slavery-related issues at the heart of secession and establishment of the Confederacy or my refusal to concede that Nathan Bedford Forrest belongs alongside Lincoln as one of Shelby Foote's "two authentic geniuses" of the Civil War. To these people, I represent a typical "Marxist/communist" professor, as several have put it, who hates the South. In contrast, my suggestion that Robert E. Lee possessed considerable military skill and wrestled painfully with multiple loyalties during the era of sectional controversy brought accusations of conservative special pleading on behalf of a slaveholder and traitor who deserved to be hanged. I have two files in my study where I preserve such sentiments—the first labeled "Hate Mail from Neo-Confederates" (one correspondent hoped I would develop a "virulent form of pancreatic cancer") and the second "Hate Mail Calling me a Neo-Confederate."[14] All such messages reminded me of advice from my graduate adviser that has guided much of my career. When I complained that recent research had forced me to change prospective conclusions, Barnes F. Lathrop curtly replied, "God damn it, Gallagher, just go where the evidence leads, and you'll be all right."[15]

All of the essays in *Civil War Times* reflect my attempt to honor Lathrop's advice, whatever the fallout when my observations diverged from prevailing orthodoxies. Because of the thousand-word limit, they are suggestive rather than exhaustive. I hope readers will find them useful, provocative, and enjoyable. Because I followed no master blueprint in writing them, I have arranged the essays in six groupings, without attention to date of original publication. Some pieces might work just as well in a different grouping. I slightly revised a few of the essays, included significantly expanded versions of two, and added two short pieces that first appeared in the *Civil War Monitor*. The original essays had no citations for quoted material. I have added endnotes, which are less detailed than would be the case in a monograph, supplied references for direct quotations, pointed readers to other pertinent material, and otherwise provided analytical context. I have changed many of the titles, usually substituting my originals for those the magazine used. A concise introductory text opens each of the book's six sections, and an appendix records the publication sequence and original titles for all the essays.

The first grouping, "Framing the War," comprises eleven pieces that deal with chronology, history and memory, and some of the new revisionist literature. Fifteen essays devoted to "Generals and Battles" come next, with particular attention to Grant, Lee, and other major figures. The third grouping, "Controversies," offers twelve essays on such topics as turning points, counterfactuals, apportioning credit for emancipation, and when the war ended. The thirteen entries in the fourth grouping, "Historians and Books," together with the thirteen in the fifth, "Testimony from Participants," evaluate important published primary and secondary accounts. The volume closes with "Places and Public Culture," the seven essays in which I examine films, preservation of battlefields, the memorial landscape, and related topics. The book lends itself to sampling, and readers might start in any of the groupings and go where their interests take them. If successful, the essays will impart a sense of how rewarding I have found my lifelong relationship with the Civil War. What better subject could a teacher or scholar investigate and try to explain?

∼ I ∼

FRAMING THE WAR

Americans have understood the Civil War, its antecedents, and its aftermath in many ways. This speaks to the interpretive richness of the era, as well as to how each generation's political and cultural concerns can spill over into historical investigation. For example, publications, commemorative programs, and media coverage during the sesquicentennial era of 2011 to 2015 reflected the preoccupation with race in contemporary American society and the impact of U.S. military involvement in the Middle East over the past quarter century.

This section explores some of the ways historians and the public have framed the four years of large-scale military conflict between the United States and the Confederacy. The first three essays deal with chronological boundaries, identifying comparative dimensions of the Civil War and the American Revolution as well as probing the relationship between history and memory. Two essays deal with the West and Indians, the second of the pair a much-expanded version of a piece titled "A Conflict Apart" that inspired spirited reactions from readers of *Civil War Times*. The next five essays take up topics that have received considerable recent attention from scholars—guerrilla operations, the dark side of the Civil War (including desertion), the degree to which the loyal citizenry exhibited militarism at war's end, and how best to interpret Lincoln's Gettysburg Address. The section closes with a look at the environmental impact of military campaigning.

LINKING AMERICA'S
TWO MOST IMPORTANT WARS

The American Revolution and the Civil War rank as our most important and destructive conflicts. Unequaled in terms of impact on the populations that experienced them, they also wielded unmatched influence on our history by establishing a fragile new republic and then subjecting it to a profoundly disruptive test of national resilience. Myriad ideological and historical ties connected the two wars, and as a pair they offer significant potential for scholarship. Yet only a few historians have pursued what seem to be obvious comparative frameworks—perhaps because each of the wars, immense in size and importance, yields apparently limitless topics.

Both sides during the Civil War looked to the founding generation and the Revolution. Confederates often compared themselves to colonists who claimed the right of self-determination, while the loyal population of the United States insisted they sought to safeguard what the founders bequeathed to ordinary citizens regarding self-governance and the opportunity to rise economically. Politicians and diplomats, whether in Washington or in Richmond, accepted the French alliance of 1778 as proof that Europe might tip the balance of power during the Civil War.

The example of sacrifice during the Revolution proved irresistible to leaders hoping to galvanize support for the respective war efforts in 1861 to 1865. During the hard winter of 1863 to 1864, for example, R. E. Lee evoked the suffering of George Washington's Continentals. The history of the Army of Northern Virginia, he told his veterans, "has shown that the country can require no sacrifice too great for its patriotic devotion." Then he compared their travails to those of an earlier generation: "Soldiers! You tread with no unequal step the road by which your fathers marched through suffering, privations, and blood, to independence." If those in the Confederate army continued to emulate the Revolutionary soldiery's disinterested service, prophesied Lee, "be assured that the just God who crowned their efforts with success will, in His own good time, send down His blessing upon yours."[1]

Robert Gould Shaw, then a member of the Seventh New York State Militia, also referred to the Revolutionary War in a letter to his mother on April 18, 1861. "The Massachusetts men passed through N. York this morning. . . ." he wrote from Staten Island just before leaving for Washington. "Won't it be grand to meet the men from all the States, East and West, down there, ready to fight for the country, as the old fellows did in the Revolution?"[2]

Perhaps most famously, Abraham Lincoln turned to what he considered the most sacred document in American history in his brief remarks at Gettysburg on November 19, 1863. "Four score and seven years ago our fathers brought forth on this continent, a new nation," declared Lincoln, in reference to the Declaration of Independence, "conceived in Liberty, and dedicated to the proposition that all men are created equal." Only by following through on the "unfinished work" of the soldiers who "gave the last full measure of devotion" at Gettysburg could loyal citizens sustain the vision, and give full meaning to the toll in military dead and wounded, of revolutionary political leaders and soldiers who had created a unique democratic republic.[3]

Many aspects of the two wars deserve comparative examination—none more so than the story of Loyalists who retained their allegiance to Great Britain in the Revolution and of Unionists in the Confederacy. Loyalists aided the war against the American rebels in many ways. Variously estimated at between a fifth and a third of the colonial population, they held political positions, contributed money, served in all military theaters, and composed the bulk of British forces on some battlefields. The notorious Lieutenant Colonel Banastre Tarleton's British Legion, which operated most famously in the southern campaigns, was a Loyalist unit. Because Britain relied heavily on Loyalists in the South between 1778 and 1783, fighting in the Carolinas and Georgia took on the character of a vicious civil war.

Southern Unionists similarly supported United States military efforts in the Confederacy. A small but significant minority of the overall Confederate population, more prevalent in the upper tier of states than in the Deep South, their numbers cannot be established with precision. They formed guerrilla bands in mountainous regions, supplied intelligence to Union armies, and assisted prisoners of war who escaped from Rebel captivity. At least one hundred thousand joined regiments recruited from the white Unionist populace (some of these troops were executed, along with black soldiers, by Nathan Bedford Forrest's forces at Fort Pillow on April 12, 1864). Elizabeth Van Lew of Richmond, the most famous woman among Unionists in the Confederacy, rendered undeniably valuable service to the United States. The landmark success for Unionists came in Virginia, where they engineered creation of the new loyal state of West Virginia in 1863.

The British government and the Lincoln administration tended to overestimate numbers of Loyalists and Unionists. The British most obviously expected too much from southern Loyalists in the last several years of the war. As for Lincoln, he initially believed that a mass of Unionists would step forward to oppose secession; in fact, Unionists in the Confederacy never provided a decisive edge to the United States on any battlefield and, though a source of considerable friction that aggravated political and military leaders, failed to compromise the Confederate war effort in a serious way. The major difference between Loyalists and Unionists lies in their postwar situations: the former supported a failed cause, lost much of their property, and emigrated in large numbers; the latter stood with the winners and often participated in the Reconstruction state governments.

An examination of Loyalists and southern Unionists would make a good start toward expanding the comparative literature on the Revolution and the Civil War. An exploration of how British and Union armies weakened the institution of slavery in the southern colonies and the Confederacy would be equally illuminating, as would a consideration of the importance of national armies in countering state and local sentiment among citizen-soldiers. With luck, scholars already may be hard at work on these and other topics.[4]

ANTEBELLUM

No person in the United States from the 1830s through the 1850s thought in terms of an "antebellum" era. Latin for "before the war," the word came into use only after the Civil War ended and participants, and then historians and other writers, sought to label the decades preceding the outbreak of fighting at Fort Sumter. A commonplace in the historical literature for many generations, it summons thoughts of a young republic lurching toward political collapse. Deployment of "antebellum" can create an impression of inevitability, of citizens increasingly obsessed with sectional differences, and of time ticking inexorably toward bloodshed on a massive scale. Indeed, the word can drain all meaning, except as prelude to four years of war, from a thirty-year swath of national events and trends.

We should be wary of such retrospective historical framing. As always with the past, America's prewar decades present an immensely complicated story rather than one pointing clearly toward secession and military conflict. An observer seeking interpretive themes between 1830 and 1860 could craft a narrative largely devoid of sectional issues. One theme involved a revolution in communications and transportation that dramatically shrank time and space. The electrical telegraph, first demonstrated by Samuel F. B. Morse in 1844, opened breathtaking possibilities. By 1861, Western Union's lines connected the Eastern seaboard and California. Railroads expanded exponentially, from slightly fewer than three thousand miles of track in 1840 to more than thirty thousand in 1860. The telegraph and trains allowed information, goods, and passengers to move much faster, increasing the pace of life and commerce in ways that left observers somewhat flabbergasted. A second theme centered on demographics. Population growth maintained a dizzying pace, averaging more than 33 percent per decade between 1830, when Americans numbered just more than 12,800,000, and 1860, when the total approached 31,500,000. Of the latter figure, more than four million were foreign born and approximately 10 percent were Catholic—major increases as percentages of the whole population and due largely to German and Irish immigration.

The observer similarly could focus on headlines dealing with significant events unconnected to sectional disputes. Toward the end of the prewar period, for example, the Panic of 1857 and the Colorado gold rush of 1858 to 1859 garnered massive attention throughout the nation. Part of a wider world economic crisis, the panic hit the North much harder than the South and caused considerable dislocation in the railroad industry, agricultural markets, and the banking sector for more than year. For many caught in its pernicious grasp, the panic far exceeded in importance the Supreme Court's Dred Scott decision of the same year. The discovery of precious metals in Colorado, which inspired the cry "Pike's Peak or Bust," lured more than one hundred thousand immigrants to the Rocky Mountain region (a roughly comparable number had flooded into California during the initial year of gold fever in 1848/49). In 1859, news from Colorado could easily overshadow John Brown's abortive raid at Harpers Ferry in October. To put it another way, most Americans of the antebellum period did not wake up every morning eager to focus on how the North and South differed. They looked first to their jobs, to their businesses, and to their families, without knowing that a gigantic war lurked in the years ahead.

New York lawyer George Templeton Strong's diary reveals that sectional issues did not always prevail. In 1857, Strong's voluminous entries contain no mention of the Dred Scott decision but accord detailed coverage to the economic collapse. "We seem floundering," he recorded on October 10. "Affairs are worse than ever today, and a period of general insolvency seems close upon us." Four days later, with "Wall Street blue with collapse," Strong exhibited great uncertainty: "Whether we've really reached the nadir, no one can tell." Toward the end of the month he lamented that the "Depression continues. . . . the tide is still running out and everything is drifting down with it, or else stuck fast already on the black mud flats of insolvency and destined to rot there and perish long before the tide comes back again."[5]

None of this is to say that sectional discord did not roil the national waters during the antebellum decades. Major disruptive moments that punctuated the timeline of North/South wrangling are well known: the Missouri controversy of 1820, the 1846–1848 war with Mexico, the Compromise of 1850, the Kansas–Nebraska Act of 1854, the caning of Charles Sumner on the floor of the Senate in 1856, Dred Scott, and John Brown's raid. Less overtly political factors such as establishment of William Lloyd Garrison's *The Liberator* in 1831, Nat Turner's rebellion the same year, publication of Harriett Beecher Stowe's *Uncle Tom's Cabin* (1852) and Hinton Rowan Helper's *The Impending Crisis of the South* (1857), and splits in major Protestant denominations such as the Baptists and Methodists further buttress a portrait of the Union heading toward disintegration.

Some people certainly predicted calamity long before the election of Abraham Lincoln. West Point cadet Stephen Dodson Ramseur of North Carolina, the son of a slaveholder, stood among these individuals. In the wake of James Buchanan's triumph in 1856, Ramseur, though a staunch Democrat, adopted a gloomy stance. Typical of many young people, who more often than older Americans tended to be less forgiving of those across the sectional divide, he believed "any man of the smallest observation can plainly see, that the Union of the States cannot exist harmoniously; that there must, & can & will be a dissolution, wise, peaceful & equitable, I hope, but at whatever cost, it must come. . . . Look out for a Stormy time in 1860," he added. "In the mean time the South ought to prepare for the worst. Let her establish armories, collect stores & provide for the most desperate of all calamities—civil war."[6]

Witnesses such as Strong and Ramseur remind us to rely on contemporary sources, in their sometimes baffling complexity, to gauge the degree to which we should understand the antebellum era as one dominated by sectionalism. Mortally wounded at Cedar Creek on October 19, 1864, Ramseur never thought in terms of an antebellum world and, unlike Strong, did not live to experience the postbellum epoch.

HISTORY AND HISTORICAL MEMORY

All my classes and other presentations combine attention to both history and historical memory. I push students to master what actually happened, while also showing that successive generations often recall and interpret historical events and personalities in starkly different ways. Memory often trumps reality, I emphasize, because people act on what they perceive to be the truth, however flawed that perception. For my Civil War–related courses, I have splendid materials at hand to illustrate the power of memory. Students view films (always outside of class time) to gauge how Hollywood has interpreted the past, writing papers that compare celluloid treatments to assigned readings and my lectures. I also conduct optional tours of various battlefields and other historic sites, where we use monuments to discuss how and why Americans have created conflicting versions of what transpired.

I address the disjuncture between history and memory in a number of other essays, including several relating to how Lost Cause writers and later enthusiasts sought to remove slavery as the bedrock of the Confederacy and one about the remarkable erosion of U. S. Grant's reputation in the middle decades of the twentieth century. That anyone could separate the Confederacy from slavery or interpret Grant as anything but a gifted soldier and widely hailed Union hero speaks to the power of memory to obscure reality.[7]

Gettysburg affords striking instances of the same phenomenon. Most obviously, the battle has become entrenched in the popular imagination as the war's great turning point. This makes sense on one level, because we know it was the conflict's bloodiest battle, the last time a major Rebel army invaded the United States, and the occasion for Abraham Lincoln's tribute to Union dead in November 1863. Yet Gettysburg, though by any yardstick an important event, was not considered decisive in breaking the rebellion. Indeed, Vicksburg's surrender loomed larger in the summer of 1863, and many in the U.S., including Lincoln, saw the Pennsylvania campaign as a lost opportunity to deliver a crippling blow to the most important Confederate army. As for the Gettysburg Address, virtually no one paid more than cursory attention during the war (the scene in Steven Spielberg's *Lincoln* showing Union soldiers quoting the speech to the president is laughably anachronistic). Had anyone polled people in the United States and the Confederacy in the summer of 1864, virtually none would have pronounced Union victory assured because of Gettysburg.

Even so, evidence of Gettysburg's supremacy in our historical imagination abounds. For example, a special sesquicentennial issue of *USA Today* termed Gettysburg "a hallowed event . . . a hinge of fate" that represented "both the high point of Confederate hopes and the turning point that led to eventual Union victory."[8] Thus did *USA Today* help sustain a hoary distortion propped up by Michael Shaara's novel *The Killer Angels*, Ken Burns's documentary *The Civil War*, and Ron Maxwell's film *Gettysburg*. In an amusing twist, *Abraham Lincoln: Vampire Hunter*, released in theaters in 2012, offers Gettysburg as not only the war's most important battle but also its last.

Perceptions regarding Joshua L. Chamberlain's role at Gettysburg also illuminate the vagaries of historical memory. As a young person during the centennial, I considered Gouverneur K. Warren the hero of Little Round Top. The dust jacket of my treasured copy of *The American Heritage Picture History of the Civil War* featured a photo of Warren's statue at Gettysburg, and Bruce Catton's text credited the New Yorker with placing troops that "saved Little Round Top." Similarly, my copy of Frederick Tilberg's *Gettysburg National Mil-*

itary Park, Pennsylvania, the NPS handbook first published in 1954 and revised in 1962, included a section titled "Warren Saves Little Round Top."[9] Neither publication mentioned Chamberlain. Nor did W. C. Storrick's *Gettysburg: The Place, the Battles, the Outcome* (1932), aimed at tourists and written by a retired superintendent of guides at the battlefield. For these authors, Warren stood first at Little Round Top, with cameos by brigade commanders Stephen H. Weed and Strong Vincent, Colonel Patrick H. O'Rorke of the 140th New York Infantry, and artillerist Charles E. Hazlett.

Thanks in large measure to Shaara, Burns, and Maxwell, Chamberlain now enjoys a position in popular culture near the front rank of all Union military heroes—not just those at Gettysburg. Events and characters prominent in Burns's series and Maxwell's adaptations of *The Killer Angels* and Jeff Shaara's novel *Gods and Generals* have received considerable attention from artists, underscoring the power of TV and films to shape the popular marketplace. A subject of no importance in post–Civil War artworks, Chamberlain became the most-painted Union military officer between the 1990s and the early twenty-first century; indeed, he and other Federal commanders at Gettysburg account for a significant proportion of all artworks on Union topics. In a few instances, figures in paintings resemble the actors in Maxwell's *Gettysburg* as much as the historical figures they represent. Chamberlain's ascendancy in the world of art, I think it safe to say, would strike William T. Sherman or Philip H. Sheridan as odd.[10]

None of this is meant to deprecate Chamberlain's service or abilities. He performed admirably at Gettysburg, but his efforts did not stand out among other competent regimental leaders. Chamberlain and his Twentieth Maine did nothing on Little Round Top to exceed what Colonel David Ireland and his 137th New York accomplished on Culp's Hill on July 2. Each successfully held one end of the Union line and suffered almost identical casualties. Yet almost no one beyond a circle of Gettysburg specialists knows anything about Ireland and his regiment.

The next students who enroll in my Civil War course will reflect on how various memory traditions have shaped their thinking about the war. As always, I will hope that a semester's work equips them to engage the vast complexity of the conflict with a sense of how history and memory often lead down different paths.

Monument to the 137th New York Infantry on Culp's Hill. Dedicated in 1888, it includes this inscription: "For Its Services in This and Many Other Great Battles of the War It Holds a Proud Position in the History of the 'Great Rebellion.'" The brigade commander's official report for Gettysburg affirmed: "The officers and men behaved admirably during the whole of the contest. Colonel Ireland was attacked on his flank and rear. He changed his position and maintained his ground with skill and gallantry, his regiment suffering very severely." (New York Monuments Commission for the Battlefields of Gettysburg and Chattanooga, *Final Report of the Battlefield of Gettysburg*, 3 vols. [Albany: J. B. Lyon, 1900], vol. 3, plate opposite 935, quotation on 942.)

OUT WEST

The West has achieved new prominence in recent literature on the Civil War and Reconstruction. The war, post-Appomattox events, and the West must be brought together, observe some authors, to expand a traditional narrative dominated by the axes of North versus South, slaveholding versus non-slaveholding, and United States versus Confederacy. What is needed, they believe, is a more comprehensive analytical framing that stretches from the Atlantic to the Pacific, includes Native Americans as well as black and white residents, encompasses borderlands with Canada and Mexico, and erases the usual chronological limits.[11]

Some definitions are necessary. "The West" as understood during the mid-nineteenth century could be expansive. Abraham Lincoln and U. S. Grant were known as "western" men, and during the Grand Review in May 1865, many observers drew distinctions between the western soldiers in Sherman's armies, most of whom hailed from what we call the Midwest, and eastern men in the Army of the Potomac. Similarly, the Iron Brigade, with regiments from Indiana, Michigan, and Wisconsin, proudly embraced its reputation as the only all-western brigade in the Army of the Potomac. The Western Theater extended from the Appalachian Mountains to the Mississippi River and from the Ohio River to the Gulf of Mexico. The Trans-Mississippi Theater, like the Western Theater a subset of the larger West, took in everything from the Mississippi River to the Pacific and from Canada to Mexico.

What most modern Americans imagine as "the West" would include the Civil War–era territories beyond the 100th meridian—everything from eastern Kansas, Nebraska, and the Dakotas to the Pacific coast. Thanks in significant measure to Hollywood's influence, this is the West associated in popular memory with gold rushes in California and Colorado, the final episodes of the long conflict between Native Americans and the U.S. Army, the building of transcontinental railroads, outlaws and lawmen in frontier towns, sodbusters and cattlemen, and the massive migration of white emigrants from eastern to western areas.

How should these various Wests fit into the history of the Civil War era?

No one can dispute the West's centrality to secession and the coming of conflict in 1860 and 1861. Debates about whether to permit slavery in federal territories provoked crises from the Missouri controversy of 1820 through the Wilmot Proviso of 1846, the Compromise of 1850, the Kansas–Nebraska explosion of the mid-1850s, and the Democratic Party's meltdowns in Charleston and Baltimore in 1860. Indeed, without friction relating to slavery in the western territories, it is difficult to imagine a secession movement that went beyond rhetorical bluster and posturing.

The war's Western Theater must be an essential part of any discussion of the war. Fighting in that region began in Kentucky, ended in North Carolina, featured storied military campaigns such as Shiloh and Atlanta, and produced the commanders who won Union victory, reelected the Republicans in 1864 (and thereby kept emancipation on the table), and headed the postwar army well into the 1880s. Whether it was as important as the Eastern Theater—in terms of morale in the Confederacy and the United States or attention in European capitals—is another question. Participants in the war, as well as later generations of Americans and a number of historians, have argued both for and against the supremacy of the Eastern Theater.[12]

The Trans-Mississippi Theater, which included noteworthy military and political action primarily in Missouri, Arkansas, and Louisiana, lagged far behind the Western and Eastern Theaters in significance. Neither the United States nor the Confederacy made it a priority when allocating material, troops, or leading generals. And events on the margins of the theater, such as Henry Hopkins Sibley's quixotic foray into New Mexico in 1862, scarcely rise to the level of inconsequential.

What about the trans-hundredth-meridian West? It remained peripheral to the fundamental issues of both the Civil War and Reconstruction. Two great goals dominated the war years: the vast majority of U.S. citizens and soldiers sought to restore the Union, while those in the Confederacy sought to establish a new slaveholding republic. Although people on both sides sometimes thought about this West (a number of Confederates hoped to find a window to the Pacific in Baja California, for example), their attention almost always displayed a more eastward interest.

The Republican agenda did feature legislation that affected later western development, most obviously the Homestead Act, the Pacific Railway Acts, and the Morrill Act, all passed in 1862. But each of these had antebellum roots, and both their wartime passage and their postwar impact can be considered part of a developmental arc that likely would have played out in some fashion absent the war.

Similarly, as I argue in the next essay,[13] the relocation of the Dakota Sioux from Minnesota after 1862, forced resettlement of the Navajo by U.S. forces under Kit Carson in 1864, and slaughter of approximately 150 Cheyenne and Arapaho at Sand Creek in 1864 were not really Civil War events—though they occurred during the war. Ample testimony underscores the degree to which people at the time separated the war over secession from clashes with Indians.

As for Reconstruction, it had a very specific meaning in the nineteenth century that had almost nothing to do with the West. The key Reconstruction documents, among them Lincoln's proclamation of amnesty and Reconstruction, the Wade-Davis Bill, the Fourteenth Amendment, and the Reconstruction Acts of 1867/68, address the problem of bringing former Confederate states back into Union and dealing with the long-term consequences of emancipation. Negotiations and treaties between the U.S. government and what Americans in the nineteenth century called the "Five Civilized Tribes" in Oklahoma also could be considered part of Reconstruction, which ended, at the latest, with the removal of token Federal forces that remained in the former Confederacy in 1877. But Reconstruction should not be conflated with the larger history of the United States between Appomattox and 1876. In the West, that larger history included, among other things, Indian wars and growth of the reservation system, accelerating white settlement, and construction of the transcontinental railroads.

It is always interesting to contemplate what an accurate survey of opinion in the past might reveal. I suspect that Americans polled in 1861 to 1865, or in 1876, would not have placed the trans-hundredth-meridian West anywhere near the center of either the war or Reconstruction.

ONE WAR OR TWO?

The United States Versus Confederates and Indians, 1861–1865

During the last weeks of August 1862, Dakota Sioux warriors cut a violent swath through much of Minnesota. Far to the southeast, Union forces battled Confederates in the campaign of Second Bull Run. "We are in the midst of a most terrible and exciting Indian war," read a telegram to Abraham Lincoln from Saint Paul on August 27. "A wild panic prevails in nearly one-half of the State. All are rushing to the frontier to defend the settlers." A week later, following defeat at Bull Run, Secretary of the Navy Gideon Welles recorded in his diary, "Our great army comes retreating to the banks of the Potomac, driven back to the entrenchments by rebels." An executive order from Lincoln the previous day had directed government clerks and employees to be "armed and supplied with ammunition, for the defense of the capital."[14]

Should these events in Minnesota and northern Virginia both be considered part of the Civil War? More broadly, should confrontations between U.S. forces and Indians from 1861 to 1865 be treated as elements of a single military conflict that also witnessed conventional operations between Union and Confederate armies?

A growing body of scholarship interprets the Civil War and military actions against Native Americans in the West as parts of one historical process. This trend exemplifies how historians, with their advantage of hindsight and access to all kinds of sources, often identify patterns by exploring seemingly disparate factors. In 2003, the distinguished western scholar Elliott West assessed martial action against the Confederacy and against Native Americans as prongs of a single U.S. state-building effort in the nineteenth century. By concentrating on the war between the United States and the Confederacy, West argued, Civil War scholars had ignored a more "powerful drive toward national consolidation . . . the integration of a divided America into a whole."[15]

Other historians have seconded this viewpoint. For example, Megan Kate Nelson, writing about Apache Pass, Arizona, posited "a Civil War that was fought over African American emancipation in the East, and American Indian subjugation in the West." Durwood Ball, an authority on the antebellum army in the West, similarly stated, "By mid-1863, the Union war had become an epic struggle to terminate the shameful social injustice of Southern slavery; that same war, when waged in the West, advanced the national program to subjugate, reduce, and concentrate those Native Americans still living freely."[16]

It is always worth asking whether new interpretive frameworks would make sense to the historical actors who lived through an era. In this case, most people in the United States almost certainly would have found it puzzling to label military operations against Confederates and those against Indians between 1861 and 1865 as the "same war." From their perspective, the war against the Confederacy involved the highest stakes—saving the republic, salvaging the promise of democracy in the western world, and guarding the legacy of the founding generation. That war dealt with a unique and existential menace and commanded nearly universal attention throughout the nation. Conflicts against Indians posed no mortal threat to the republic. Concerned with expanding and developing the nation's continental empire and protecting white settlers, they continued long-standing policies and actions and largely affected only those individuals directly involved.

Beyond this profound disparity in degree of threat to the nation, numbers and motivation for service help explain why the loyal population separated the two spheres of military action. The war to save the Union placed more than 2.2 million citizen-soldiers into uniform, the majority of them true volunteers, and cost billions of dollars. "What saved the Union," noted U. S. Grant admiringly in the 1870s, "was the coming forward of the young men of the nation. . . . as they did in the time of the Revolution, giving everything to the country." The Indian wars always had been, and going forward past Appomattox would remain, primarily the bailiwick of the tiny regular army. Its ranks contained men who took up arms as a profession, with no specific crisis to meet. William Tecumseh Sherman, as general in chief of the army after the war, got at the matter of scale when he spoke of infantry units deployed as garrisons in western posts: "To call them an Army is simply a misnomer. They are little squads of men strung along a frontier of fifteen hundred or sixteen hundred miles." Such soldiers and their mission would never be equated, by the Civil War generation, with the armies of the Potomac, the Tennessee, or the Cumberland.[17]

It is most fruitful to interpret wartime struggles that pitted Indians against the U.S. Army and territorial military units as part of a much longer chronological trajectory. Three of the most written about episodes involved the uprising and relocation of the Dakota Sioux from Minnesota in 1862 and 1863, the forced resettlement of Navajos by U.S. forces under Brigadier General James Henry Carleton in 1863 and 1864, and the slaughter of approximately 150 Cheyenne and Arapaho people, including many women and children, at Sand Creek, Colorado Territory, in 1864. These kinds of incidents would have occurred, at some place and in some fashion, even in the absence of the four-year slaughter triggered by sectional wrangling and waged by large national armies. They fit within a framework that connects innumerable episodes from the Tidewater and Pequot wars of the seventeenth century to the conflicts between Native Americans and the U.S. Army during the post–Civil War decades.

Continuities across time abound. During the summer of 1863, in Cañon de Chelly, Colonel Christopher "Kit" Carson's command destroyed crops on which Navajos, as he put it, "depended entirely for subsistence" during the upcoming winter.[18] Carson's actions recalled attempts to deny Indians sustenance and shelter that went back to "feed fights" of the colonial era or, nearer the Civil War, to Colonel William J. Worth's actions during the Second Seminole War in 1841 and 1842. The relocation of the Dakota Sioux in Minnesota and, more famously, the Long Walk of eight thousand to nine thousand Navajos from modern-day Arizona to the Bosque Redondo near Fort Sumner, New Mexico Territory, recalled the "removal" of the Five Civilized Tribes, as they were called in the nineteenth century, from the Old Southwest to what is now Oklahoma.

Wartime friction with Indians also inspired debates about methods that had arisen in earlier eras. One side, usually dominated by white voices from frontier areas, called for unrestrained war against Indians. For example, Colonel John M. Chivington, who led the Colorado and New Mexico units at Sand Creek, pronounced himself "fully satisfied that to kill them is the only way we will ever have peace and quiet." Others decried such brutal methods, as when Congressman Thaddeus Stevens of Pennsylvania remarked, in May 1864, "In nine cases out of ten, Indian wars have been produced by the provocations of the whites." Going back to the late eighteenth century, insisted Stevens, overwhelmingly "the breach of faith has come from the white man."[19]

Political leaders, soldiers, and the press habitually treated the two arenas of warfare as distinct. Reactions to the violence in Minnesota illustrate this point. Inside Lincoln's cabinet, Second Bull Run and Antietam prompted numerous discussions. But the fighting in Minnesota in August and September, which resulted in more than five hundred dead white civilians and the mass hanging of thirty-eight Indian men at Mankato later that year, received scarcely any mention. Indeed, the best-known aspect of the Minnesota drama related to Lincoln's commuting death sentences of more than 250 Indians. Secretary of the Navy Welles devoted portions of just two entries in his voluminous diary to the Sioux uprising, both of which commented about executions.

John G. Nicolay, sent by Lincoln to Minnesota, separated events there from the war against the Confederacy. In messages to Lincoln and Secretary of War Edwin M. Stanton on August 26 and 27, he referred to the bloodshed as an "Indian war" that had wreaked havoc among settlers. "Compared with the great storm of rebellion which has darkened and overspread our whole national sky," wrote Nicolay a few months later, "the Indian war on our northwestern frontier has been a little cloud 'no bigger than a man's hand.'" He went on to sketch a long historical arc unconnected to efforts to suppress the rebellion. Linking the violence in Minnesota to "similar events in our history," Nicolay suggested that from "the days of King Philip to the time of Black Hawk, there has hardly been an outbreak so treacherous, so sudden, so bitter, and so bloody."[20]

Lincoln's annual message to Congress in December 1862 aligned with Nicolay's observations. Early in the message, he alluded to the "civil war, which has so radically changed for the moment, the occupation and habits of the American people." Later in the text, he informed Congress that the "Territories of the United States, with unimportant exceptions, have remained undisturbed by the civil war" and also mentioned "Indian tribes upon our frontiers . . . [who] have engaged in open hostilities against the white settlements in their vicinity." Lincoln referred to the fighting in Minnesota as "this Indian war," during which "not less than eight hundred persons were killed by the Indians and a large amount of property destroyed."[21]

The Lincoln administration briefly considered sending paroled Union soldiers to augment local forces in Minnesota—a sure sign of separating military action against the Confederates from that against Indians. Under a cartel between the United States and the Confederacy that governed prisoners of war, paroled men could not return to service until they had been exchanged for soldiers captured by the other side. Yet Secretary Stanton, in response to a plea from Minnesota's governor, embraced the idea of "the paroled prisoners being sent to the Indian borders" as an excellent one that "will be immediately acted upon." Lincoln backed Stanton on September 20, urging that paroled soldiers be moved "to the seat of the Indian difficulties . . . with all possible despatch."[22]

Discussion of the issue continued for a month. General in Chief Henry W. Halleck sent three communications to the president on October 3 and 4, the last of which advised, "After full consultation with the Secretary of War and Colonel [Joseph] Holt it is concluded that the parole under the cartel does not prohibit doing service against the Indians." The cartel, Halleck had stated in his initial reply, stipulated only that parolees not "bear arms against the Confederate States during the war or until exchanged." Attorney General Edward Bates weighed in on October 18 with a contrary opinion: "It is the plainly declared purpose of the Cartel to prevent the use of prisoners paroled . . . in the discharge of any of the duties of a soldier." Thus did four top officials, all lawyers who never would have used non-exchanged parolees to fight Confederates, seriously discuss utilizing such men in what they deemed an Indian war.[23]

Editorial choices in *Harper's Weekly* manifested a sharp distinction between the Indian war in Minnesota and operations against the Confederacy. During September, the newspaper contained multiple stories and illustrations concerning Second Bull Run and Confederate invasions of Kentucky and Maryland. Two passages totaling fifteen lines covered Minnesota—one of which underscores attitudes about the relative importance of the Indian and Confederate wars. Because of escalating chaos, Governor Alexander Ramsey requested an extension to meet the state's quota for troops in August. *Harper's Weekly* printed the president's perfunctory response: "Attend to the Indians. If the draft *can not* proceed, of course it *will not* proceed. Necessity knows no law. The Government cannot extend the time." Lincoln's reply signaled that the nation needed men to fight Rebels, and Ramsey could deal with Indians on his own.[24]

Many soldiers serving in remote western areas expressed disappointment at being so far from what they considered the real war. Early in 1862, an Iowan affirmed that deployment in Dakota Territory "is not the height of our ambition. We are anxious to take an active part in this struggle for national existence, and distinguish ourselves . . . in maintaining our country's rights and restoring peace and harmony to its now torn and distracted States." Similarly, a member of the Fourth Minnesota Infantry, a unit initially assigned to garrisons on the frontier, recalled how men in the regiment considered duty against Indians far less important than crushing the Confederacy and held out hope for a chance to help save the nation. "Our men believed that the war would be a long one," he observed in designating the effort to defeat the Confederacy the principal conflict, "and that they would have the opportunity to see all the fighting that they would desire."[25]

It is difficult to imagine duty more removed from the seat of decisive military events than at many posts along the western frontier. Typical was Fort Garland, which stood in the shadow of 14,351-foot Blanca Peak in the Sangre de Cristo range and guarded the eastern entrance to Colorado's remote San Luis Valley. In October 1862, an inspector sent north from Santa Fe reported that 209 officers and men of the First New Mexico and Second Colorado Volunteers occupied the fort. The inspecting officer pronounced the New Mexicans "very deficient" in skirmish drills and "sadly deficient" in target practice. Officers "appeared sober but wanting in energy & industry," and the First Colorado suffered from "laxity of discipline." Moreover, the inspector found the guard duty "very negligently attended to" and the fort's layout "scarcely defensible." In sum, the garrison at Fort Garland, lackadaisical and without pressing business, seemingly marked time in an isolated world of its own.[26]

Witnesses whose service spanned the Civil War and postwar years reveal how soldiers explained the transition from a war to save the Union to a war against Indians. George A. Forsyth, a volunteer who fought throughout the Civil War and held a commission in the postwar U.S. Army, addressed how quickly the change took place: "Scarcely had the echoes of the guns at Appomattox Courthouse died away," he wrote, "when the demands of the West for protection from the warlike Indians on the great plains forced themselves upon the attention of Congress." Only with Confederate surrender could "the urgent needs of the Western frontier, which had necessarily been neglected during the civil war, became once again one of the absorbing questions of the hour."

Like Forsyth, George W. Baird juxtaposed the wars against Rebels with those against Indians. Colonel of the Thirty-Second United States Colored Troops Infantry during the Civil War and later an officer in the regular army, Baird spoke in 1906 before members of the Military Order of the Loyal Legion of the United States. He tied the postwar regular army's efforts against Indians to the professional soldiers of Arthur St. Clair and "Mad Anthony" Wayne, who fought the battles of the Wabash and Fallen Timbers in the early days of the republic. Aware that MOLLUS meetings focused on the Civil War, Baird remarked that he would talk about "a war not less perilous, calling for rather more than less of heroism, than the war of the rebellion." Giving full credit to both the "heroic little army of the frontier" and "the great national force of the period this order commemorates," Baird lamented that the former "had no Homer to celebrate them in immortal verse."

A third witness, George H. Holliday, "served through the war of the Rebellion" and remained in uniform when "his regiment, with a few other volunteer regiments, was ordered to the Rocky Mountains to assist in protecting the frontier." Many of Holliday's comrades in the Sixth West Virginia Cavalry believed they had done their full duty by helping defeat the Confederacy. They had enlisted "at the 'first call'" to save the Union, "had 'seen her through,'" and reacted with "wrath and indignation" to the prospect of participating in a different war against Indians in the West. During 1861 to 1865, wrote Holliday in language that echoed Forsyth's: "The Government had been sorely taxed in her efforts to put down the Rebellion, and the red men of the plains had had their own way to a great extent." Once "the war in the South had come to an end," the United States could turn its attention to Indians, "who had been so unruly while the 'Great Father' was chastizing his subjects in the South."[27]

Congressional handling of veterans' benefits showcased how Indian wars stood apart from the nation's four-year effort to defeat the Rebels. Citizen-soldiers who saved the Union received far better treatment than their counterparts who labored in frontier garrisons and mounted operations against Native Americans. As late as the 1920s and 1930s, the latter sought equal treatment. In 1927, a report in the House of Representatives recommended raising the upper limit of pensions for Indian war veterans from twenty dollars to fifty dollars per month—and covered anyone "who served 30 days or more in any military organization" from January 1859 through December 1898 "under the authority, or by the approval of the United States or any State of Territory, in any Indian war or campaign."[28]

A hearing in January 1936 revealed that inequities lingered. Congressman John W. McCormack of Massachusetts, who served in World War I and later became Speaker of the House of Representatives, complained that Civil War veterans could receive one hundred dollars per month while Indian war veterans were limited to half that sum, despite service "rendered in opening up the great frontier." Another member of Congress remarked that Indian war veterans occupied "a class by themselves in the history of our country" and deserved to be treated better. The cost of fairness would not have been great. At their peak in 1896, Indian war veterans and their widows on the pension rolls numbered 6,955—compared to almost a million Civil War pensioners. By January 1936, just 3,661 men, with an average age of seventy-four, remained on the rolls.[29]

Anyone seeking to characterize the relationship between the Confederate and Indian wars of 1861 to 1865 should take seriously participants' testimony. Algernon S. Badger will contribute a final word about nineteenth-century attitudes. A native of Massachusetts who finished the Civil War as lieutenant colonel of the First Louisiana Cavalry (Union), Badger speculated in the summer of 1865 that some "cavalry will undoubtedly be sent up on the Indian frontier as the Indians are committing numerous depredations." Badger had no desire "to chase Indians," he told his father. "After the work of the past four and a half years, it would seem boys play."[30]

UNCONVENTIONAL WARFARE

Guerrillas did not play a major role in shaping the military outcome of the Civil War. First to last, conventional armies composed of citizen-soldiers waged operations that dictated swings of national morale, determined control over the most important waterways and logistical areas of the Confederacy, and, ultimately, decided the fate of slavery. Of more than three million men who served, the overwhelming majority fought in regular units commanded by duly appointed officers. The outcome of the Seven Days battles, which brought Robert E. Lee to the fore and did much to place emancipation on the table for the United States, had more to do with how long the war lasted than all guerrilla activities during the entire conflict combined. The depredations of outliers such as William Clarke Quantrill and "Bloody Bill" Anderson, as well as the headline-grabbing but vastly overrated exploits of John Singleton Mosby, scarcely influenced any campaign in a meaningful way. Expanding the definition of "guerrilla" to include officers such as John Hunt Morgan, as sometimes happens, does not change the picture. (Nathan Bedford Forrest and Earl Van Dorn cannot be termed guerrillas or irregulars by any reasonable definition of the term.)

This is not to say that guerrilla activities should be ignored. The few thousand genuine guerrillas contributed to chaotic social conditions in a number of places, most obviously in parts of Missouri and areas radiating out from the spine of the Appalachian Mountains. Civilians suffered amid an escalating drama of brutality, reprisals, and freebooting lawlessness. The Confederacy sought to manage its guerrilla problem with the Partisan Ranger Act of April 1862, only to repeal it less than two years later as irregular groups proved resistant to any type of discipline. Early guerrilla activity in Missouri also helped to inspire Francis Lieber's attempt to codify the rules of war, signed by President Lincoln and issued as General Order No. 100 in April 1863. "Gen Halleck called upon me, after my correspondence with him, to write a pamphlet on guerrillas," Lieber wrote to Charles Sumner in May 1863, "which I did. . . . At last I wrote to Halleck that he ought to issue a Code on the Law of Nations so far as it relates to the armies in the field. I was approached, and here is the thing."[31]

Some historians believe the Confederacy should have pursued a wide-scale guerrilla resistance. They argue that Confederate manpower within this context would have lasted almost indefinitely, that the northern public lacked the commitment to suppress dedicated guerrillas, that the Confederacy could have relinquished considerable territory without materially damaging its cause, and that the Revolutionary War demonstrated how a guerrilla war for national liberation could succeed.

If subjected to the realities confronting the Confederacy, however, a guerrilla-based "war of liberation" seems an anachronistic pipe dream. Such a policy would have required Confederates to repudiate their obvious military leaders. Robert E. Lee, Albert Sidney Johnston, Joseph E. Johnston, P. G. T. Beauregard, and other West Point trained soldiers represented an ideal of the gentleman as military officer that held great appeal in the antebellum South. Considering the antebellum efforts to replicate West Point at the Virginia Military Institute, the Military College of South Carolina, and elsewhere, it is inconceivable that Confederates would have shunned prominent West Pointers in favor of unknown men who would command small bands of partisans.

Guerrilla war also would have been inappropriate for the kind of nation Confederates hoped to establish. They envisioned taking their place among the roster of recognized western states, a goal that demanded creation of formal governmental institutions—including a national army and navy. In his inaugural address, Jefferson Davis spoke to his fellow citizens of "the position which we have assumed among the nations of the earth."[32] European recognition could prove decisive. Would Great Britain and France have recognized a fledgling Confederacy that relied on guerrilla units rather than on a formal army? Would harassment of Federal armies, rather than victories such as the Seven Days and Second Bull Run, have persuaded Europeans that the Confederacy seemed destined to achieve independence—as Saratoga had pointed the way toward American independence in 1777?

Supporters of the guerrilla option often cite the American Revolution as a precedent but emphasize the wrong dimension of that earlier struggle. Although partisans such as Thomas Sumter and Francis Marion earned success in the Revolution, Confederates looked for their models to George Washington, who always placed the broad interests of the nascent nation above local needs, and the Continental Army, which loomed large in the memory of Saratoga, Yorktown, and other benchmark military events. As Beauregard wrote in the summer of 1861, "Washington and the Revolution should always be present in our minds."[33]

The threat of social chaos in a slave-based society stood as the most important obstacle to a Confederate policy of guerrilla war. The approach of Union forces understandably provoked alarm among Confederates about the consequences for their slaves. Late antebellum fears of insurrection and reactions to Union invaders strongly suggest that Confederates would have opposed a guerrilla strategy that accelerated the process by which slaves came into contact with Federal armies. Having seceded in large measure to protect their slave-based society, it strains credulity to believe Confederates would select a strategy calculated to undermine their economic and social control over millions of black people.

Ironically, Jefferson Davis supplied the opening for historians to broach the subject of guerrilla war. On April 4, 1865, he addressed the Confederate citizenry. "We have now entered upon a new phase of a struggle," stated Davis, because the fall of Richmond had rendered "our army free to move from point to point, and strike in detail the detachments and garrisons of the enemy; operating in the interior of our own country, where supplies are more accessible, and where the foe will be far removed from his own base, and cut off from all succor in case of reverse."[34] For many historians, Davis seemed belatedly to recognize the merits of a guerrilla strategy. Often overlooked is his explicit mention of "our army," by which he meant Lee and the Army of Northern Virginia. Davis envisioned not a "people's war" but an unleashed Lee taking the offensive against whatever pieces of the Federal army he could find.

THE DARK TURN—LATE NINETEENTH-CENTURY STYLE

It has become fashionable among scholars to emphasize the "dark side" of the Civil War. Troubled by what they consider a literature gone stale with old questions and topics, these historians seek to revitalize the field by examining the conflict's often disturbing underside. Among the genres that come under fire as repetitive and unfruitful are books that revisit storied campaigns and commanders, especially the ones that deploy words such as "heroism" or "gallantry" in narrating tactical events. That kind of drum-and-bugle history too often cloaks the war in romantic trappings, insist the dark side advocates, as do studies that find a soaring purpose in a war for Union, or even one for Union and emancipation. The overlooked war, they counter, featured cruelty, atrocities, cowardice, brutal guerrilla activity, and physical and mental wounds that left veterans profoundly damaged. A striking example of how succeeding generations fashion their own interpretations of seismic historical events, the turn toward the dark side reflects the impact of the American military experience in Vietnam and, more recently, in the Middle East.

Late in the nineteenth century, a handful of authors anticipated some of the directions this new scholarship has taken. Frank Wilkeson and Ambrose Bierce, both Union veterans, illustrate this point. A New Yorker whose father wrote for the *New York Times,* Wilkeson lost his older brother, Bayard, to a mortal wound at Gettysburg. Frank subsequently enlisted as a teenager and saw action with the Eleventh New York Light Artillery in the Overland campaign and at Petersburg. His *Recollections of a Private Soldier in the Army of the Potomac* opens with an unsparing portrait of men who accepted bounties to enlist. "If there was a man in all that shameless crew who had enlisted from patriotic motives," he writes dismissively, "I did not see him. There was not a man of them who was not eager to run away." Yet "dishonest Congressmen who desire to secure re-election by gifts of public money and property to voters," continues Wilkeson, "say they were brave Northern youth going to the defence of their country."[35]

An entire chapter of his *Recollections* deals with severe wounds. During action on May 5 in the Wilderness, a young soldier's "head jerked, he staggered, then fell, then regained his feet." Wilkerson noticed that a "tiny fountain of blood and teeth and bone and bits of tongue burst out of his mouth." A round had passed through the man's jaws, and "the lower one was broken and hung down." Adopting an almost clinical tone, Wilkeson adds: "I looked directly into his open mouth, which was ragged and bloody and tongueless." At the North Anna River, an infantryman passed between the guns and caissons of the Eleventh New York battery. "A solid shot, intended for us, struck him," recalls Wilkeson. "His entire bowels were torn out and slung in ribbons and shreds on the ground. He fell dead, but his arms and legs jerked convulsively a few times. It was a sickening spectacle."[36]

Wilkeson also chronicles how the war's destructive hand crushed civilians. Deployed to the Tennessee/Alabama border area later in the war, he encountered white refugees who had suffered from guerrilla activity. "Defenceless women and children . . . starved out of their homes" had been given shelter in camps set up by the Union army. "Their features were as expressionless as wood" and "their eyes lustreless." Gaunt, unwashed, and infested with vermin, "all were utterly poor. It seemed that they were too poor to ever again get a start in life."[37]

Ambrose Bierce also enlisted while in his teens, joining the Ninth Indiana Infantry and seeing action in many of the most famous battles in the Western Theater. Badly wounded in the head at Kennesaw Mountain, he later served as a staff officer before leaving the army in early 1865.

Bierce achieved considerable postwar fame as an author and wrote both fiction and nonfiction pieces about the war. *Ambrose Bierce's Civil War*, edited by William McCann, offers a convenient selection of his work that reveals why Bierce has been described as, among other things, sardonic, bitter, cynical, disenchanted, and misanthropic.

Bierce offers a fascinating discussion of why "brave troops could retreat while their courage was still high." Discussing action at Pickett's Mill in

May 1864, he explains that where both sides fight without cover "each has its 'dead-line,' and between the two is a clear space—neutral ground, devoid of dead, for the living cannot reach it to fall there." At Pickett's Mill, Union corpses littered the ground in front of the enemy's line, "a third were within fifteen paces, and not one within ten." The perception on the part of the "still courageous soldier" that he cannot cross that last bit of ground explains why he would withdraw without coming into actual contact with his foe: "He sees, or feels, that he *cannot*."[38]

Bierce also takes occasion to describe terrible deaths. In his short story "Chickamauga," a soldier comes upon a dead woman—"the white face turned upward, the hands thrown out and clutched full of grass, the clothing deranged, the long dark hair in tangles and full of clotted blood." Close inspection reveals that the "greater part of the forehead was torn away, and from the jagged hole the brain protruded, overflowing the temple, a frothy mass of gray, crowned with clusters of crimson bubbles—the work of a shell."[39]

Grimly humorous passages abound in Bierce's fiction and nonfiction pieces. Two examples will suffice. The battle of Franklin, where the Army of Tennessee lost a dozen generals, proved "a great day for Confederates in the line of promotion." And in the midst of chaos at Chickamauga, when Bierce offered to guide General James S. Negley to the action, the general rejected him "a little uncivilly." "His mind, I think," remarks Bierce, "was in Nashville, behind a breastwork."[40]

Anyone who explores the dark side of the war should consult Wilkeson and Bierce. Yet even they occasionally slip into a different voice, as when Bierce, recalling fallen comrades at Chickamauga, confesses that for all who struggled there, "the place means much."[41]

RECKONING WITH CONFEDERATE DESERTION

Historians examining Confederate defeat often describe desertion as both a symptom and a cause. As conditions behind the lines worsened, loved ones begged soldiers to return home. Thousands of men did so, a fact that many scholars use to portray eroding morale across the Confederacy. At least 105,000 out of a total of perhaps 850,000 soldiers eventually deserted, enough to affect the performance of the armies and hasten Confederate defeat. Scholars have accorded far more attention to Confederate than to Union desertion, and they often treat it as an indicator of weak national sentiment in the incipient slaveholding republic.

By way of comparison, approximately 210,000 of 2.2 million U.S. soldiers deserted, and another 120,000 evaded conscription. Estimates of the number of northerners who fled to Canada during the war to escape enrollment officers, dodge the draft, or desert from their units run as high as eighty-five to ninety thousand. Thousands more fled to areas such as mountainous central and western Pennsylvania, where they hoped to place themselves beyond the reach of the federal government.

It is important to remember that the presence of United States armies on Confederate soil generated a type of desertion in Rebel forces largely unknown among Federals—one not necessarily indicative of weak will or unhappiness with the Confederacy. A soldier in the Army of Tennessee informed his wife, in mid-July 1864, that "a great many Tennesseeans and up[country] Georgians are leaving the army and say they are going back home. . . . They know that their families are left behind at the mercy of the Yankees, and it is hard to bear." If the Confederate army retreated beyond his home county, admitted this man, "I could not say that I would not desert and try to get to you."[42] Thousands of Confederates left the ranks when they marched close to the areas where their families lived, but later returned to their units.

Should these men be reckoned deserters who cared nothing about which side prevailed in the war? Many Confederate officers acknowledged different types of deserters. Jubal A. Early, a tough disciplinarian, professed no toleration for desertion during the war, "and never failed to sanction and order the execution of sentences for the extreme penalty for that offence . . . but some palliation was to be found for the conduct of many of those who did desert, in the fact that they did so to go to the aid of their families, who they knew were suffering for the necessaries of life."[43]

At the least, historians should avoid portraying Confederate desertion as a linear problem of constantly increasing gravity. One careful study of Virginia describes a bulge of desertions in 1862 that probably represented, at least in part, anger at implementation of the conscription act, which extended the service of thousands of men who originally had signed on for one year. After this initial wave, rates dropped off until the final eight months of the war. This pattern should caution against the use of desertion to demonstrate a deep-seated and pervasive absence of identification with the Confederate cause.

Dealing with desertion illuminates the challenge of pinning down statistics and comprehending exactly what they indicate. Surviving Confederate records contain many vexing gaps, a problem compounded by uncertainty in fathoming how best to read surviving documents. For example, one historian has observed, "Had it not been for the two-thirds of soldiers who were absent by September 1864, the Confederacy might well have been able to offset the North's population advantage."[44] This passage doubtless would leave most readers with an impression of catastrophic desertion by the early autumn of 1864.

Were two-thirds of the men absent in the fall of 1864?[45] Desertion unquestionably grew in severity as the war headed into its final eight months, but a closer look at the critical evidence—inspection returns—muddies the picture. The "consolidated abstract from returns of the Confederate Army on or about December 31, 1864" gives these numbers: Present for Duty, 154,910; Aggregate Present, 196,016; Aggregate Present & Absent, 400,787. These totals might seem to suggest that only 38.7 percent of the men were ready for duty and that the rest must have gone off somewhere. In fact, the first two categories (roughly one half of the whole) include those literally present as well as all men detailed for duty elsewhere, under arrest in camp, sick in field hospitals, and in other categories. In the third category, the absent would include prisoners of war, men on furlough, and those in general hospitals due to illness or battlefield wounds—categories that do not necessarily support a portrait of armies experiencing crises of morale.

The inspection report dated August 19, 1864, for the Tenth South Carolina Infantry, a unit in the Army of Tennessee, pinpoints the difficulty of extracting unequivocal numbers from manuscript sources. The report lists 208 men present for duty; 255 as the aggregate present, with 39 of them on special, extra, or daily duty, and 8 sick; and 529 as aggregate present and absent, with 14 on detached service, 2 on leave, 156 absent sick, and 7 absent without authority. The sum of 255 + 14 + 2 + 156 + 7 equals only 434—95 short of 529. The report also has a column for prisoners of war, listing another 96 men, producing a grand total of 530, one more than the aggregate present and absent (perhaps the clerk was tired or not very good at arithmetic). Some of those on detached service, on leave, or absent sick could have deserted and the regimental officers not yet known it; some of the 96 prisoners also could have taken the oath or joined the United States Army to fight Indians on the frontier. But without doubt, most of the 274 or 275 soldiers not among the "present" or "aggregate present" should be considered loyal soldiers.

Confederate military and civilian leaders, newspaper editors, and citizens in their private diaries and letters left ample testimony about the problem of desertion. There is no question it weakened the war effort and, in many cases, reflected an indifference toward the Confederate nation. But a careful look at patterns, numbers, and circumstances reveals that, as is almost always the case with history, the phenomenon was far more complex, and its impact less certain, than often assumed.

THE GRAND REVIEW

The Grand Review in Washington, D.C., on May 23–24, 1865, featured more than 150,000 soldiers from George G. Meade's Army of the Potomac and William T. Sherman's armies of the Tennessee and Georgia. The men marched down Pennsylvania Avenue amid throngs of onlookers, for whom the seemingly endless ranks bespoke the impressive military power of a mobilized populace, citizen-soldiers who had risked all in a brutal war and stood as exemplars of disinterested patriotic sacrifice. These troops had come forth in "tribute to free government . . . ," affirmed one newspaper, "representatives of every loyal State, to struggle, shoulder to shoulder, for their common country. They were our friends and brothers and sons, our fellow-citizens, our *people*."[46]

The Grand Review affords a striking example of tension between contemporary meanings and subsequent analysis of a historical event. For veterans who marched in the review and spectators who watched and cheered, the two-day spectacle marked a victory that had preserved the Union, ensured the vi-

Spectators along Pennsylvania Avenue watch mounted officers leading infantry units, with sun glinting off the soldiers' musket barrels, during the Grand Review. (Library of Congress, Prints and Photographs Division, LC-DIG-cwpb-02806.)

ability of democracy, and vanquished forces of Southern oligarchy inimical to the intent of the founding generation. U.S. armies had shouldered the burden of suppressing the rebellion, and those on parade in Washington could claim more achievements on storied battlefields than any others. During the past year, these armies had captured Atlanta and Richmond, cut a swath through Georgia and the Carolinas, and forced the Army of Northern Virginia and its famous commander to surrender. The state and national flags at the head of regiments, many of them little more than tattered remnants, summoned emotional images of both the nation's constituent parts and its triumphant whole.

Americans who regarded the Grand Review in such terms could not have anticipated that future generations would take a far different view. Much recent scholarly literature finds in the events of May 23 and 24 a template for what was wrong with the war's winning cause. Too militaristic, too avowedly nationalist, and, most troubling, too white, the review laid bare the flawed nature of Union triumph. Strip away the waving flags and chest thumping and what remained was a soon-to-be-reunited nation that looked much like the racist, exclusionary United States of the prewar era.

How should we reconcile these conflicting interpretations of the Grand Review? The answer to that question opens inquiry into topics such as how the review was planned and, in a broader sense, the meaning of Union and the relationship between the loyal citizenry and the men who campaigned in U.S. armies.

The absence of black troops in the review is easily explained. Put together quickly (as late as May 16, General in Chief Ulysses S. Grant did not know whether it would take place), the review was limited to forces close to Washington—Meade's and Sherman's, which contained no black units. Could organizers have scheduled the event to make certain black troops were present? The answer must be yes. They also could have waited to summon from other theaters representative white units with as much claim to a place in the parade or, perhaps most obviously, arranged for some of the navy's fifty thousand sailors to participate. Instead, working on a short timetable, planners opted to stage the event with the republic's greatest and most famous armies.

It is worth noting that black units had been included in processions at Lincoln's second inauguration and at his funeral in Washington—facts that undercut any notion of a conspiracy to ban them from the Grand Review. The *New York Times*, a solidly Republican sheet, pronounced "very silly, and scarcely worthy of notice" the idea that black units had been barred from the review. The nation's leading abolitionist newspaper found the charge that "brave colored troops [had been] debarred from participation in the late military review" to be groundless. "There have been no negro troops in the Army of the Potomac for nearly a year," observed the *Liberator*, which accurately described how Sherman's black pioneers "marched shoulder to shoulder, in the review, with their white comrades, under the same flag."[47]

The modern complaint about the nationalism displayed on May 23 and 24 seems scarcely worth addressing. More than a third of a million Union soldiers had perished in an effort to restore the nation, a democratic republic with a franchise quite narrow by current standards—women and most black men could not vote—but breathtakingly broad within a mid-nineteenth-century transatlantic context. Participants and observers predictably cheered the nation's survival as a democratic beacon in a world yet to embrace the idea of government by the people. The Democratic *New York Herald*, which boasted a robust domestic circulation and the largest European readership among all American newspapers, captured the triumphal character of most reactions to the Grand Review. Blue-clad soldiers, noted the *Herald*, "have secured the perpetuity of that Union upon which the hopes of the oppressed of all climes and countries depend. They are the champions of free governments throughout the world."[48]

Finally, grousing about the review as a militaristic ritual completely misses a crucial point. The deeply antimilitaristic American tradition, rooted in opposition to professional British soldiers during the colonial and revolutionary eras, stood out sharply in coverage of the event. Victory belonged to citizen-soldiers who wanted nothing more than to put aside their weapons and return to civilian life. "These are only dutiful American *citizens*," commented one newspaper that articulated a common theme, "coming home to disband after a long successful work in behalf of their country!" One reporter quoted an Englishman in the crowd who affirmed he never had seen a more impressive military parade and thought "the grandeur of it all is that these men are citizens." A Baltimore paper placed the veterans' work "alongside the events of the Revolutionary generation," singling out "the significance of the transition from the soldier to the citizen. The soldier of yesterday is the citizen of to-day."[49]

The Grand Review represented a moment to look back and ahead—to the military labors of more than two million men who donned blue uniforms during the war and to a reinvigorated republic in which veterans and fellow citizens would play out their lives.

REVISITING THE GETTYSBURG ADDRESS

An early scene in Steven Spielberg's film *Lincoln* suggests that the Gettysburg Address resonated powerfully with the loyal citizenry of the United States. Set at night, the sequence depicts the president with Union soldiers who are preparing to embark on the campaign against Wilmington, North Carolina, in the last winter of the war. Lincoln initially speaks with a pair of black men, but their conversation is interrupted when two white infantrymen walk up. Both had been present at Gettysburg in November 1863, they say, and heard Lincoln's dedicatory remarks for the military cemetery. To the president's obvious discomfort, they begin to quote the language of his address but falter when they reach the last part. Lincoln instructs them to get on with the process of boarding and then turns back to the black men, one of whom, as he walks away, recites the final section of the address that calls for "a new birth of freedom." Just more than a year after Lincoln delivered his speech, viewers would conclude from this scene, it already had become so well known in the United States that soldiers, black and white, had memorized it.

Most people who watched *Lincoln* probably found all this entirely plausible. After all, the Gettysburg Address is the best-known presidential speech in American history. The most influential book on the address, Garry Wills's *Lincoln at Gettysburg: The Words that Remade America*, argues that the "vast throng of thousands" who streamed away from Evergreen Cemetery on November 19, 1863, ventured "into a different America. Lincoln had revolutionized the Revolution, giving people a new past to live with that would change their future indefinitely." Far more important than the Emancipation Proclamation, which had been "only a military measure, an exigency of war," the remarks at Gettysburg set a goal for "a nation trying to live up to the vision in which it was conceived."[50]

Whether most citizens in 1863 would have equated Lincoln's phrase "a new birth of freedom" with emancipation could be the subject of another essay, but for now I will note that Wills and many others who have written about the address accord very little attention to its contemporary reception. Their readers likely assume that such a famous speech must have been widely discussed. In fact, Lincoln's brief remarks occasioned surprisingly little comment before his death. Edward Everett's long oration, which is usually treated as a long-winded prelude to Lincoln's profound comments, gained far more attention at the time.

Testimony from within the cabinet and the president's inner circle illustrate this phenomenon. Treasury secretary Salmon P. Chase mentioned Lincoln's departure for Gettysburg on November 18, but in letters dated November 19, 23, and 25 ignored the content of the address. Chase told his daughter Kate that he did not accompany the president because too much work crowded his desk. Secretary of the Navy Gideon Welles, though "strongly urged by the President to attend the ceremonials at Gettysburg," begged off, pleading that he "could not spare the time."[51] Welles's extensive diary offers no comment on the substance of the speech. Both Chase and Welles expressed far more interest in the president's upcoming message to Congress, which would reference both emancipation and black military service.

John Hay, Lincoln's young secretary, made the journey to Gettysburg but provided only a perfunctory description of the program: "Mr Everett spoke as he always does perfectly—and the President in a firm free way, with more grace than is his wont said his half dozen lines of consecration and the music wailed and we went home through crowded and cheering streets." Another attendee in Gettysburg, Commissioner of Public Buildings Benjamin Brown French, similarly praised Edward Everett, who brought "his audience to tears many times during his masterly effort." As for the president, he uttered "a few brief, but most appropriate words" to dedicate the cemetery.[52]

Newspapers apportioned far less space to Lincoln's remarks than to Everett's two-hour oration. Advance copies of the latter went to papers in some large cities, which allowed them to publish the entire text accompanied by editorial comment. The brief text of Lincoln's speech arrived late in the day by telegraph, leaving time only for a hasty typesetting and publication with little or no evaluation. For example, the *New York Times* printed Lincoln's remarks without analysis, preceded by "The President then delivered the following dedicatory speech" and followed by "Three cheers were then given for the President and the Governors of the States." *Frank Leslie's Illustrated Newspaper* handled the text similarly, placing it deep inside the issue under the headline "The Gettysburg Celebration"—just after "To My Little Brother," a forgettable poem, and an article titled "A Japanese Legend."[53]

Contrary to what the scene in *Lincoln* depicts, soldiers seem to have manifested virtually no curiosity about Lincoln's words. Typical was Lieutenant Frank A. Haskell, a member of Brigadier General John Gibbon's staff, who attended the program on November 19. The author of a famous account of the battle written immediately after Lee retreated from Pennsylvania, Haskell tersely dismissed events at the dedication in a letter to his brother on November 20: "We had little interest in the ceremonies, and I shall not attempt to describe them." A Pennsylvania sergeant, like Haskell present on November 19, pronounced Everett's speech "elegant" but said nothing about Lincoln's.[54]

Senator Charles Sumner of Massachusetts offered a retrospective judgment about the importance of the Gettysburg Address in a eulogy delivered in Boston on June 1, 1865. He applauded how the president had given his life to make good on the promise of the Declaration of Independence. The speech "uttered at the field of Gettysburg, and now sanctified by the martyrdom of its author, is a monumental act. . . . The world noted at once what he said, and will never cease to remember it."[55]

Sumner was only partly correct—the world had not taken much notice in late 1863. But United States victory in the war, the accomplishment of emancipation as part of that victory, and Lincoln's assassination and civic apotheosis all helped elevate the speech to a position that stands out boldly, if anachronistically, in Spielberg's *Lincoln*.

ENVIRONMENTAL SHOCKS

By the summer of 1863, the war's profound impact on environmental resources stood out across much of the Confederacy and in loyal states subject to military activity. The mere presence of an army disrupted natural patterns and agricultural rhythms. Wherever an army camped for any length of time, thousands of campfires resulted in the destruction of many acres of woods and forests, substituting moonscapes for previously lush vegetation. Even one night's appearance by an army, whether friendly or hostile, could bring the loss of a farm's fencing, crops, and animals. As the war progressed, much of the Confederacy's heartland experienced catastrophic damage from armies

"Stripping a rail fence for fires." Alfred R. Waud's sketch depicts how the presence of soldiers from either army, even for a single day or night, could cause serious damage on farms. (Library of Congress, Prints and Photographs Division, LC-DIG-ppmsca-21020.)

bent on destruction or simply seeking food and fodder for soldiers, as well as for the thousands of horses and mules that labored alongside them. When armies went into winter quarters, the environmental dislocation escalated in any area within reach of troops seeking firewood, building materials for huts, food, and other materials.

William Tecumseh Sherman and Philip H. Sheridan most often come to mind when considering how armies wreaked havoc on Confederate agriculture and the animals and structures that supported it. "I have destroyed over 2,000 barns filled with wheat, hay and farming implements," Sheridan famously reported from the Shenandoah Valley in 1864, "over 70 mills, filled with flour and wheat; have driven in front of the army over 4,000 head of stock, and have killed and issued to the troops not less than 3,000 sheep."

Sherman spoke more concisely in a letter to his wife near the outset of the Atlanta campaign: "We have devoured the land and our animals eat up the wheat & corn fields."[56]

Three witnesses provide testimony about the environmental changes wrought long before Sherman's and Sheridan's operations. In late June 1863, a British officer named Arthur James Lyon Fremantle traveled through central Virginia with Lee's army and wrote about the countryside around Sperryville, a village near the eastern slope of the Blue Ridge Mountains. The nearby presence of two armies for more than a year—there had been no battle in the area—left the region "completely cleaned out." Many acres lay "almost uncultivated, and no animals are grazing where there used to be hundreds. All fences have been destroyed, and numberless farms burnt, chimneys alone left standing." Fremantle concluded, "It is difficult to depict and impossible to exaggerate the sufferings which this part of Virginia has undergone." Two Union accounts demonstrate that Middle Tennessee presented a comparably bleak picture. Known in the prewar years for its agricultural bounty, the region had been overrun by Federal armies in 1862 and subjected to intense foraging. "This is a dreary, desolate, barren and deserted looking country," stated an officer, well before the midpoint of the war. A cavalryman, writing in April 1863, adopted language similar to Fremantle's: "It is really sad to see this beautiful country here so ruined. There are no fences left at all. There is no corn and hay for the cattle and horses, but there are no horses left anyhow and the planters have no food for themselves."[57]

The cavalryman in Tennessee would have been particularly alert to the absence of horses. The contending sides probably used close to 1,100,000 horses and 750,000 mules—for the cavalry and artillery, to pull supply wagons and ambulances, and to support construction or repair projects associated with campaigning. Losses among horses and mules cannot be determined with precision, but they were terrible. Diseases swept through horse depots and armies, and the plague of equine glanders claimed tens of thousands of victims. In the fall of 1863, the Army of the Cumberland alone, while besieged in Chattanooga, lost ten thousand animals dead or so disabled they could no longer work. The following spring, Union armies ordered that all livestock abandoned on the march should be shot to prevent Rebels from capturing and returning them to service. Charles Francis Adams Jr., a Union cavalryman whose great-grandfather and grandfather had been presidents of the United

States and whose father was minister to the Court of Saint James (ambassador to Great Britain, in modern parlance), spoke to how horses suffered. "The air of Virginia is literally burdened today with the stench of dead horses, federal and confederate," he informed his mother in May 1863. "You pass them on every road and find them in every field, while from their carrions you can follow the march of every army that moves."[58]

The built environment inevitably bore the marks of military disruption. Private homes and outbuildings, as well as mills, factories, railroad facilities, and other structures more directly tied to the war efforts, suffered damage or destruction. Among the first was Judith Henry's modest home on the battlefield of First Bull Run, which stood near the center of combat on July 21, 1861, and by the summer of 1862 had been reduced to a crumbling chimney and fragments of wood framing. Fredericksburg, Charleston, Petersburg, Vicksburg, Atlanta, and other Confederate towns and cities endured artillery bombardments that left many dwellings in ruins. North of the Potomac River, Confederate cavalry torched hundreds of structures in Chambersburg, Pennsylvania, on July 30, 1864. *Harper's Weekly* published several engravings of

Fredericksburg, Virginia, from Stafford Heights on the left bank of the Rappahannock River, February 1863. Before the midpoint of the war, Fredericksburg already showed the effects of a long-term presence of more than 125,000 Union soldiers. Ruins of the Richmond, Fredericksburg & Potomac Railroad bridge and ground stripped of vegetation along the riverfront dominate this view, taken a short way upstream from George Washington's birthplace. (Library of Congress, Prints and Photographs Division, LC-DIG-ppmsca-35083.)

the destruction and reported that Chambersburg's "burned district covers all the business portion of the town and some of the finest private residences."[59] Guerrilla depredations in every military theater took a toll on private as well as public buildings and other property, most notoriously when Confederates under William C. Quantrill sacked Lawrence, Kansas, in August 1863.

A visitor to Fredericksburg, Virginia, in late 1864 captured the degree to which a protracted military presence transformed many areas. By that time, the Army of the Potomac and the Army of Northern Virginia had waged four huge battles within a few miles of Fredericksburg, and many smaller actions and periods of Union occupation had further affected the local population and environment. The visitor noted that "few trees remain upon the hills . . . [and] not a fence nor an inhabited house. . . . The rich plains bear no crops now but crops of luxuriant weeds. . . . There are no hands at work in the fenceless fields—no signs of animated life about the deserted houses." Around Fredericksburg, he summed up, "All is still as death for miles and miles under the sweet and autumnal sun."[60] That person could not know that Fredericksburg, whose residents, white and black, were buffeted by the war, would not return to its 1860 population until 1900.

II

GENERALS AND BATTLES

The success of the Century Company's *Battles and Leaders of the Civil War* in the 1880s foreshadowed the perennial interest those aspects of the conflict have inspired. These fifteen essays focus on important commanders, seven Union and five Confederate, during the war and in long-running debates about performance and reputations. Essays on Ulysses S. Grant and on his partnership with William Tecumseh Sherman lead off, followed by a pair on Robert E. Lee's generalship and struggles with conflicting loyalties, one on the complicated relationship between Lee and Joseph E. Johnston, and a fourth assessing attrition among top officers in the Army of Northern Virginia. George B. McClellan, behind only Grant and perhaps Sherman in terms of Union generals' impact on the war, follows next, after which come essays on James Longstreet in memory, Stonewall Jackson's importance to the Confederate people, and Jackson and Jubal A. Early as commanders in the Shenandoah Valley. The section devoted to leadership concludes with essays on Philip H. Sheridan in the Shenandoah Valley, George G. Meade's awkward role as commander of the Army of the Potomac, and John F. Reynolds and John Sedgwick as examples of how a dramatic death can affect reputation. Two campaign-centered essays round out this section, one on Henry H. Sibley's operations in New Mexico Territory in 1862 and one on Gettysburg as understood in the early twenty-first century.

TRACKING U. S. GRANT'S REPUTATION

Ulysses S. Grant's life and career dramatically illustrate the vagaries of historical memory. His imposing stature between the end of the Civil War and the early decades of the twentieth century cannot be disputed. Second only to Lincoln as a savior of the nation and praised by many former Confederates for his demeanor at Appomattox, he became the first four-star general in United States history before winning two terms as president. A courageous effort to complete his memoirs while battling terminal cancer further enhanced his reputation. More than a million spectators watched his funeral procession, which stretched for several miles through the streets of New York City on August 8, 1885. Twelve years later, the dedication of his tomb on Morningside Heights above the Hudson River also drew a million people, among them President William McKinley. Then and now the largest tomb in North America, it remained New York City's leading tourist site until the Great Depression. The national capital unveiled its memorial to Grant on April 27, 1922, the centenary of his birth. The third-largest equestrian statue in the world, it took more than twenty years to complete and occupies perhaps the most desirable site in the city—at the foot of Capitol Hill, facing down the Mall toward the Lincoln Memorial.

By the time of the statue's dedication in Washington, shrill criticisms of Grant as a military butcher, a drunk, and a president surrounded by corruption clouded his reputation. Many former Confederates had labored with great effect to diminish Grant's stature through the use of numbers and casualties. They insisted he had defeated Robert E. Lee only because of overwhelming advantages of men and matériel, casting him as a brutally effective officer who fed Union soldiers into a meat grinder until outnumbered Confederates capitulated. Jubal A. Early, a Confederate lieutenant general and leading Lost Cause controversialist, set the tone soon after the war, claiming that Grant

"General U. S. Grant Monument and Tomb, New York." Grant's tomb appeared on innumerable postcards, including this one mailed from New York City to Wilkes-Barre, Pennsylvania, in 1906. (Collection of Joan Waugh.)

"merely possessed the most ordinary brute courage, and had the control of unlimited numbers and means." "Shall I compare Lee to his successful antagonist?" asked Early. "As well compare the great pyramid which rears its majestic proportions in the valley of the Nile, to a pigmy perched on Mount Atlas." Winston Churchill seconded Early when he wrote, in *A History of the English-Speaking Peoples*, of Grant's "unflinching butchery" and insisted that "More is expected of the high command than determination in thrusting men to their doom."[1]

Other evidence suggests the degree to which Grant's reputation dropped throughout the twentieth century. William S. McFeely's Pulitzer Prize–winning *Grant: A Biography*, published in 1981 and highly influential for two decades, portrayed a man of "no organic, artistic, or intellectual specialness" who "became general and president because he could find nothing better to do."[2] Filmmakers in the late twentieth and early twenty-first centuries apparently concurred with McFeely's dubious conclusion that Grant lacked "specialness." Lee appeared prominently in *Gettysburg* (1993) and *Gods and Generals* (2003), but Grant enjoyed no comparable cinematic turn. He fared even less well in prints and sculptures marketed to Civil War enthusiasts. Advertisements in popular magazines devoted to the conflict reveal that between the 1960s and the early 2000s, readers could choose from nearly ten items devoted to Lee for every one depicting Grant.

Much like consumers in the Civil War art market, tourists selecting Civil War–related destinations have exhibited relatively little interest in Grant. His tomb fell into neglect by the early 1990s—defaced by graffiti, extensively vandalized, a gathering place for drug users. Descendants of the general threatened to remove his and Mrs. Grant's remains for reinterment elsewhere, which helped prod the National Park Service into making needed repairs. The tomb, partly refurbished, was rededicated on its centennial in 1997, but it remains to be seen whether visitation will climb to anything like its past high level.

There is a zero-sum dimension to many assessments of Grant and Lee as commanders, as if conceding ability to one somehow diminishes the other. Both were gifted generals whose martial talents place them among the greatest American soldiers. Both presided over campaigns that resulted in huge casualties—significantly more, as a percentage of his army's strength, in Lee's case. Indeed, the "Grant the Butcher" characterization simply does not stand up to scrutiny. In the five major operations he oversaw before facing Lee in 1864's Overland campaign (Belmont, Forts Henry and Donelson, Shiloh, Vicksburg, and Chattanooga), Grant's losses totaled roughly 35,000 killed, wounded, and missing. Lee's pre–Overland campaign losses (Seven Days, Second Bull Run, the Maryland campaign, Fredericksburg, Chancellorsville, and Gettysburg), in comparison, approached 90,000. In the Overland and Petersburg campaigns, when Federal armies outnumbered Confederates by about two to one, Grant suffered another 126,500 casualties to Lee's 71,000. With these numbers as a yardstick, Lee must be reckoned the bloodier general—in an absolute sense in the first years of the war and a relative sense during the 1864–1865 campaigns. I offer this observation not as a criticism of Lee (many historians have misused numbers to assail his generalship) but rather to counter the idea that Grant stood out among Civil War commanders as a callous butcher.

Grant's stock has gone up significantly in scholarly literature over the past twenty-five years. Largely favorable studies from Brooks D. Simpson, Jean Edward Smith, Josiah Bunting III, Joan Waugh, Ronald C. White, and, most recently, Ron Chernow reveal the shallowness of the virulently anti-Grant literature. And yet, as recently as 2004, a short biography, though virtually worthless in quality of research and soundness of argument, asserted that most Americans know only two things about Grant: "his reputation as a drinker" and "the fact that his portrait, with a glum, seedy, withdrawn, and slightly guilty expression, like that of a man with a bad hangover, . . . is on the fifty-dollar bill."[3]

Long-term change will come only when the best new scholarship makes its way into popular conceptions of Grant. Only then will there be a chance for the hero of Vicksburg and Appomattox to resume his place among the most celebrated and attractive figures in United States history.[4]

THE SUPREME PARTNERSHIP

Ulysses S. Grant and William Tecumseh Sherman formed the most important and successful military partnership of the Civil War. As general in chief of United States armies and commander of what would now be called an army group, Grant and Sherman worked on a larger canvass than R. E. Lee and Stonewall Jackson—the Confederacy's preeminent team—and proved indispensable to saving the Union. Both Ohio-born leaders had experienced personal and professional setbacks during the antebellum years, but during the Civil War they discovered they could rely on each other. Abraham Lincoln and the loyal citizenry of the United States relied on them as well. As the president explained in March 1864, Grant's elevation to lieutenant general represented the "nation's appreciation of what you have done and its reliance upon you for what remains to do in the existing great struggle . . . I scarcely need to add that with what I here speak for the nation goes my own hearty personal concurrence." A newspaper account of the Grand Review in Washington at the close of the war captured the pervasive opinion across the North that Grant's and Sherman's veterans, more than 150,000 of whom had marched down Pennsylvania Avenue, "are the champions of free governments" who "have saved the world as they have saved the Union."[5]

Success during the war did not come immediately—especially for Sherman. He failed as an independent commander in late 1861, magnifying Rebel threats and suffering a crippling loss of confidence. On January 1, 1862, he confessed to his wife that "the idea of having brought disgrace on all associated with me is so horrible to contemplate that I cannot really endure it."

Only subsequent service under Grant retrieved his reputation. The mercurial Sherman, who never underestimated his own intelligence and talents, readily acknowledged Grant's dominant position in the relationship. "I am a damned sight smarter than Grant," he told James Harrison Wilson in 1864. "I know a great deal more about war, military history, strategy, and grand tactics than he does; I know more about organization, supply and administration and about everything else than he does; but I'll tell you where he beats me and where he beats the world. He don't care a damn for what the enemy does out of his sight but it scares me like hell!"[6]

Sherman's assessment got to the heart of Grant's greatness—steady confidence, imperturbable will, and tenacity that, together with a willingness to shoulder ultimate responsibility, provided a calming framework within which Sherman thrived. Grant grasped his friend's strong points from the outset, writing to his wife in January 1865, "I am glad to say that I appreciated Sherman from the first feeling him to be what he has proven to the world he is." The two men developed unshakable trust in each other. "I knew wherever I was that you thought of me," Sherman wrote Grant, in reference to their 1862–1863 campaigns, "and if I got in a tight place you would come if alive."[7]

They fought together from the spring of 1862 until the end, directing storied campaigns in the Western and Eastern theaters and presiding over the surrenders of the two principal Rebel armies in April 1865. Grant learned to allow his lieutenant wide latitude and praised him often. When Sherman's critics suggested the idea for the March to the Sea had originated with others, for example, Grant settled the matter with one sentence in his *Personal Memoirs*: "The question of who devised the plan of march from Atlanta to Savannah is easily answered: it was clearly Sherman, and to him also belongs the credit for its brilliant execution." For his part, Sherman recognized in Grant a rare ability to draw the best from lieutenants. "General Grant possesses in an eminent degree that peculiar & high attribute of using various men to produce a Common result," he observed in late summer 1863, "and now that his Character is well established we can easily subordinate ourselves to him with the absolute assurance of serving the Common Cause of our Country."[8]

Both men wrote memorable accounts of the war. The two thick volumes of *Personal Memoirs of U.S. Grant* reveal the strategic vision, willingness to experiment, and daring that brought success at Vicksburg, in Chattanooga, and finally against Lee in Virginia. Grant's tribute to Zachary Taylor helps illuminate his own success: "General Taylor was not an officer to trouble the administration much with his demands, but was inclined to do the best he could with the means given him. . . . No soldier could face either danger or responsibility more calmly than he. These are qualities more rarely found than genius or physical courage." Similarities between Grant and "Old Rough and Ready" also impressed Sherman, who wrote during the Vicksburg campaign, "Grant is as honest as old Zack Taylor."[9]

Grant and Sherman agreed that victory required laying a hard hand on Confederate civilians as well as defeating Rebel armies. Grant's orders to Sherman following the fall of Atlanta allowed Federals to live off the land to a considerable extent. "You will, no doubt, clean the country where you go of railroad tracks and supplies," instructed Grant, as his lieutenant prepared to strike toward Savannah. "I would also move every wagon, horse, mule, and hoof of stock, as well as the negroes." As often was the case, Sherman deployed more colorful language to make a similar point. He intended to persuade Confederate civilians that their government was helpless to defend them, and possible accusations of brutality would not dissuade him. "If the people raise a howl against my barbarity & cruelty," he stated, after ordering civilians to evacuate Atlanta, "I will answer that War is War, & not popularity seeking."[10]

No artist ever produced a painting of Grant and Sherman that achieved the iconic status of E. B. D. Julio's *The Last Meeting of Lee and Jackson,* an engraving of which hung in countless southern homes following Appomattox and kept alive the pair's reputation as Confederate paladins. But few who celebrated the United States' victory in the conflict needed such an artistic reminder of the Union's transcendent military partnership. The nation stood as Grant's and Sherman's imperishable monument, a restored republic for which they, more than anyone else but Abraham Lincoln, could claim credit.

R. E. LEE AS A GENERAL

Robert E. Lee has occupied a remarkable position in the American memory of the Civil War. Few people in April 1865, whether in the Confederacy or the

United States, would have predicted his rise to national popularity. Leaders in failed civil wars typically suffer drastic consequences, but by the early twentieth century Lee stood alongside Abraham Lincoln as one of the conflict's two most beloved figures. His towering reputation among ex-Rebels made sense. His acceptance throughout the rest of the United States was more surprising. Lee has appeared on six United States postage stamps—most recently in 2015. Arlington House was designated the Lee Mansion National Memorial by Congress in 1925. Nine years later, President Franklin D. Roosevelt captured the prevailing sentiment about Lee. "All over the United States of America we regard him as a great leader of men and a great General," Roosevelt told a crowd in Dallas, adding, "I believe that we recognize him as something even more important than that. We recognize Robert E. Lee as one of the greatest American Christians and one of our greatest American gentlemen."[11]

The trajectory of Lee's reputation through much of the twentieth century offers an interesting contrast to that of Ulysses S. Grant's. As Grant increasingly suffered caricature as a drunk, a butcher, and a corrupt politician, Lee remained widely admired as a brilliant Christian soldier who accepted defeat gracefully and called for postwar reconciliation. As I noted in my essay on Grant, Lee's aggressive generalship yielded horrific casualties; indeed, he must be reckoned the bloodiest general in United States history if measured by the percentage of his men killed or disabled. Yet, unlike Grant, he suffered no loss of reputation among his contemporaries as a consequence. Confederates mourned the thousands of soldiers killed or maimed while serving under Lee, but they directed little criticism toward him. A British visitor to Richmond in March 1865 surely spoke the truth when he described Lee as "the idol of his soldiers & the Hope of His Country" who inspired an "almost fanatical belief in his judgement & capacity."[12]

The harshest critiques of Lee as a bloody commander came in the late twentieth century. Thomas L. Connelly's *The Marble Man: Robert E. Lee and His Image in American Society* (1977) and, more especially, Alan T. Nolan's *Lee Considered: General Robert E. Lee and Civil War History* (1991) emphasized high casualties in the Army of Northern Virginia. Nolan argued that offensive tactics and strategy hurt morale within the army and undermined the Confederacy's national military effort. Lee's critics sometimes point to the defensive victory at Fredericksburg as a model he should have followed, rather than pressing the tactical offensive at the Seven Days, Chancellorsville, Gettysburg, and elsewhere (though how anyone hoping to replicate the victory at Fredericksburg could guarantee a supply of minimally gifted opponents such as Ambrose E. Burnside goes unaddressed).

No one can dispute the costly nature of Lee's generalship or the fact that he sometimes made questionable military decisions. The attacks at Malvern Hill and on the third day at Gettysburg, the decision to fight at Antietam, and other episodes invite criticism. If examined without reference to how his operations influenced Confederate and Union politics and morale, Lee's mistakes and massive casualties can be interpreted as evidence of a decidedly mixed record.

The fundamental question should be whether Lee's leadership yielded a good return on the high investment of Confederate blood. Here we must look beyond numbers killed and wounded and ground lost or won to examine the Confederate home front and morale in the Army of Northern Virginia. With the exception of Fredericksburg, Lee's operations between June 1862 and May 1863 included offensive strategic and tactical components and per-suaded the Confederate people that their largest army was dictating the action rather than merely waiting for Union forces to strike. Civilians applauded Lee's efforts and increasingly saw him as their equivalent of George Washington during the American Revolution. By the midpoint of the war, Lee and his army had become the most important national institution in the Confederacy.

Within his army, Lee's daring leadership helped forge an unshakable bond with the men. Wartime writings by Lee's soldiers betray remarkable devotion to their general. Lee experienced a typical reaction at a review of James Long-street's First Corps in April 1864. "As he rode up to the colors, and the men caught sight of his well known figure," reported one witness two days after the event, "a wild and prolonged cheer, fraught with a feeling that thrilled all hearts, ran along the lines and rose to the heavens. . . . Many persons became almost frantic with emotion."[13]

It is worth noting that most defensive campaigns also failed to conserve Confederate manpower. Not counting surrendered troops at places such as Vicksburg (whose numbers dramatically increased the defender's losses, a phenomenon seldom noted by scholars critical of Lee's offensive tendencies), strategically defensive campaigns often resulted in roughly equal casualties on both sides. The reason was simple. Generals on the defensive usually had to attack in order to avoid a siege, and their tactical counteroffensives seldom occurred under favorable conditions. Joseph E. Johnston's retreat up the Virginia Peninsula in 1862 offers a case in point. While falling back toward the Confederate capital, Johnston fought a delaying action at Williamsburg and later, with his back against Richmond, launched a clumsy tactical offensive at Seven Pines. Confederate casualties approached eight thousand for the campaign while Union losses fell short of 7,500.

Far from pursuing a strategy that shortened the Confederacy's life, Lee crafted victories in 1862 and 1863 that convinced a majority of his people that independence could come as long as the Army of Northern Virginia remained in the field. That belief held firm until the last stages of the war and, more than any other factor, explains why Confederates fought as long and as hard as they did. For Lee, as with Grant, numbers should not be the principal yardstick by which we judge their actions and establish their historical reputations.

ROBERT E. LEE'S MULTIPLE LOYALTIES

Robert E. Lee's decision to leave the United States Army and cast his lot with Virginia has inspired a great deal of examination by historians and others. The most influential writer has been Douglas Southall Freeman, whose four-volume *R. E. Lee: A Biography* (1934–1936) remains by far the most detailed reckoning of Lee's life. Freeman described Lee's decision in a chapter titled "The Answer He Was Born to Make," which argued that anyone hoping to understand Lee need only know that Virginia always remained paramount in his thinking. This idea has made its way into the broader world of people interested in the Civil War, manifesting itself in such disparate places as the film *Gods and Generals*, which portrays Lee as preeminently a Virginian, and the work of historians who insist that Lee's strategic vision during the Civil War suffered from a fixation on Virginia.

Lee's loyalty to Virginia is beyond question. In the critical period between April 19 and April 22, 1861, I believe it *was* the most important of his loyalties. Letters to Winfield Scott, his sister Anne, and his brother Smith written on

April 20, the day he resigned from the United States Army, emphasized that he could not retain a position that might require him to engage in coercion against his native state. Yet, while devotion to Virginia likely explains Lee's decision to resign and to accept command of the state's forces two days later, other powerful allegiances must be considered in assessing his life and actions.

Lee undoubtedly possessed a strong loyalty to the United States. Indeed, some might think, from his background, that Unionism would have pointed the way toward a different "answer he was born to make." His idol was George Washington, whose actions as general and president underscored a belief that the national whole transcended state and local interests. Lee's father, like Washington, was a Federalist. In 1798, "Light-Horse Harry" Lee had opposed the Virginia and Kentucky resolutions, with their strong claim for state power, arguing that the Constitution rested on support of the people and not the state governments.

Lee himself had rendered notable service to the republic in Mexico and as an engineer and superintendent of West Point. He also opposed secession during the winter of 1860/61, affirming to his sister, Anne, a "devotion to the Union" and "feeling of loyalty and duty of an American citizen." Earlier that year, in a letter to his son, William Henry Fitzhugh ("Rooney"), he insisted that the framers meant for the Union to be perpetual and pronounced it "idle to talk of secession." He lamented the possibility that Washington's "noble deeds [would] be destroyed and that his precious advice and virtuous example so soon forgotten by his countrymen."[14]

Lee also had a strong sense of being part of the slaveholding South—a regional attachment too often overlooked. In letters and comments addressing his decision to resign from the army, he mentioned the South as well as Virginia. His political philosophy stood strikingly at odds with the virulent rhetoric of secessionist Fire-Eaters, yet well before resigning he wrote to Rooney that the "South in my opinion has been aggrieved by the acts of the North. . . . I feel the aggression, & am willing to take every proper step for redress."[15]

Often portrayed as opposed to slavery, Lee in fact embraced the peculiar institution as the best means for ordering relations between the races and resented northern attacks against the motives and character of slaveholders. "There is no sacrifice I am not ready to make for the preservation of the Union," he averred in January 1861, "save that of honour." As a member of the slaveholding aristocracy of Virginia and the South, his sense of honor dictated that he stand with those of his blood, class, and section. He hated the idea of disunion but rejected the idea of a country "that can only be maintained by swords and bayonets"—precisely the scenario he imagined in the wake of Abraham Lincoln's call for 75,000 volunteers after the firing on Fort Sumter.[16]

Those who cling to the idea of Lee as preeminently devoted to his state must come to terms with a fourth important loyalty. Amid the stresses of war, Lee quickly and decisively adopted a national as opposed to a state-centered stance. His most important loyalty during the conflict was to the Confederate nation. From the opening of the conflict until the final scenes at Appomattox, he urged Confederate soldiers, politicians, and civilians to set aside state and local prejudices in their struggle to establish a new nation. This stance is especially noteworthy from a man who described himself in an early postwar interview as "a firm and honest believer in the doctrine of State rights."[17]

Lee articulated his views about the relative importance of state and national concerns in a letter to Andrew G. McGrath, South Carolina's secretary of state, in late December 1861. Though the war was only eight months old, Lee took the long view, turning his attention to the topic of subordinating state to nation. "The Confederate States have now but one great object in view," he explained to McGrath, "the successful issue of their war of independence. Everything worth their possessing depends on that. Everything should yield to its accomplishment."[18] During the ensuing years of war, Lee called for national conscription, supported government impressment of goods and enslaved labor, and otherwise betrayed a dominant national loyalty.

The full scale of the approaching war, and the demands it would make on the Confederate people, did not dominate Lee's thinking when he penned his letter of resignation on April 20, 1861. Virginia, the slaveholding South, and the pain of severing ties to a nation his father and other relatives had done a great deal to establish surely preoccupied him. But within a few weeks, his loyalties to Virginia and the slaveholding South began a transmutation into ardent Confederate purpose that marked the most important period of his life.

A ONE-SIDED FRIENDSHIP

In April 1870, Robert E. Lee and Joseph E. Johnston, both sixty-three years old, gray, and grizzled, sat for a photographer in Savannah, Georgia. Lee had about six months to live, Johnston nearly twenty-one years. In two of three poses from the session, Lee looks directly across a small table at the man he considered a nearly lifelong friend, while Johnston avoids eye contact by focusing on some papers next to Lee's hand. I always have believed these images to be very revealing about the two men. Lee engages Johnston forthrightly, as one would a friend; Johnston seems reluctant to reciprocate. Perhaps that was because Johnston had nourished a deep envy of Lee for years and worried that the truth might flicker across his eyes if he met Lee's directly.

The two men's careers intersected frequently. Both graduated from West Point in the class of 1829—Lee stood second and entered the engineers; Johnston ranked thirteenth and joined the Fourth Artillery. Both earned brevets for gallantry to major, lieutenant colonel, and colonel during the war with Mexico. Johnston was second in command of the Regiment of Voltigeurs during heavy fighting around Mexico City, and Lee served on Winfield Scott's staff. Lee ended his antebellum service as colonel of the First Cavalry, a line rank Johnston never achieved, though he was named brigadier general of the Quartermaster Corps in June 1860. When both joined the Confederate army in 1861, Lee ranked third among the full generals—behind Samuel Cooper and Albert Sidney Johnston—and Joseph Johnston was fourth.

His position junior to three other Confederate officers sent Johnston into a fury that poisoned his relationship with Jefferson Davis and affected his entire Confederate military service. Unable to rise above what he considered a professional slight, he seemed to relish every opportunity to revisit it. This preoccupation with rank surfaced long before 1861. In 1843, Lee noted his friend's concern for advancement. "Joe Johnston is playing Adjt. Genl. in Florida, to his heart's content," observed Lee with no hint of disapproval. "His plan is good, he is working for promotion. I hope he may succeed."[19]

Three years later, as Scott's remarkable campaign against Mexico City came to a close, Lee wrote about Johnston with humor and affection. Johnston had been wounded during the assaults against Chapultepec (he seemed to receive

R. E. Lee and Joseph E. Johnston, "From a Photograph Taken after the War." This full-page engraving of the photograph, published in *Battles and Leaders of the Civil War*, reached a very large audience. (Robert Underwood Johnson and Clarence Clough Buel, eds., *Battles and Leaders of the Civil War*, 4 vols. [New York: Century, 1887–88], vol. 1, p. 228.)

wounds on almost every battlefield, noted Scott), and Lee described his friend as "fat ruddy & hearty." "I think a little lead, properly taken is good for a man," he suggested playfully. "I am truly thankful however that I escaped all internal doses, & only re[ceive]d some external bruises, contusions & cuts."[20]

Although Lee regretted assignment to desk duty as head of Virginia's state forces early in the Civil War, he applauded Johnston's successes in the field. In the wake of First Bull Run, where Johnston and P. G. T. Beauregard shared highest Confederate honors, Lee hastened to congratulate his friend. "I almost wept for joy," he wrote Johnston on July 24, 1861, "at the glorious victory achieved by our brave troops on the 21st & the feelings of my heart could hardly be expressed on learning the brilliant share you had in its achievement."[21]

Johnston never managed to muster equivalent generosity of spirit regarding Lee. Serendipity in the form of a Federal artillery round at the battle of Seven Pines on May 31, 1862, cost Johnston command of the army defending Richmond and elevated Lee to the position in which he would become the most famous and important Confederate. As Lee led the Army of Northern Virginia to a series of victories in 1862 and 1863, Johnston recuperated and eventually ended up in the Western Theater, whence he found opportunities to deprecate his friend's accomplishments in the East. Although no evidence proves that Lee knew the depth of "Old Joe's" bitterness toward him, others surely did, including Robert Garlick Hill Kean, who monitored and commented on many aspects of Confederate military affairs from his position in the Bureau of War in Richmond. On April 12, 1863, Kean wrote of both Johnston's obsession with rank and antipathy toward Lee: "He is a *very little man*, has achieved nothing, full of himself, [and] above all other things, eaten up with morbid jealousy of Lee and of all his superiors in position, rank, or glory."[22]

Johnston's *Narrative of Military Operations, Directed, During the Late War Between the States, by Joseph E. Johnston, General, C.S.A.* betrays an animus toward Lee. In defending his Fabian strategy against William Tecumseh Sherman during the Atlanta campaign, Johnston manifested sarcasm and envy regarding Jefferson Davis and Lee. "I supposed that my course would not be disapproved by him [Jefferson Davis]," observed Johnston archly, "especially as General Lee, by keeping on the defensive, and falling back toward Grant's objective point, under circumstances like mine, was increasing his great fame."[23]

No source better illustrates Johnston's attitude toward Lee than Robert M. Hughes's *General Johnston*. The work of the general's approved biographer, this book not surprisingly praises its subject. Sensitive to the fact that Johnston's retreats and failure to win dramatic victories had elicited criticism from the Confederate people, Hughes reflects some of Johnston's attitude toward Lee in a passage that combines distortion and mean-spiritedness: "With the general public, during and since the war, the commander whose lot it was to organize armies for others and relinquish their leadership just as they became veterans who could win Fredericksburgs and Chancellorsvilles, obtains but little credit. The public imagination must be inflamed by the brilliancy of actual combat, and thinks little of the strategy which secures equal results without bloodshed, except to ridicule and condemn it."[24]

Hughes got one thing right: many Confederates deplored Johnston's penchant for retreating. As one young South Carolina woman wrote in 1865, "The last news from Johnston was that he retreated to Raleigh. This arch-retreater will probably retreat till perhaps he retreats to Gen. Lee, who may put a stop to this retrograde movement."[25] Such unflattering comparisons to Lee during and after the war proved particularly galling to Johnston. I wonder if, as the old men sat opposite one another in Savannah and the photographer arranged his shot, years of imagined unfairness weighed on Johnston's mind.

ATTRITION IN LEE'S HIGH COMMAND

Stonewall Jackson's wounding at Chancellorsville on May 2, 1863, represents the most famous example of attrition among officers in the Army of Northern Virginia. Robert E. Lee treated the passing of his famous lieutenant as a calamity. "You will have heard of the death of General Jackson," he wrote to his son Custis shortly after the battle. "It is a terrible loss. I do not know how to replace him." Many historians have argued that the event shaped the war's outcome. Robert K. Krick, an eminent chronicler of Lee's army, held nothing back when he described the shots that felled Jackson as "the smoothbore volley that doomed the Confederacy."[26] Untold admirers of "Old Jack" implicitly have seconded Krick's opinion by endlessly raising the unanswerable question, "What if Jackson had been at Gettysburg?"

Although Jackson's death must be reckoned a heavy blow, his presence at Gettysburg might have made no difference. Similarly, his continued service in the Army of Northern Virginia might not have appreciably affected a conflict that dragged on for nearly two more bloody years. Still, it is beyond dispute that Lee never found an adequate replacement for Jackson, though Jubal A. Early, who assumed command of the Second Corps in late May 1864, showed considerable aptitude for semi-independent operations and conducted a campaign in the Shenandoah Valley that in many ways compared favorably with Jackson's fabled operations there in 1862.

Whatever its full impact, Jackson's death should be framed as symptomatic of the larger phenomenon of casualties among generals in the Army of Northern Virginia. Losses sometimes exceeded 25 to 30 percent in a single campaign, and the search to find replacements occupied much of Lee's attention. More than two dozen brigadier generals were killed or mortally wounded during Lee's tenure, and some of the army's most accomplished or promising major generals—among them William Dorsey Pender, Robert E. Rodes, and Stephen Dodson Ramseur—joined that grisly list.

The top echelon of subordinate leaders also suffered heavily. Indeed, stable and successful performances among Lee's principal lieutenants occurred only between the reorganization of the army after the Seven Days and the Chancellorsville campaign. For those nine and one half months, James Longstreet (always Lee's senior subordinate) led the army's Right Wing and then the First Corps, Jackson the Left Wing and then the Second Corps, and "Jeb" Stuart the cavalry. Lee used each of these gifted soldiers well, making the most of their disparate talents, granting wide latitude, and reaping strategic and tactical benefits on a number of storied battlefields.

That fruitful period ended with the Pennsylvania campaign of June and July 1863. After Chancellorsville, Lee's second major reorganization of his army's high command required three rather than two corps commanders for the infantry and left Stuart in charge of the mounted arm. Longstreet retained the First Corps, Richard S. Ewell took over a smaller Second Corps, and Ambrose Powell Hill headed the new Third Corps. All four of these men, together with Lee, exhibited weaknesses during the Gettysburg campaign, and neither Ewell nor Hill gave evidence of real aptitude for directing a corps. Although the months between Gettysburg and the opening of the Overland campaign in May 1864 witnessed little action in Virginia, both Hill and Ewell suffered further lapses that deepened Lee's concerns about their fitness for corps-level responsibility.

The maelstrom of the Overland campaign proved catastrophic for the army's high command. More than a third of all general officers became casualties during six weeks of unrelenting combat, and the corps structure rapidly fractured. On May 6, just two days into the campaign, Longstreet received a wound that probably would have killed a less hardy man. While seeking to maintain offensive momentum along the Plank Road, he came under fire from some of his own troops in an incident eerily reminiscent of what had befallen Jackson almost exactly one year earlier and just a few miles away. A staff officer noted "the sadness in [Lee's] face, and the almost despairing movement of his hands when he was told that Longstreet had fallen."[27] Six days later, Stuart succumbed to a wound in the stomach from action at Yellow Tavern. Hill and Ewell each failed at critical moments, forcing Lee to intervene directly in the action on May 6 at the Widow Tapp farm in the Wilderness and on May 12 in the Mule Shoe at Spotsylvania—resulting in the two most famous "Lee to the rear" episodes. Hill's health also proved to be serious a problem.

The crisis of command in May and June 1864 far exceeded that which followed Jackson's death. The structure instituted after the Seven Days lasted until Chancellorsville, and that created in May 1863 continued for more than a year. In contrast, the roster of top lieutenants present on May 5, 1864, the first day of the Wilderness, changed drastically within a single month. The effect of an unraveling high command stood out starkly at the North Anna River in late May. U. S. Grant maneuvered his Union forces into awkward positions on both sides of the river. Lee recognized his opponent's vulnerability but could do nothing about it. Confined to his cot by illness, he trusted none of his corps commanders to oversee attacks. In 1863, Jackson or Longstreet could have handled the duty; a bit later, Lee might have assigned Early the responsibility. But in late May, with Longstreet absent and both Ewell and Hill bitter disappointments, Lee watched helplessly as the opening passed.

By the middle of June, when the armies settled into a siege at Petersburg, new officers led three of the four corps (counting the Cavalry Corps) and a third of the divisions in the army. Losses among brigadiers and field grade officers had been catastrophic. Ironically, the siege operations Lee feared above all other things represented the best hope to manage an army with dwindling resource of command. The sheltering works at Petersburg would ameliorate errors in judgment that might have proved more disruptive in the open field.

LITTLE MAC

George Brinton McClellan invites markedly contradictory assessments of his personality and career. One of the more controversial figures of the Civil War, he has admirers and detractors in profusion. Book titles reflect the striking contrast of opinions. In 1957, Warren W. Hassler published *General George B. McClellan: Shield of the Union,* an appreciative treatment that portrayed its subject as "not only a most able organizer, drillmaster, and disciplinarian" but also "a soldier of superior strategic and tactical ability as compared with many of the other prominent generals on both sides." In contrast, fifty years later Edward H. Bonekemper III offered *McClellan and Failure: A Study of Civil War Fear, Incompetence and Worse,* which suggested that "Little Mac" "has not yet received the ignominy that he so richly deserves."[28] Careful studies by Stephen W. Sears, Joseph L. Harsh, and Ethan S. Rafuse have occupied more moderate interpretive ground, conveying the complexity of the thirty-five-year-old officer who found himself general in chief of all United States armies and commander of the republic's largest and most important field force in the autumn of 1861.

McClellan's actions and statements pose daunting obstacles to anyone hoping to reach unbiased conclusions. He repeatedly manifested scorn for his commander in chief, refused to accord Winfield Scott—a soldier far McClellan's superior in every way—the respect he deserved, and exhibited unlovely ambition, narcissism, and lack of self-awareness in quite stunning proportion. All these qualities were on display in the wake of Antietam, a hard-won victory that could have been much more decisive had McClellan proved willing to risk anything in pursuit of a much smaller and badly mauled Army of Northern Virginia.

Three days after the battle, McClellan sent a most revealing letter to his wife. "I feel some little pride," he wrote with self-congratulatory understatement, "in having with a beaten and demoralized army defeated Lee so utterly, & saved the North so completely." He then turned to characteristic whining about how others failed to appreciate his earlier service: "Well—one of these days history will I trust do me justice in deciding that it was not my fault that the campaign of the Peninsula was not successful." As for the future, only recognition of his superior talents would redeem the republic. "The only safety for the country & for me" would be in getting rid of General in Chief Henry W. Halleck and Secretary of War Edwin M. Stanton. "I am tired of fighting against such disadvantages," he said in his best martyr's tone, "& feel that it is now time for the country to come to my help, & remove these difficulties from my path. . . . Thank Heaven for one thing—my military reputation is cleared—I have shown that I can fight battles & *win* them! I think my enemies are pretty effectively killed by this time! May they remain so!!"[29]

The war, it seems from reading many such letters from McClellan's pen, was really about allowing the long-suffering hero to win the war despite tormentors in the Lincoln administration and in the army's hierarchy. The general would take comfort in knowing that some twenty-first-century authors and denizens of social media sites, quick to defend him against what they describe as small-minded critics, match his own soaring flights of self-congratulatory rhetoric untethered to any reasonable assessment of historical evidence.

Yet it must be admitted that McClellan possessed formidable talents, rendered superior service to the nation, and earned his soldiers' love. He built the nation's most important army from the wreckage of green units that lost the battle of First Bull Run, instilling a sense of pride in the men who would contest more of the conflict's bloody battles than any other U.S. forces. That he also compromised the Army of the Potomac's performance by creating a culture of caution that persisted even after the advent of U. S. Grant in the spring of 1864 should not diminish McClellan's good work in the summer and fall of 1861.

The incredible bond between McClellan and his soldiers has always fascinated me. Only that between Lee and his soldiers exceeded it, I believe, and in the Army of Northern Virginia's case there was the variable of multiple victories against long odds, which McClellan's relationship with his men lacked. Why did officers and men in the Army of the Potomac embrace their young commander enthusiastically and maintain their affection for so long? A crucial factor lay in a shared vision of the war's overarching purpose. First to last, McClellan and the soldiers waged a war to smash the rebellion, restore the Union, and protect it from future internal threats such as that posed by secession crisis of 1860 to 1861.

The famous Harrison's Landing letter that McClellan handed to Abraham Lincoln in July 1862 underscores this point. Dated July 7, 1862, it has provoked a good deal of criticism of McClellan because it seems to highlight his penchant for addressing political questions when he should have been smiting the Rebels militarily. After retreating unnecessarily following the battle of Malvern Hill, runs a common argument, McClellan sought to divert attention from his military failures by lecturing Lincoln on the issue of emancipation. The letter called for a restrained war that did not seek to destroy the slavery-based social structure of the Confederate states. "Military power should not be allowed to interfere with the relations of servitude," argued McClellan, "either by supporting or impairing the authority of the master; except for repressing disorder as in other cases." War should be waged for the sole purpose of restoring the Union—adding emancipation to the equation would be harmful. "A declaration of radical views," insisted McClellan, "especially upon slavery, will rapidly disintegrate our present Armies."[30]

Although McClellan exaggerated the degree to which emancipation would weaken the nation's armies, he correctly gauged the sentiment of the vast majority of Federal soldiers—in July 1862 and throughout the conflict. The alignment of general and rank-and-file regarding the centrality of Union helps explain their remarkable bond. As McClellan noted in his farewell order to the Army of the Potomac, "We shall also ever be comrades in supporting the Constitution of our country & the nationality of our people."[31]

HOW LEE'S "OLD WAR-HORSE" GAINED A NEW FOLLOWING

Two dramatic scenes stand out in James Longstreet's Confederate career. The first occurred on the evening of September 17, 1862, after a day of ghastly combat at Antietam that almost shattered the Army of Northern Virginia.

Upon seeing Longstreet, R. E. Lee, who earlier had described his senior lieutenant as "the staff in my right hand," extended a warm greeting. "Ah! here is Longstreet," he said with evident relief that "Old Pete" appeared unhurt after the day's carnage, "here's my old *war-horse*."[32]

That affectionate nickname stuck to Longstreet, who on the afternoon of July 3, 1863, found himself in the second of the two scenes. As Confederate infantrymen arrayed along Seminary Ridge awaited orders to advance, he met with Colonel Edward Porter Alexander, who oversaw Rebel batteries that had been firing at Federals along Cemetery Ridge. Manifestly upset, Longstreet spoke to his talented young artillerist, with slight pauses between each statement: "I don't want to make this attack—I believe it will fail—I do not see how it can succeed—I would not make it even now, but that Gen. Lee has ordered & expects it."[33] Soon the Confederate brigades advanced in what became the most famous assault in American history.

Longstreet ended the war as a widely admired general who deserved a position alongside Stonewall Jackson as one of the two best Confederate corps commanders. That reputation soon underwent a drastic change. Unlike most former Confederates, Longstreet criticized Lee publicly, embraced reconciliation quickly and wholeheartedly, and became a Republican. Reaction across much of the South, swift and furious, cast him as a traitor to his old chief and to all who had fought for the short-lived slaveholding republic. Jubal A. Early led the way among the first wave of detractors, establishing a tradition followed by John B. Gordon and several generations of later critics. Longstreet had failed Lee at Gettysburg, these writers argued, proved a balky subordinate on other fields, and lied about events and comrades in his memoirs, titled *From Manassas to Appomattox* and published in 1896, and in other postwar publications.

Longstreet defended himself but proved no match for his tormentors. Although he remained popular among veterans of his First Corps, he finished his life as a pariah in the South. Hundreds of monuments soon sprouted across the southern landscape, many of them honoring soldiers far less important and accomplished than Longstreet, but none honored Lee's "old war-horse."

That changed in the summer of 1998, when supporters dedicated an equestrian statue on Seminary Ridge at Gettysburg. Far from an artistic success in the minds of many, the statue nonetheless announced Longstreet's official rescue from perdition within the world of Civil War memory.

Favorable treatment in Ron Maxwell's film *Gettysburg* undoubtedly boosted support for the General Longstreet Memorial Fund, which raised money through the 1990s to commission this statue by artist Gary Casteel. Located on Seminary Ridge and dedicated in July 1998, the statue features a larger-than-life Longstreet on a somewhat oddly proportioned "Hero," the general's horse. Some visitors treat the statue as a shrine to Longstreet, placing coins in Hero's upturned left-front hoof and small Confederate flags at the base. (Copyright Chris Heisey, reproduced with permission.)

Several forces came together to bring this turnaround. Longstreet's admirers, some of whom rallied in support of the statue under the slogan "It's About Time," had long faced a difficult task. Biographers such as Hamilton J. Eckenrode and Bryan Conrad, whose *James Longstreet: Lee's War Horse* (1936) remained the standard work for many years, had been very harsh. No historian had hurt Longstreet more than Douglas Southall Freeman. In his Pulitzer Prize–winning *R. E. Lee: A Biography*, Freeman presented a devastating portrait of Longstreet as a sulking, minimally gifted soldier. Between the 1950s and the mid-1990s, four biographies helped to rehabilitate Longstreet. Donald B. Sanger and Thomas Robson Hay's *James Longstreet: I. Soldier; II. Politician, Officeholder, and Writer* (1952) offered a positive treatment based largely on published materials, while Wilbur Thomas's *General James "Pete" Longstreet: Lee's "Old War Horse," Scapegoat for Gettysburg* (1979) mounted a no-holds-barred defense of its subject. William Garrett Piston's *Lee's Tarnished Lieutenant: James Longstreet and His Place in History* (1987) dealt at length with the Lost Cause assault on Longstreet's reputation, setting the stage for Jeffry D. Wert's *General James Longstreet, The Confederacy's Most Controversial Soldier: A Biography* (1993), a well-researched, carefully argued study that portrayed a gifted officer who did his best for the Confederacy.

The greatest impetus for Longstreet's popular rehabilitation came from Michael Shaara's novel *The Killer Angels* (1974), which won the Pulitzer Prize and inspired director Ron Maxwell's cinematic treatment titled *Gettysburg* (1993). Both the novel and the film depict Longstreet as a modern soldier who understood the killing power of Civil War weapons, preferred the tactical defensive, and sought to avoid useless effusions of blood such as the Pickett-Pettigrew assault. Juxtaposed against a tired and impatient Lee, whose aggressive instincts set up the climactic horror of the attack, Longstreet functions as the most perceptive and attractive character on the Confederate side. Indeed, the novel and film align very well with Longstreet's own accounts of Gettysburg.

Longstreet surely deserves to be defended against critics influenced by the Lost Cause warriors, but modern readers should not get carried away with notions of him as a farseeing modern officer. A solid subordinate who reached his level of competence at the corps level and functioned best under Lee's sure leadership, he had his share of bad days. Few generals mounted less-effective assaults than Longstreet's against Fort Sanders at Knoxville on November 29, 1863, and his performance at Seven Pines in 1862 was equally dismal. In terms of tactical understanding, he fit comfortably within the framework of mid-nineteenth-century thinking. His operational and strategic imagination was far inferior to Lee's in every way.

At his best on the tactical offensive while in Lee's army, he delivered powerful blows at the Seven Days, Second Bull Run, and on May 6, 1864, at the Wilderness. He marched his men efficiently (Lost Cause writers shamelessly claimed otherwise), looked after them in camp, habitually brought units to the battlefield in excellent condition, and handled them impressively once fighting commenced. His courage was unquestioned, and Lee's reliance on him was such that news of Longstreet's wounding at the Wilderness proved deeply troubling. "I grieve to announce that Lieut Genl Longstreet was severely wounded," he wrote with evident feeling to Secretary of War James A. Seddon a few hours after fighting ceased in the Wilderness.[34] Lee's continuing high opinion through the rest of the war best counters those who would diminish Longstreet's well-earned stature.

STONEWALL JACKSON AND THE CONFEDERATE PEOPLE

Stonewall Jackson inspirited the Confederate people on many occasions. He played a major role in celebrated victories while exhibiting the audacious generalship his fellow citizens craved. His 1862 Valley campaign catapulted him to a position of unrivaled fame in the Confederacy (R. E. Lee would surpass him late in 1862 or early in 1863). He followed up his success in the valley with a stirring march around John Pope's flank in August 1862, the capture of Harpers Ferry in September 1862, and the famous flank march on May 2, 1863, beyond Joseph Hooker's exposed right flank at Chancellorsville. All these accomplishments were *offensive* in nature and fit the model of what most Confederates considered superior military leadership. Jackson's boldness and insistence on inflicting the greatest possible damage to the enemy, together with his well-known Christian piety, made him a perfect soldier for the Confederate people.

The Valley campaign illustrates Jackson's impact on southern morale. Timing and command style meant everything in terms of why this operation, modest by Civil War standards, resonated so powerfully. Between May 8 and June 9, when Jackson's campaign unfolded, Confederate fortunes reached a critical low point. Federals had captured New Orleans and Nashville, won victories at Forts Henry and Donelson and at Shiloh, secured southern Missouri with a success at Pea Ridge, blunted a minor Confederate offensive in the far west at Glorieta Pass, and placed a hundred-thousand-man army at the vital rail center of Corinth, Mississippi. In the Eastern Theater, the CSS *Virginia* had been scuttled and the largest Union army approached Richmond, the fall of which likely would end the war. The Confederate people hungered for good news from the battlefield.

Jackson supplied it, with five small engagements that loomed large because of when they came and how they were achieved. Through rapid movement, daring, and aggressiveness, "Old Jack" triumphed at McDowell (May 8), Front Royal (May 23), First Winchester (May 25), Cross Keys (June 8), and Port Republic (June 9). As a quintet, these clashes scarcely added up to one real battle, but Jackson had taken the war to the enemy when all other Confederate generals seemed to be retreating and suffering defeats. Had Richmond fallen during the ensuing Seven Days campaign, the valley operations would be an insignificant footnote in Civil War military history. But the Confederate capital did not fall, and Jackson's victories, which raised hopes in the hearts of countless Confederates, assumed almost mythical status.

Four quotations underscore how news from the valley hit the Confederate home front. The *Charleston Daily Courier* offered a breathless, and inaccurate, accounting on June 18, 1862, inviting "attention to the following summary of the achievements of Gen. Thos. J. Jackson ('Stonewall'). With a handful of citizen soldiers . . . he has, in little more than sixty days, marched over five hundred miles, fought about twelve battles—five of which were pitched battles—defeated four generals—routed four armies—captured millions of dollars worth of stores, &c., and killed, wounded and secured as prisoners, almost as many of the enemy as he had soldiers under his command! These are startling assertions, but they are literally true!"

Judith McGuire, a refugee living in Richmond, expressed feelings typical of many Confederates upon learning of events at Cross Keys and Port Republic. "General Jackson is performing prodigies of valor in the Valley," she observed on the evening of June 9. "He has met the forces of Fremont and Shields, and *whipped them in detail.*" Three days later, McGuire compared Jackson's campaign with failed operations in the West. "We are more successful in Virginia than elsewhere," she observed, adding that the "whole Mississippi River, except Vicksburg and its environs, is now in the hands of the enemy, and. . . . Memphis has fallen!"[35]

The *Richmond* [Daily] *Dispatch,* on June 11, 1862, suggested that aggressive maneuvering and fighting by "glorious 'Stonewall' in the Valley cannot fail to raise a high old panic among the functionaries of Washington. . . . The result of these splendid victories is too evident to need comment; and it is therefore unnecessary to urge that immediate reinforcements be sent to Jackson, that he may be able to follow up the advantages already gained."

From eastern North Carolina on June 11, diarist Catherine Ann Devereux Edmondston noted that "Jackson has gained another victory in the Valley of Va. He has beaten Shields & holds Fremont in check, who fears to attack him singly." Edmondston then got to the heart of why so many Confederates loved Jackson: "He is the only one of our generals who gives the enemy no rest, no time to entrench themselves." In contrast, she deprecated the efforts of Joseph E. Johnston and his successor R. E. Lee outside the capital. "Matters before Richmond look gloomy to us outsiders," she wrote sadly. "McClellan advances, entrenching as he comes. Why do we allow it?"[36]

The reputation for cold-blooded effectiveness won in the valley clung to Jackson for the rest of the war. It pervaded accounts of his activities and showed clearly in reporting about the rearguard action at Shepherdstown, Virginia, on September 19–20, 1862. An aftershock to Antietam, this fight claimed just more than 650 Union and Confederate casualties and compelled a Federal retreat across the Potomac. The Confederate press described it as a bloody Union defeat, a theme picked up by civilians. "On the 19th a division of the enemy crossed over to Shepherdstown," wrote a woman in Fredericksburg, Virginia, with typical hyperbole. "Jackson captured or killed the whole of them. The Potomac was damned [*sic*] up with their bodies." Judith McGuire similarly estimated that "ten thousand Yankees crossed at Shepherdstown, but unfortunately for them, they found the glorious Stonewall there. . . . We succeeded in driving a good many of them into the Potomac. . . . The account of the Yankee slaughter is fearful."[37]

Neither questionable performances at the Seven Days and Fredericksburg, nor a striking absence of tactical skill even in his victories, diminished Jackson's reputation among Confederates. He was their Stonewall—purposeful, destructive to the enemy, and Lee's right arm. Death in the wake of Chancellorsville cemented his place as the second most important figure in the Confederate pantheon.

STONEWALL AND OLD JUBE IN THE VALLEY

Stonewall Jackson's Shenandoah Valley campaign of 1862 has been widely hailed as a brilliant military event. Jubal A. Early's operations in the valley during 1864 conjure more negative images of multiple defeats and destruction of the region's agricultural productivity. Jackson certainly performed well, winning a series of small victories between May 8 and June 9, 1862, that inspirited the Confederate people at a time of widespread pessimism. Early's activities in the valley, though ending in undeniable failure, measure up well against Jackson's. Several comparative dimensions of the two operations suggest why.

The quality of Union leadership heavily favored Jackson. Nathaniel P. Banks, a politician turned general, compiled a record of unbroken futility in theaters from the Shenandoah Valley to Louisiana's Red River. John C. Frémont mirrored Banks's ineptitude in the valley, a record matched or only modestly improved upon by other Federals, such as Robert H. Milroy and James Shields. Perhaps most important, no Union officer exercised overall control in the valley in 1862, which virtually guaranteed problems of coordination.

Although Early's opponents proved equally inept during the first phase of his Valley campaign (David Hunter and Lew Wallace came to grief, respectively, at Lynchburg and the Monocacy), Philip H. Sheridan brought impressive military gifts to the climactic phase of operations in 1864. Sheridan stumbled tactically at both Third Winchester and Fisher's Hill, but he possessed an ability to rally troops rivaled by few other Civil War officers. "God *damn* you, don't cheer me! There's lots of fight in you men yet!" he shouted to Union soldiers upon reaching the battlefield at Cedar Creek, after his army had been driven from successive positions.[38] His fiery example more than once brought impressive results in the Shenandoah.

Sheridan also understood how to use his superior strength, pressing Early relentlessly and carrying out U. S. Grant's orders to destroy the valley's logistical riches. Talented subordinates assisted Sheridan, including George Crook, Horatio G. Wright, and George A. Custer. "Little Phil" also wielded overall control in the valley, answering only to Grant, who gave him a free hand, and to the secretary of war. During his entire Confederate career, Jackson never faced an opponent of Sheridan's caliber.

Jackson enjoyed an edge over Early in the troops he both commanded and faced. On the Confederate side, he possessed a slight advantage in numbers and quality of soldiers. He led slightly more than seventeen thousand men for most of the campaign, almost all of them original volunteers who had willingly gone to war. Early's Army of the Valley counted approximately fifteen thousand soldiers at its peak and often fought with considerably fewer. These Confederates served well but were neither as fresh nor as well supplied as Jackson's men. Early did have talented subordinates in Robert E. Rodes, John B. Gordon, Stephen Dodson Ramseur, and Joseph B. Kershaw (Rodes and Ramseur lost their lives during the campaign), whose accomplishments in the valley exceeded those of Richard S. Ewell, Richard Taylor, and Jackson's other principal lieutenants. Neither Jackson nor Early enjoyed competent cavalry support.

As for Federal troops, Jackson fought against much weaker foes. Writers frequently state that he defeated more than sixty thousand of the enemy, but there never were nearly that many Union troops *together* in the valley. The number sixty thousand includes troops with Irvin McDowell or other commanders stationed far from the Shenandoah. Union strength in a single force seldom reached even twenty thousand against Jackson, and the soldiers often suffered from low morale, exhibited little confidence in their leaders, and contended with problems of supply.

Early labored under far more difficult circumstances. He fought a Federal army of thirty-five to forty-five thousand directed by the aggressive Sheridan, including the veteran Sixth Corps and the competent Nineteenth Corps. Even after their brilliant flanking movement at Cedar Creek, Old Jube's troops assaulted more numerous Federals. Jackson receives well-earned plaudits for placing the bulk of his small army in a position to strike fragments of the Union forces; no Confederate commander, including Jackson, could have duplicated that achievement against Sheridan in September and October 1864. And Jackson's tactical efforts at McDowell, First Winchester, and Port Republic add no luster to his reputation.

The scale of marching and fighting offers a final useful point of comparison. Cartographer Jedediah Hotchkiss served under both Jackson and Early, and by his careful reckoning, Early's soldiers marched more than 1,500 miles, a distance about two and one half times greater than Jackson's men covered in 1862. Casualties tell a similar story. Jackson's six largest engagements—First Kernstown, McDowell, Front Royal, First Winchester, Cross Keys, and Port Republic—resulted in approximately 5,500 Union and 2,750 Confederate casualties (prisoners accounted for half of the U.S. total). Of the six, only First Winchester and Port Republic properly should be called battles. The rest ranked as large-scale skirmishes with fewer than one thousand casualties for each side. In contrast, Early's six largest engagements—Lynchburg, the Monocacy, Second Kernstown, Third Winchester, Fisher's Hill, and Cedar Creek—produced more than fifteen thousand Union and about ten thousand Confederate casualties. Third Winchester and Cedar Creek each cost Sheridan approximately as many men in one day as were lost by all of Jackson's opponents combined in 1862.

Against weak opponents leading second-line troops, Jackson won a series of small victories and accomplished the strategic goals laid out by Robert E. Lee. Against equally weak Union officers in June and July 1864, Early also won victories and achieved Lee's strategic goals. He managed far less success against Sheridan, though for three months he denied the services of more than forty thousand Federals to Grant on the Richmond/Petersburg front.

Could Early have duplicated Jackson's fabled performance in the spring of 1862? Probably not—though he almost certainly would have bested the undistinguished Union commanders. Would Jackson have defeated Sheridan in 1864? Again, probably not, because Sheridan had the ability and numbers to vanquish any opponent laboring under the handicaps imposed on Jubal Early. Both Jackson and Early deserve high marks for their work in the valley. But if forced to choose one or the other operation to command, most reasonable people would choose to be in Jackson's rather than in Early's position.

SHERIDAN MAKES HIS NAME
IN THE VALLEY

Abraham Lincoln spoke to a crowd on October 21, 1864, about news from the Shenandoah Valley, proposing "three hearty cheers for Sheridan." The next day, Major General Philip Henry Sheridan, architect of several victories that culminated at Cedar Creek on October 19, received a message from the president. "With great pleasure," wrote Lincoln, "I tender to you and your brave army, the thanks of the Nation, and my own personal admiration and gratitude, for the month's operations in the Shenandoah Valley." Shortly thereafter, William Tecumseh Sherman acknowledged how success in the valley had boosted Sheridan's reputation: "Grant Sheridan & I are now the popular favorites."[39]

In the preceding essay, I contrasted the performances of Stonewall Jackson and Jubal A. Early in their Shenandoah campaigns of 1862 and 1864, and included a few observations about Sheridan. Here I want to assess more closely the Federal commander's actions against Early in 1864.

U. S. Grant assigned Sheridan three major tasks: clear Confederate forces from the lower valley, destroy the region's capacity to send food and other matériel to Lee's army, and disrupt the Virginia Central Railroad, which crossed the Blue Ridge Mountains between Staunton and Charlottesville and connected with the Orange and Alexandria line in the Piedmont.

Sheridan commenced his offensive on September 19 and within a month extinguished any credible Confederate military threat in the lower valley. Victories at Third Winchester on the nineteenth, at Fisher's Hill three days later, and at Cedar Creek, each of which ended with flanked Confederates in full retreat, demonstrated that Sheridan could thrash the Rebels seemingly at will. He did equally well with Grant's second task, laying waste to large stretches of the valley between Staunton and the Potomac River as well as to much of the Luray Valley east of the Massanutten Range.

The third of Grant's goals, disruption of the Virginia Central, went unmet. After driving Early well up the valley after Third Winchester and Fisher's Hill, Sheridan seemed positioned to disrupt the railroad and move across the Blue Ridge toward Charlottesville and Gordonsville. But in a message to Grant on

October 12, he objected "to the opening of the R. R. and an advance on the old Rapidan line, on account of The waste of fighting force to protect R. Rds, and the additional waste of force, as some would have to be left in this valley." In the end, Grant did not press the issue and continued to see Sheridan as "one of the ablest of Generals."[40]

Numbers admittedly played a crucial role in Sheridan's success. His army benefited from a numerical edge over Early's—of at least two to one and sometimes nearly three to one. In later accounts, Confederates habitually inflated Union strength and undercounted their own. Sheridan did the opposite in his memoirs. "The Confederate army at this date was about twenty thousand strong . . . ," he observed of the campaign's first phase, and the "force that I could take with me into the field at this time numbered about 26,000 men." Although clearly disingenuous in this reckoning, Sheridan came closer to the truth than did Grant. The commanding general's memoirs advanced the unsupportable claim that each side initially fielded about thirty thousand troops. Only "the superior ability of the National commander over the Confederate commander," remarked Grant in a clear jab at Early, brought Union success.[41]

Accepting preponderant numbers as a starting point, a fair estimate of Sheridan's leadership in the valley yields far more positive than negative factors. The Army of the Shenandoah boasted the highest percentage of mounted units in any major U.S. force, and Sheridan coordinated cavalry operations with those of his infantry and artillery as well as any army commander during the war. Not content to have cavalrymen screen his movements and seek out the enemy, he repeatedly employed their repeating firepower to demoralize and break Confederate infantry. This use of infantry and cavalry at Third Winchester and Cedar Creek represented a unique feature of the 1864 Valley campaign.

Sheridan's personal behavior in battle also produced striking results. His dramatic presence rallied Federals at Third Winchester, and his ride along the lines before the climactic assault at Cedar Creek greatly inspired the men. When Sheridan appeared on the field, wrote a Federal surgeon shortly after Cedar Creek, "his arrival infused new courage into our soldiers. . . . He remarked that 'Early should that day get the *damndest thrashing* he ever got,' and the battle turned to our favor; and such a victory as we had *that day* I never saw." A soldier in the Twenty-Ninth Maine Infantry agreed that "our Brave Sheridan wrung a *great victory* from the very jaws of defeat. . . . He rode right

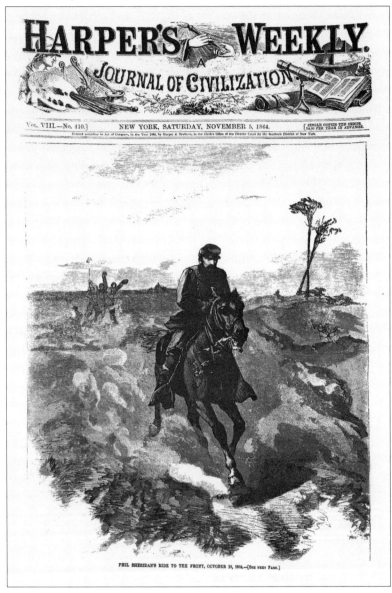

HARPER'S WEEKLY.

JOURNAL OF CIVILIZATION

Vol. VIII.—No. 410.] NEW YORK, SATURDAY, NOVEMBER 5, 1864. [SINGLE COPIES TEN CENTS. $4.00 PER YEAR IN ADVANCE.

Entered according to Act of Congress, in the Year 1864, by Harper & Brothers, in the Clerk's Office of the District Court for the Southern District of New York.

PHIL SHERIDAN'S RIDE TO THE FRONT, OCTOBER 19, 1864.—[SEE NEXT PAGE.]

"Phil Sheridan's Ride to the Front, October 19, 1864." *Harper's Weekly* devoted its front page to Sheridan, crediting him with "the victory of the day" at Cedar Creek and quoting U. S. Grant about his lieutenant. "Turning what bid fair to be a disaster into a glorious victory," affirmed the general in chief, "stamps SHERIDAN what I have always thought him, one of the ablest of Generals." (*Harper's Weekly*, November 5, 1864, pp. 705–6.)

on the feild told the boys they wasn't half whipped Turned on the Rebels drove them from our works way beyond fishers Hill."[42]

Sheridan did suffer tactical lapses. He sent the Sixth and the Nineteenth Corps through the Berryville Canyon at Third Winchester on a single road, where they predictably became bogged down, and left the Eighth Corps far behind without orders before committing it to action. At Fisher's Hill, he exhibited a poor grasp of terrain by suggesting an assault against Early's well-protected right flank astride the Valley Pike. George Crook proposed a movement around the Confederate left, where a thin line of dismounted cavalry posed the weakest of obstacles. Sheridan embraced Crook's idea and implemented it on September 22—then, much to Crook's displeasure, claimed credit for the tactical success.

Overall, Sheridan proved himself a skilled officer who implemented most of Grant's strategic design and helped reelect Lincoln in November. He relied on his superior strength to overcome tactical mistakes as well as to deliver powerful blows. Although he never devised a plan equal to Early's surprise attack at Cedar Creek, his soldiers and northern newspapers generally credited him for all triumphs, often slighting his subordinates. A major general's commission in the regular army gave tangible expression to gratitude from military and civilian superiors. More than that, Sheridan's Shenandoah campaign placed him behind only Grant and Sherman in the Union pantheon, and he followed them as the third general to wear four stars in the U.S. Army.

POOR GEORGE GORDON MEADE

On July 14, 1863, Abraham Lincoln drafted a letter to Major General George Gordon Meade, whose Army of the Potomac recently had mauled the Army of Northern Virginia in the battle of Gettysburg. "I am very—*very*—grateful to you for the magnificent success you gave the cause of the country at Gettysburg," wrote the president, who nonetheless expressed "deep distress" at Robert E. Lee's successful return to Virginia. "I do not believe you appreciate the magnitude of the misfortune involved in Lee's escape," continued Lincoln, who predicted that Meade's failure to press the Rebels ruthlessly meant "the war will be prolonged indefinitely." Lincoln never sent the letter—did not need to send it—because earlier that day Major General Henry W. Halleck had conveyed the president's "great dissatisfaction" with Meade's lethargic pursuit of Lee.[43] The unsent letter has plagued Meade for more than a century and a half, creating a widely held impression that he bungled a chance to end the war and saddling him with a reputation for indecisiveness.

Meade commanded the Army of the Potomac for the majority of its turbulent history. George B. McClellan christened the army, built it into a formidable force in the months following First Bull Run, led it during the 1862 Richmond and Maryland campaigns, and always remained first in the hearts of thousands of its soldiers. In the half year following McClellan's removal on November 7, 1862, Ambrose E. Burnside and Joseph Hooker presided over humiliating defeats at Fredericksburg and Chancellorsville, and Hooker's problematic actions as Lee marched into Pennsylvania in June 1863 brought his tenure to an end. Meade replaced Hooker on June 28, just three days before the armies collided at Gettysburg, and retained his position until the end of the war.

Meade's promotion made sense within the intensely political climate that habitually enveloped the Army of the Potomac. A dependable brigade and division leader in the 1862 campaigns, he took charge of the Fifth Corps after the battle of Fredericksburg. At Chancellorsville, Meade performed adequately, though Hooker's inept generalship afforded him and his corps limited opportunity to excel. Why did the Lincoln administration choose a man with modest experience at the corps level to head the army? The absence of enemies in Congress certainly played a role. Unlike McClellan and his Democratic military clique, or the openly ambitious and politically active Hooker, Meade had kept a low profile, offended no key members of the Joint Committee on the Conduct of the War, or otherwise made himself a target for partisan infighting (political opponents appeared in profusion in the wake of Gettysburg).

News of Meade's ascension pleased much of the army, though he was largely unknown to many of its soldiers. Even some who admired him doubted the wisdom of a change in the midst of an active campaign. A senior artillery officer in the First Corps, for example, believed Meade had "the longest and clearest head of any officer in this army" but thought the timing "a very dangerous experiment on the eve of a battle."[44]

"The Surrender at Appomattox." George G. Meade's absence stands out in this illustration from *Battles and Leaders of the Civil War*. Several Union generals and members of Grant's staff (all identified for readers), but not the officer who had commanded the Army of the Potomac since late June 1863, crowded into Wilmer McLean's parlor to observe the historic scene. (Robert Underwood Johnson and Clarence Clough Buel, eds., *Battles and Leaders of the Civil War*, 4 vols. [New York: Century, 1887–88], vol. 4, p. 228.)

Meade turned out to be a competent army commander, but it is hard to construct a scenario, absent Grant's presence, within which he could have delivered ultimate victory over Lee. Few generals faced situations as potentially frustrating. He inherited the republic's largest army while Lee and his veteran troops maneuvered on United States soil. Then he "commanded" a force most loyal citizens considered Grant's for the last year of the war. Meade endured undeserved criticism after Gettysburg, watched helplessly as Grant received virtually all the credit for winning the war in Virginia, yet went about the daily business of running the army.

His role in the war has inspired a relatively small literature—a tiny one, in fact, compared to what has poured forth relating to McClellan. Freeman Cleaves's admiring *Meade of Gettysburg* (1960) remains the most complete biography. Ethan S. Rafuse's very brief *George Gordon Meade and the War in the East* (2003) contains a number of useful insights, and Tom Huntington's *Searching for George Gordon Meade: The Forgotten Victor of Gettysburg* (2013) combines scholarship and a travelogue of the author's visits to places associated with Meade. *Meade's Headquarters, 1863–1865: Letters of Colonel Theodore Lyman from the Wilderness to Appomattox* (1922; paperback edition titled *With Grant and Meade from the Wilderness to Appomattox*, 1994), edited by George R. Agassiz, includes a superb store of observations and anecdotes from the pen of a literate and incisive officer close to the general. Equally valuable is *Meade's Army: The Private Notebooks of Lt. Col. Theodore Lyman* (2007), edited by David W. Lowe.

The essential title for any study of Meade is *The Life and Letters of George Gordon Meade, Major-General United States Army*, a two-volume set compiled with connecting text by his son George Meade and edited for publication by his grandson of the same name. Understandably favorable to its subject and marred by imperfect editing, this set nevertheless offers invaluable evidence regarding Meade's personality, his opinions on a range of subjects, and his service during both the war with Mexico and the Civil War. Meade emerges as an honest, patriotic, and sometimes dyspeptic officer increasingly concerned with a lack of public recognition for his contributions after Gettysburg. In a letter to his wife, written on June 21, 1864, Meade notes that, in the fighting at Petersburg on June 16 to 18, "I had exclusive command, Grant being all the time at City Point, and coming on the field for only half an hour on the 17th, and yet in Mr. Stanton's official despatch he quotes General Grant's account, and my name is not even mentioned. I cannot imagine why I am thus ignored." After a cruel twist of fate denied Meade a place in Wilmer McLean's parlor on April 9, he wrote the next day to his wife about the final campaign in Virginia: "I don't believe the truth ever will be known, and I have a great contempt for History. Only let the war be finished, and I returned to you and the dear children, and I will be satisfied."[45]

Until we get a comprehensive biography that fully exploits the rich store of Meade's manuscript papers, *Life and Letters* helps illuminate the contributions of one of the Union's most important soldiers.

REYNOLDS AND SEDGWICK

Major generals John Fulton Reynolds and John Sedgwick died in striking circumstances that undoubtedly burnished their reputations as successful Union corps commanders. On July 1 at Gettysburg, Reynolds accompanied the leading units of his First Corps into action. Positioned behind the Iron Brigade's Second Wisconsin near the eastern fringe of McPherson's Woods, he urged his troops to stop the approaching Confederates. "Forward men," he shouted, "forward for God's sake, and drive those fellows out of the woods." Turning to look back toward Seminary Ridge, he went limp in the saddle after a minié ball entered the back of his neck, and he was dead before hitting the ground. Sedgwick's story on the second day of the battle of Spotsylvania could be conjured from a novelist's imagination. Steadying a portion of his Sixth Corps line opposite Laurel Hill on the morning of May 9, he noticed some men dodging as Confederate musket rounds struck nearby. "I am ashamed of you," he told them. "They can't hit an elephant at this distance." He repeated those words, with a good-natured laugh, after a sergeant dropped to the ground for safety. A moment later, an unmistakable thud told observers that Sedgwick had been hit, incurring a mortal wound just below his left eye.[46]

William Swinton, who covered the Army of the Potomac for the *New York Times,* anticipated the tenor of many subsequent evaluations of the two generals. Reynolds's death, wrote Swinton in *Campaigns of the Army of the Potomac,* was "a grievous loss to the Army of the Potomac, one of whose most distinguished and best-loved officers he was; one whom, by the steady growth of the highest military qualities, the general voice of the whole army had marked out for the largest fame." As for Sedgwick, the "loss of this lion-hearted soldier caused the profoundest grief among his comrades, and throughout the army, which felt it could better have afforded to sacrifice the best division." Edward J. Nichols's *Toward Gettysburg: A Biography of General John F. Reynolds* quotes Winfield Scott Hancock, the Comte de Paris, Joseph Hooker, and others proclaiming Reynolds the best soldier in the army. In *General John Sedgwick: The Story of a Union Corp Commander,* Richard Elliott Winslow III pronounces his subject "a steadfast soldier who contributed much to ultimate Union victory" in the course of playing a "crucial role during the Civil War."[47]

Did Reynolds and Sedgwick merit such praise? As corps chiefs, the answer must be no. At Fredericksburg, his initial battle as head of the First Corps, Reynolds's penchant for overseeing details relating to his artillery rendered him ineffectual in directing the activities of key subordinates such as George G. Meade. One careful student of the battle concludes that Reynolds's dallying among the guns "made him completely ineffective when Meade sought critical reinforcements."[48] At Chancellorsville, Reynolds and his corps saw almost no action, suffering fewer than three hundred of the army's more than seventeen thousand casualties. His actions at Gettysburg on July 1 were solid but scarcely sufficient to warrant extravagant praise.

Sedgwick's terrible wound in the West Woods at Antietam, where his division was butchered, kept him out of the Fredericksburg campaign. Promoted to command of the Sixth Corps, he played an important role at Chancellorsville, where his corps absorbed the heaviest casualties in the army. Sedgwick's actions on May 1 to 5 certainly lacked aggressiveness and have inspired a good deal of criticism. Edward Porter Alexander, the most astute of all Confederates who wrote about the war in the Eastern Theater, pulled no punches: "I have always felt surprise that the enemy retained Sedgwick as a corps commander . . . , for he seems to me to have wasted great opportunities, & come about as near to doing nothing with 30,000 men as it was easily possible to do."[49] At Gettysburg, Sedgwick's corps, the army's largest, played only a minor part in the fighting and lost just 212 men killed or wounded.

Sedgwick put in a mixed performance during the battle of the Wilderness, earning praise from U. S. Grant for his bravery but receiving harsh critiques from others for allowing John B. Gordon's successful flank attack on May 6 against the Sixth Corps. "This stampede," wrote Theodore Lyman of Meade's staff regarding Gordon's routing of two Union brigades, "was the most disgraceful thing that happened to the celebrated 6th corps during my experience of it." Lyman also thought some of Sedgwick's other actions "amounted to nothing."[50]

There is no doubt that both Reynolds and Sedgwick inspired a good deal of admiration. A pair of officers, one from each general's staff, offer useful testimony on this point. Stephen Minot Weld met the ambulance carrying Reynolds from the field on July 1, which triggered a surge of emotion. "He was the best general we had in our army," wrote Weld in his diary. "Brave, kindhearted, modest, somewhat rough and wanting polish, he was a type of the true soldier. I cannot realize that he is dead." Sedgwick's nickname—"Uncle John"—revealed the degree to which his soldiers thought of him as a leader who looked after their welfare. Thomas W. Hyde captured the bond between the general and his men. Referring to Sedgwick as "our friend, our idol," Hyde described the feeling when news of the general's death settled in: "Gradually it dawned upon us that the great leader, the cherished friend, he that had been more than a father to us all, would no more lead the Greek Cross of the 6th corps."[51]

Such heartfelt tributes should not obscure that neither Reynolds nor Sedgwick crafted a sterling record as a corps commander. Both fit comfortably within the culture George B. McClellan created in the Army of the Potomac. That culture prized caution, seldom sought to deliver a killing blow to the enemy, and accepted, almost preferred, inaction to any movement that might yield negative results. Dramatic deaths lifted Reynolds and Sedgwick to a special position in the pantheon of Union generals. As Edward J. Nichols admitted in his biography of Reynolds, "A hero's death sits well with posterity."[52]

TOWARD SANTA FE AND BEYOND
Confederates in New Mexico

Twenty-five hundred Texans led by Brigadier General Henry Hopkins Sibley moved up the Rio Grande Valley in the early months of 1862. Sibley hoped to establish a Confederate presence in the territory of New Mexico, gain access to the mineral wealth of Colorado, and, if all went well, push on toward California. "By geographical position, by similarity of institutions, by commercial interests, and by future destinies New Mexico pertains to the Confederacy," he announced from Fort Bliss at the outset of the operation. He and his troops came as friends, Sibley assured New Mexicans, "to liberate them from the yoke of military despotism."[53] The Sibley Brigade—grandly denominated the Army of New Mexico by its commander—covered an immense distance, traversing a sere landscape that changed, as the column reached Santa Fe and the foothills of the Sangre de Cristo Mountains, to more striking countryside featuring stands of piñon and larger evergreens. Along the way, the invaders fought battles at Valverde (February 21), Apache Canyon (March 26), and Glorieta or Pigeon's Ranch (March 28).

Although Confederates gained tactical success in two of the battles, they could not sustain their strategic offensive. Exposed in northern New Mexico, unable to provision his troops locally, and far from sources of supply in Texas, Sibley, who drank heavily throughout the campaign, ordered a retreat. The exhausted survivors of his little army reached El Paso in early May, closing the book on their brief invasion of New Mexico and ending any chance for future Confederate success in the Southwest. Thus did events tied to the farthest geographic reach of Confederate ambition contribute to a catastrophic string of southern failures during a period that included Forts Henry and Donelson, Pea Ridge, Shiloh, and the loss of Nashville, New Bern, and New Orleans.

A short shelf of books allows readers to master the details and impact of the operation. Martin Hardwick Hall's *Sibley's New Mexico Campaign,* the first scholarly study, argues that Sibley lacked the means to achieve long-term success in New Mexico—never mind threaten Colorado or California. Hall deems the Rebel effort "a gallant, but essentially impractical, effort to accomplish a great objective with woefully inadequate resources." Jerry Thompson's *Henry Hopkins Sibley: Confederate General of the West* devotes three of its thirteen chapters to the invasion. Mincing no words, Thompson asserts that Sibley "must rank as one of the worst generals to serve the southern Confederacy." The foray into New Mexico left his command "shattered and defeated, as much or more by the vastness and the sterility of the land and by inadequate and incompetent leadership as by the Union Army."[54]

Donald S. Frazier's *Blood & Treasure: Confederate Empire in New Mexico* places the campaign within the context of antebellum southern expansionism. "For more than thirty years prior to Sibley's campaign," notes Frazier, "Southern writers, statesmen, and warriors had urged the occupation and development of the American Southwest. . . . In 1861, the time and conditions for a Southern empire had arrived." Sibley concocted a blueprint for conquering the Southwest but oversaw a campaign that achieved nothing and ravaged the morale of Sibley's Brigade: "The will to fight had been crushed, replaced by the overwhelming desire to go home." As for the general himself, "One feeling was universal to these weary veterans," observes Frazier, "no one trusted Sibley."[55]

On the climactic engagement, Don E. Alberts's *The Battle of Glorieta: Union*

Victory in the West provides details about a clash that, while marked by dramatic tactical ebb and flow, should be considered a large-scale skirmish. As is often the case in tactical studies of small engagements, hyperbole sneaks into the text. "In saving New Mexico Territory for the Union," remarks Alberts, "the regular and volunteer soldiers took severe casualties, as had their Rebel enemies." What were the casualties? "Approximately two hundred, mostly from combat," reports Alberts, which would accord with losses from a few minute's action at places such as Shiloh or Antietam.[56]

Two firsthand Confederate accounts yield excellent material. *Westward the Texans: The Civil War Journal of Private William Randolph Howell* (1990), edited by Jerry D. Thompson, and *Rebels on the Rio Grande: The Civil War Journal of A. B. Peticolas* (1984), edited by Don E. Alberts, contain entries relating to battles, attitudes among Sibley's soldiers, the terrain between El Paso and Santa Fe, and the often harsh weather. Peticolas also produced a number of crudely delightful drawings of structures and physical features in New Mexico.

The Federal side of the story emerges from two other titles. The classic Union account is Ovando J. Hollister's *Colorado Volunteers in New Mexico, 1862*. Written from the perspective of a common soldier, Hollister's text mixes descriptions of events and places with insights about service in the ranks. "Patriotism has a good sound," he writes, "but soldiering as a private calls for the genuine article." Flint Whitlock's *Distant Bugles, Distant Drums: The Union Response to the Confederate Invasion of New Mexico* never exaggerates the scale of operations, informing readers at the outset that action in New Mexico was "the second-smallest campaign of the Civil War in terms of number of combatants. No more than 7,000 men total were involved in the four main battles . . . and fewer than 300 were killed in combat." He then does an excellent job of bringing to life figures such as Governor William Gilpin of Colorado Territory, Major John M. Chivington of the First Colorado, and Colonel E. R. S. Canby, who commanded the Department of New Mexico.[57]

Sibley issued a congratulatory order to "Soldiers of the Army of New Mexico" toward the end of the campaign. Praising their valor in battle and steadfastness during the trip back to Texas "through mountain passes and over a tracless [sic] waste," he predicted the campaign would be "duly chronicled, and form one of the brightest pages in the history of the Second American Revolution."[58] Typically exaggerated, Sibley's words nonetheless remind us that the Rio Grande valley in early 1862 merits continuing attention.

GETTYSBURG IN PERSPECTIVE

Most Americans see Gettysburg as the great turning point of the Civil War. The sesquicentennial underscored this fact, with newspapers and magazines that reached very large audiences casting the battle as decisive in crushing Confederate chances for independence. For example, the editors of *BBC History Magazine* published a special 150th Anniversary Edition booklet that pronounced Gettysburg "the last chance for the Confederacy" and "the pivotal battle of the war." A special issue of *National Geographic* similarly affirmed that "the Union began to gain the upper hand only in July 1863 with its victory at Gettysburg, the bloodiest battle ever fought in North America." *Time*'s 150th Anniversary Tribute made the same point in its subtitle: *Gettysburg: A Day-by-Day Account of the Greatest Battle of the Civil War.*[59]

But in trying to understand Gettysburg's importance within the context of the war, we must remember not to read into the battle everything we now know. By July 1863, there already had been many ghastly battles, and nobody knew whether another one, even more horrific than Gettysburg, lay somewhere ahead. Similarly, no one knew whether the Army of Northern Virginia would mount another major invasion of the United States. Neither could they anticipate that Abraham Lincoln would go to Gettysburg in November 1863 to deliver what eventually would be perceived as an immortal address (virtually no one at the time paid much attention to Lincoln's brief speech). The vast outpouring of writings about the battle, which by a recent count number more than six thousand, lay in the future, as did the battlefield's development as a major attraction for people interested in American history and the war's battlegrounds.

A fair assessment of Gettysburg's impact in the summer and early autumn of 1863 is that both sides saw it as an important but not decisive battle. Admittedly, many people in the United States rejoiced upon first hearing about Lee's retreat. It seemed, as New York diarist George Templeton Strong observed on July 6, that the "rebels are hunted out of the North, their best army is routed, and the charm of Robert Lee's invincibility broken." Yet Strong soon echoed Lincoln's unsent letter, dated July 14, 1863 (quoted in my essay on Meade), in lamenting that Robert E. Lee's army had escaped across the Potomac. "Newspapers brag far too loudly about our having 'broken the backbone' of the rebellion . . . ," Strong noted on August 8. "The vertebrae of Southern treason still cohere, as we may yet learn to our terrible cost, especially if Lee reinforce[s] himself with the debris of rebellion from the Southwest."[60]

Strong's assessment aligned almost perfectly with Abraham Lincoln's. On July 14, in the letter written but never sent to General Meade, the president confessed to being "distressed immeasurably" by the failure to capitalize on a "golden opportunity" to trap the Army of Northern Virginia north of the Potomac River.[61] Although somewhat unfair to Meade, who strained under very difficult circumstances, this attitude nonetheless took much of the gloss off the victory at Gettysburg. It soon became all too clear throughout the loyal states that the conflict would drag on, with no end in sight and no certainty as to the outcome.

Confederate testimony from 1863, as opposed to postwar writings by ex-Rebels that elevated Gettysburg to a position of special importance, suggests a pervasive view that the battle had not delivered a catastrophic blow to hopes for independence. Many in the Confederacy did lament the high casualties (in North Carolina, excessive losses among that state's units at Gettysburg fueled antiwar feeling), and some criticized Lee's generalship. Yet most concluded that Lee's foray into Pennsylvania and subsequent retreat represented only a temporary setback with few long-term consequences for either the Army of Northern Virginia or the Confederacy. Confederates typically drew a sharp distinction between Gettysburg, with its high casualties but striking southern success on July 1, and Vicksburg, an unequivocal disaster that cost the Confederacy an entire army and control of the Mississippi River.

Many civilians quickly judged Gettysburg as less ruinous than Vicksburg. Writing on July 9, 1863, South Carolinian Emma Holmes termed U.S. Grant's capture of John C. Pemberton's army "a terrible blow to our cause" that would "prolong the war indefinitely." But when early notices of a triumph in Pennsylvania gave way to descriptions of Lee's retreat, Holmes observed calmly, "It certainly does not appear to be the great victory at first announced, though a very great battle."

"Lee has recrossed the Potomac, in admirable order, and the army in splendid trim and spirits without loss," she noted on July 17, in her last entry devoted to the Pennsylvania campaign. "His retreat from Gettysburg was strategic, to draw Meade's army from the high hills behind which they took refuge." A physician serving with the military in Richmond pronounced both Vicksburg and Gettysburg "serious blows" but immediately clarified his relative assessment of the two: "The latter was not a defeat—an accident only prevented it from being the ruin of the Yankees." Although the "accident" went unidentified in this letter, the surgeon unquestionably considered Vicksburg a more harmful reverse.[62]

Many historians have quoted from the diary of Confederate ordnance chief Josiah Gorgas to support the idea of Gettysburg as a ruinous turning point. "Events have succeeded one another with disastrous rapidity," wrote Gorgas on July 28, 1863. "One brief month ago we were apparently at the point of success. Lee was in Pennsylvania, threatening Harrisburgh, and even Philadelphia. Vicksburgh seemed to laugh all Grant's efforts to scorn." Thirty days later, Lee had retreated and Vicksburg, as well as Port Hudson, Louisiana, had fallen. "Yesterday we rode on the pinnacle of success—today absolute ruin seems to be our portion," stated an apparently shaken Gorgas. "The Confederacy totters to its destruction." Yet anyone who reads Gorgas's diary in August and early September 1863 finds a rapid shift in attitude regarding Gettysburg's long-term impact. All seemed quiet on Lee's front, he recorded on August 24, "and his army appears to be nearly in its original good condition." By September 6, Gorgas alluded to the army's "excellent condition" and speculated that Lee might invade Maryland again.[63]

Whatever the precise breakdown of Union and Confederate opinion in 1863, one thing is certain: As the armies of Lee and Grant engaged in the bloody Overland campaign of May and June 1864 and then settled into siege warfare at Petersburg, virtually no one, in the United States or in the Confederacy, would have insisted that Gettysburg had been a watershed. It by then amounted to scarcely more than a distant memory, as civilian morale in the United States dropped to its lowest point of the war and Confederates maintained high hopes that a Democratic triumph in the autumn elections would boost chances for southern nationhood.

III

CONTROVERSIES

Few episodes or eras in United States history equal the Civil War's potential to stir controversy. This became apparent immediately after Appomattox, when the wartime generation argued about personalities, political events, and decisions on battlefields. These kinds of debates continue today, some taking the form of scholarly exchanges among historians and others occurring in the public arena. The dozen essays in this section consider controversial topics, starting with two devoted to the challenge of studying the Confederacy and the tension between academic and popular approaches to the war. Three pieces then address the meaning of Union for the loyal citizenry of the United States, how imperfectly modern Americans understand it, and how it intersected with attitudes toward emancipation. I allocated this much attention to the topic because I believe the concept of Union lay at the heart of the war's meaning for those who were willing to fight rather than allow secessionists to destroy the nation. The next four essays feature turning points, the relative importance of different military theaters, and Lee's decision to attack on the third day at Gettysburg, one of the most debated tactical choices on any of the Civil War's battlefields. This section closes with essays on counterfactual speculation, the concept of a long Civil War that has become increasingly prominent in academic circles, and the place of occupation in the conflict's military narrative.

LET THE CHIPS FALL WHERE THEY WILL

Historians interested in the Confederacy navigate in perilous interpretive waters. The subject of their interest began its brief and stormy existence as a breakaway republic devoted to protecting slavery. Mississippi's secession convention put the matter bluntly: "Our position is thoroughly identified with the institutions of slavery—the greatest material interest of the world. . . . A blow at slavery is a blow at commerce and civilization." Vice President Alexander H. Stephens famously agreed, observing in the spring of 1861 that the Confederacy's "foundations are laid, *its corner stone rests, upon the great truth that the negro is not equal to the white man*. . . . This, our new Government, is the first, in the history of the world based upon this great physical and moral truth."[1] Four brutal years of conflict saw the Confederacy mount a prodigious national defense that killed approximately one-fourth of its white military-age males, ravaged its economy, brought the destruction of slavery, and ended in absolute defeat. Along the way, Robert E. Lee and his Army of Northern Virginia carved a record of accomplishment against the odds that resonated powerfully among fellow citizens and invited praise from subsequent generations of Americans.

Following the trail of evidence relating to the Confederacy often leads to conclusions that upset two very different groups of readers—those who romanticize the Rebel republic and try to distance it from the institution of slavery, and those, mostly from the academic world, who bridle at anything they construe as even mildly positive about the Confederates and their nation. Broadsides aimed at me, many of them quite remarkable in their intensity, have come from both directions.

I will start with those from people who jealously protect the Confederacy's image. Like Lost Cause writers after the war who played down the importance of slavery (for example, Stephens claimed that it had not been the Confederate cornerstone, that the conflict was between "the principles of Federalism, on the one side, and Centralism, or Consolidation, on the other"),[2] they choose to ignore the overwhelming preponderance of evidence from the secession crisis and war years. Shortly after I published *The Confederate War,* in 1997, I received a number of communications deploring my characterization of the Confederacy as a "slaveholding republic." It was a nation devoted to state rights, these critics blustered, and I had willfully twisted history to defame the Confederacy. I can only imagine that these individuals have never read the Confederate constitution carefully. The pseudo scholarship seeking to prove that thousands of black men "served" in Confederate armies represents another facet of the effort to get Rebels right on slavery. If there were thousands of black Confederate soldiers (I have seen estimates as high as one hundred thousand), I can only wonder why no one told General Lee. I feel certain he would have requested that some of these men be sent to his army.

Critiques of Nathan Bedford Forrest can also trigger overwrought reactions from Lost Cause devotees. Shelby Foote's inexplicable statement that the "Wizard of the Saddle" ranks alongside Abraham Lincoln as one of the "two authentic geniuses" of the Civil War cries out for refutation. Forrest established himself as a very good cavalry officer who often operated on the fringes of major campaigns; however, nothing in his career, which contains many unsavory elements, justifies the label "genius." My comment to this effect on a television call-in program in 2006 brought a cascade of angry calls and e-mails. One of the latter pronounced me a "social Marxist historian" who "deliberately ignored" the truth of history.

The Confederate War also inspired a very different type of criticism. In the book, I argued that many Confederates demonstrated robust devotion to their slave-based republic, developed feelings of national community, and sacrificed more than any other large group of white people in United States history. The last of these three is uncontrovertibly true; the other two can be debated, though I, not surprisingly, believe the evidence supports my conclusions. I was careful to distinguish between "Confederates" and "southerners," the former being white people in the Confederacy who represented a subset of the latter, which included white and black people in the border states and black people in the Confederacy. Upset with my comments about the level of Confederate commitment, some reviewers and other scholars labeled me a "neo-Confederate"— which in academia is a synonym for "racist." As one put it, my analysis of the "Confederate military and civilian experience veers dangerously close to hagiography of an entire culture."[3]

My goal in *The Confederate War* (and in some of my other scholarly work) was to challenge the idea that lack of will, absence of a sense of national community, fractures along lines of race and class and gender, and flawed military strategy doomed the Confederacy. I insisted that United States armies led by U. S. Grant and William Tecumseh Sherman had much to do with the war's outcome, and that vanquished Confederates were not confused about this in the spring of 1865. I also observed that Robert E. Lee and his army, through their storied campaigns, inspired people behind Confederate lines until very deep into the war. These conclusions strike me as obvious for anyone who reads widely in the evidence, assesses relative rates of human and matériel loss, and compares the Confederate experience to that of other segments of white American society. For some, however, conceding determination and nationalist sentiment to many Confederates is tantamount to endorsing their effort to establish a slaveholding republic. It is a wonderfully perverse reaction that can be summed up this way: "You are what you write about."

Perhaps the safe play would be to forego additional work on the Confederacy, to shift to a bland topic unlikely to arouse anyone's ire. I leave that strategy to others. I will continue to explore what remains for me a complex and fascinating field, to encourage others to do so as well, and to let the interpretive chips fall where they will.

TWO WAYS TO APPROACH ONE WAR

Two Civil Wars await anyone seeking to understand our transformative national trial. In the one dominated by nonacademic historians, armies maneuver against one another, seeking strategic advantage. Once engaged in combat, soldiers in these armies ensure the lasting fame of mundane places on the American landscape. They fight for control of ghastly entrenchments at Spotsylvania's "Bloody Angle," shed blood profligately in D. R. Miller's cornfield at Antietam, and introduce their societies to a new scale of slaughter near a backwoods Methodist church called Shiloh. This Civil War also features celebrated American military commanders. Ulysses S. Grant carries out a brilliant campaign of indirect aggression against Vicksburg, reducing that Rebel stronghold overlooking the Mississippi River on July 4, 1863. Far to the east, two months earlier, Robert E. Lee and Stonewall Jackson lead the Army of Northern Virginia to victory against long odds in the clutching woods around Chancellorsville. Sixteen months after Chancellorsville, William Tecumseh Sherman delivers a powerful blow to the Confederacy when he captures Atlanta. Told and retold by every generation since Appomattox, this Civil War— marked by honor and hubris, triumph and failure, and gallantry and perfidy on an epic scale—comes closer to serving as an American *Iliad* than any other element of our national past.

The second of our two Civil Wars emanates, for the most part, from scholars in an academic setting. Here the focus is on the home fronts, and compelling political issues stand out sharply. For example, how and when will emancipation be accomplished? Who should get credit for removing the stain of slavery that mocked the founding generation's noble language? Will Republicans enact their legislative program? And does their agenda anticipate the emergence of a capitalist behemoth destined to achieve world power status in the twentieth century? In this Civil War, small farmers in the Confederacy grow disenchanted with a government that seems to favor the wealthy, as do coal miners in Pennsylvania's northeastern regions. Women on both sides struggle to find their roles amid changing conceptions of what it means to be a patriotic mother, and sometimes, battling economic hardship, those in the Confederacy take to the streets to demand more food. This war offers a jumble of advocates and victims, all of whom act out parts in a drama largely devoid of battles and generals. For readers drawn to a gripping narrative played out against the boom of cannons and the rattle of musketry, this Civil War neither fires the imagination nor evokes comparisons with Homer. Other readers, however, will find a family's struggle amid the turbulence of war or a slave's successful escape to freedom as powerfully moving as anything on battlefields.

Both these Civil Wars form part of a complicated story that cannot be comprehended by mastering only one. Yet the historical literature has evolved in a way that often conspires against anyone who would engage both wars—who would, more especially, strive to know how the two intersected and influenced one another. The root of the problem lies in the fact that far too many nonacademic historians care for little beyond commanders and battles and soldiers in the ranks, while almost all academic historians nourish a resolutely dismissive attitude toward military history in general and Civil War campaign history in particular.

Because most Americans receive their first introduction to the conflict through battles and generals, I believe military history affords the best way to bring the two wars together in a fashion likely to attract the broadest audience. A certain kind of military history, framed to explain how battles influenced the home fronts and how, in turn, politics and public opinion shaped the Union and Confederate war efforts, will be required to accomplish the task. Success will depend on wooing readers who begin with popular treatments of battles and campaigns, piquing their interest in the other war, and providing a bridge that will carry them across the chasm between academic and nonacademic history.

Some of our best Civil War historians have made excellent progress toward making such connections. Among books from academic scholars, James M. McPherson's *Battle Cry of Freedom* devotes a number of chapters to battles and campaigns—always with an eye toward explaining their larger impact. "Most of the things that we consider important in this era of American history," McPherson asserts, such as "the fate of slavery, the structure of society in both North and South, the direction of the American economy, the destiny of competing nationalisms in North and South, the definition of freedom, the very survival of the United States—rested on the shoulders of those weary men in blue and gray who fought it out during four years of ferocity."[4] Among nonacademic historians, Bruce Catton provides a model for those who seek beautiful writing and gripping military description that also places battles and campaigns within a broader framework.

Tactics and strategy certainly deserve ample attention, but the final meaning of a military operation usually lies beyond the battlefield. Anyone drawn to the Seven Days campaign should know not only that George B. McClellan gave way before Lee's hammer blows at Gaines's Mill and elsewhere, but also that Confederate national morale surged upward with news of Lee's success at Richmond. Similarly, no comprehension of Lincoln's reelection in 1864 is possible without linking civilian morale, voter expectations, and the military campaigns of Sherman in Georgia and of Philip H. Sheridan in the Shenandoah Valley.

None of this is meant to imply that all Civil War studies should deal with both home front and battlefield. There will always be a place, and a market, for close tactical examinations of battles (or, in the case of huge engagements such as Gettysburg, phases of battles). Similarly, a study of legislative infighting relating to the Homestead Act need not devote attention to key military actions at the time. But a diet of books on only the military or only the nonmilitary aspects of the conflict will leave any reader with a poor appreciation of the conflict's daunting complexity.

THE UNION IN MEMORY

On April 20, 1861, a mass of citizens turned out in New York City to support the Union. This impressive gathering, which appropriately took place at Union Square, prompted diarist George Templeton Strong to suggest, "Few assemblages have equalled it in numbers and unanimity." Men, women, and children carried flags or wore cockades, the Stars and Stripes hung from most buildings, and impromptu renderings of "The Star-Spangled Banner" echoed through the streets. "The city," observed Strong, "seems to have gone suddenly wild and crazy."[5]

This outpouring of pro-Union sentiment illuminated why the loyal citizenry chose to fight rather than accept Confederate independence. In a conflict that stretched across four years and claimed more than 800,000 U.S. casualties (360,000 of them dead), the nation experienced huge swings of civilian and military morale before crushing Rebel resistance. Union always remained the paramount goal, a fact clearly expressed by Abraham Lincoln in speeches and other statements designed to garner the widest popular support for the war effort. What Walt Whitman said of Lincoln and Union in the wake of the president's assassination applied equally to most loyal Americans. "UNIONISM, in its truest and amplest sense, form'd the hard-pan of his character," wrote the poet, who defined it as "a new virtue, unknown to other lands, and hardly yet really known here, but the foundation and tie of all, as the future will grandly develop."[6] That hardpan of unionism held millions of

"The Great Meeting in Union Square, New York, to Support the Government, April 20, 1861" appeared in *Harper's Weekly* two weeks after the event. The *New York Herald* estimated on April 21 that 250,000 people had jammed the square and adjacent streets, "truly and literally an uprising of the people in their majesty . . . a grand demonstration in favor of the perpetuity of that 'union of States, union of hearts and union of hands,' which called into being the most glorious and perfect fabric of government that has ever existed. . . . No one can henceforth breathe a doubt concerning the loyalty of the Empire City to the Union, let its preservation cost what it will." (*Harper's Weekly*, May 4, 1861, p. 277.)

Americans to the task of suppressing the slaveholders' rebellion, even as the human and material cost mushroomed.

Whitman celebrated a Union that carried great meaning for loyal citizens who joined him in equating it with "the Nation." It represented the cherished legacy of the founding generation, a democratic republic with a constitution that guaranteed political liberty and afforded individuals a chance to better themselves economically. From the perspective of loyal Americans, their republic stood as the only hope for democracy in a western world that had fallen more deeply into the stifling embrace of oligarchy since the failed European revolutions of the 1840s. Slaveholding aristocrats who established the Confederacy, believed untold unionists, posed a direct threat not only to the long-term success of the American republic but also to the broader future of democracy. Should armies of citizen-soldiers fail to restore the Union, forces of privilege on both sides of the Atlantic could pronounce ordinary people incapable of self-government and render irrelevant the military sacrifices and political genius of the Revolutionary fathers. Secretary of State William Henry Seward encapsulated much of this thinking in one sentence pertaining to the Republican Party's wartime agenda: "Their great work is the preservation of the Union and in that, the saving of popular government for the World."[7]

As we approach the sesquicentennial of the Civil War, the meaning of Union to mid-nineteenth-century Americans has been almost completely lost. Americans typically are reluctant to believe that anyone would risk life or fortune for something as abstract as "the Union." A war to end slavery seems more compelling, something powerfully reinforced for millions of viewers in the film *Glory*. Slavery, emancipation, and the actions of black people, unfairly marginalized for decades in writings about the conflict, have inspired a huge and rewarding literature since the mid-1960s. No longer can any serious reader fail to appreciate how African Americans figured in the political, social, and military history of the war. This has been one of the most heartening developments in the field of Civil War scholarship since the successes of the civil rights movement in the 1950s and 1960s.

Unfortunately, a concentration on emancipation and race sometimes suggests that Union victory had scant meaning apart from them. Historical context is crucial on this point. Anyone remotely conversant with American democracy as practiced in 1860 knows that it denied women, free and enslaved African Americans, and other groups basic liberties and freedoms most northerners routinely attributed to their republic. Almost 99 percent of residents in the free states were white in 1860, and their racial views offend our modern sensibilities. Yet a portrait of the nation that is dominated by racism, exclusion, and oppression obscures more than it reveals. Within the mid-nineteenth-century western world, the United States offered the broadest political franchise and the most economic opportunity. Vast numbers of immigrants believed that, however difficult they might find the circumstances, relocation in the United States promised a brighter future. As one Irish-born Union soldier wrote, "This is my country as much as the man that was born on the soil." If the Union lost the war, he added, "the first test of a modern free government in the act of sustaining itself against internal enemys" would fail and would allow European aristocrats to claim "that such is the common end of all republics."[8]

During the last months of the war, Lincoln and William Tecumseh Sherman spoke to the centrality of Union. The president's fourth annual message to Congress, dated December 6, 1864, mentioned the proposed Thirteenth Amendment to abolish slavery, which had passed the Senate eight months earlier but failed to garner the requisite two-thirds majority in the House of Representatives. The issue should be revisited, Lincoln argued, in light of Republican success in the recent national elections. Those returns represented "the voice of the people now, for the first time, heard upon the question." Lincoln framed his call for another vote in the House with reference to what he knew to be the bedrock of sentiment among loyal Americans. "In a great national crisis, like ours, unanimity of action among those seeking a common end is very desirable—almost indispensable. . . ." he observed. "In this case the common end is the maintenance of the Union," and the amendment stood "among the means to secure that end." Five and one half months later, in the wake of United States victory, Sherman echoed Lincoln's words in a congratulatory order to veterans he had led in Georgia and the Carolinas. "Three armies had come together from distant fields, with separate histories," he said, "yet bound by one common cause—the union of our country, and the perpetuation of the Government of our inheritance."[9]

Maintenance of the Union, as Lincoln and Sherman made clear, always ranked first among war aims for most citizens in the United States. Republicans and many Democrats eventually accepted emancipation as a useful tool to help defeat the Rebels and punish the slaveholding class that most northerners blamed for secession and the outbreak of war. Most also came to believe that only a Union without slavery would be safe from internal threats in the future. Except among abolitionists and some Radical Republicans, however, liberation of enslaved people took a backseat to saving the Union. This fact does not drain all value from a war for constitutional law and a democratic republic on the northern model. For the wartime generation, Union promised liberty, freedom, and opportunity that, while restricted in many ways even with emancipation, would expand as the republic moved through the nineteenth century and into the twentieth. That expansion often proceeded at a depressingly slow pace—even stopped altogether at various points—but likely would have been far more problematic if the Confederacy had succeeded, slavery had survived in some of the loyal states, and the specter of additional groups of states separating themselves from a diminished Union had lingered on the political landscape.

Without an appreciation of why loyal citizens believed a Union that guaranteed democratic self-government was worth great sacrifice, no accurate understanding of the Civil War era is possible. A sesquicentennial that fails to make this clear will have failed in a fundamental way.

THE UNION ARMY AND EMANCIPATION

Abraham Lincoln invited the audience at his second inaugural address to join in gratitude for what Union armies had accomplished when he said, early in the speech, "The progress of our arms, upon which all else chiefly depends, is as well known to the public as to myself; and it is, I trust, reasonably satisfactory and encouraging to all."[10] The "all else" included emancipation, the topic to which the president devoted what became the most quoted sections of his speech.

What Lincoln realized about emancipation also should be apparent in the early twenty-first century—namely, that among contributory elements including the Emancipation Proclamation, congressional legislation, and the actions of hundreds of thousands of African Americans in the Confederacy, the impact of United States military forces stood out as the absolutely essential factor.

Historians over the past thirty years have dealt with the Union army's role in bringing emancipation in a fascinating way. The most prominent debate features those who identify slaves as the primary actors and those who concede that Lincoln should not get all the credit but insist that he should get a good deal of it. Advocates of both positions typically nod toward the Union army as a critical agent in the process—and then ignore it while focusing either on slaves who fled to Union lines or on Lincoln's actions.

The Freedmen and Southern Society Project at the University of Maryland has offered the most powerful case for self-emancipation in a series of volumes of rich documentary evidence. Once disentangled from the idea that the Emancipation Proclamation and the Thirteenth Amendment are the keys, goes the argument, "the story of slavery's demise shifts from the presidential mansion and the halls of Congress to the farms and plantations that became wartime battlefields. And slaves—whose persistence forced federal soldiers, Union and Confederate policy makers, and even their own masters onto terrain they never intended to occupy—become the prime movers in securing their own liberty."[11]

This interpretation removes black people from their position as passive recipients of freedom, embedded in the old image of Lincoln as the Great Emancipator. Any fair assessment of the evidence leaves no doubt that both enslaved people and Lincoln played important parts in the drama of emancipation—so also, of course, did Congress, with the Confiscation Acts and other legislation.

But there can be no doubt that none of the other actors would have been successful on a broad scale without the United States Army. No matter how desperately slaves wanted to be free, the chance to escape was negligible un-

Black refugees crossing the Rappahannock River into Union lines during the campaign of Second Bull Run in August 1862. The presence of United States military forces provided a crucial element in the process of emancipation across much of the Confederacy. (Library of Congress, Prints and Photographs Division, LC-DIG-cwpb-00219.)

less a Union military force had reached their area. In the heartland of Alabama, almost anywhere in Texas, and in many other parts of the Confederacy where Union forces established no sustained presence, freedom remained no more than a tantalizing mirage. Similarly, without the projection of Union military power, Lincoln's proclamation and congressional acts were mere words on paper to both slaves and slaveholders in the Confederacy.

The number of soldiers in United States Colored Troops units from the various Confederate states underscores the importance of Union military forces. Federal armies exercised the greatest control for the longest time along stretches of the Mississippi River and in parts of West and Middle Tennessee. The Confederate states credited with sending the most black men into Federal service all bordered the Mississippi: Louisiana sent 24,052, which constituted 31 percent of its black men between the ages of eighteen and forty-five; Tennessee 20,133—39 percent; and Mississippi 17,869—21 percent. In contrast, Texas, which experienced almost no Union incursions, contributed forty-seven—a statistically insignificant .001 percent of its 36,202 black men in the crucial age group. Georgia, which had the second-largest slave population in 1860 but relatively little long-term Union occupation, accounted for just 3,486 enlistees—4 percent of its total pool. And Virginia, where the Army of Northern Virginia prevented Union forces from establishing long-term control over most of the state until 1865, contributed only 5,919—6 percent of its 101,428 military-age black males.

People at the time grasped the correlation between the arrival of Union military forces and the opportunity for slaves to escape from bondage. I will quote just one of countless examples. Robert Gould Shaw, then a captain in the Second Massachusetts Infantry, wrote to his mother on September 25, 1862. News of Lincoln's preliminary proclamation of September 22 had made its way to the home front and the armies. "So the 'Proclamation of Emancipation' has come at last, or rather, its forerunner," Shaw observed. "I suppose you are all very much excited about it. For my part, I can't see what *practical* good it can do now. Wherever our army has been, there remain no slaves, and the Proclamation will not free them where we don't go."[12]

The men in Union armies did not present what we would consider an ideal collective portrait for a liberating force. White soldiers were racists by our standards—as was virtually everyone else in the mid-nineteenth century.

Moreover, the vast majority of white troops supported emancipation for what seem to be the wrong reasons. They did not embrace it as a stand-alone war aim of intrinsic value. First to last, the mass of the loyal soldiers (and civilians) supported a war for Union. Emancipation represented a tool to help realize the great goal of Union, to punish the oligarchic southern slaveholders who had caused all the trouble in the first place, and to remove any future threat arising from an institution that had, in one way or another, menaced the viability of the nation from the moment of the Constitutional Convention until 1860.

Whatever the attitudes of its troops, the Union army must be considered a bright thread in the tapestry of emancipation. Slighting the role of citizen-soldiers—whether to emphasize the movement toward freedom of hundreds of thousands of African Americans, or Lincoln's continuing importance, or some other factor—prevents true understanding of one of the transformative moments in American history.

UNION VETERANS CLAIMED THEY FOUGHT FOR A HIGHER CAUSE

It has become widely accepted that reconciliation quickly spread across North and South after Appomattox, and that white Americans from both regions agreed to play down the importance of slavery and emancipation in an effort to heal wartime scars. Speeches delivered by Union veterans at Gettysburg in the late 1880s afford a perfect opportunity to test this idea about postwar attitudes. A number of loyal states placed regimental monuments on the field in the 1880s, most of which involved ceremonies with one or more lectures. Speakers alluded to reconciliation with their former Rebel opponents in many instances, but they also celebrated the Union and its citizen-soldiers, deprecated the Confederacy and oligarchic slaveholders, and spoke of emancipation as a salutary outcome of the conflict.

Joshua Lawrence Chamberlain participated in the dedication of the Twentieth Maine Infantry's modest marker on Little Round Top in October 1889. "The organization of the army of the Union was a counterpart of that of the Union itself. . . ." he told the crowd, with an eye toward the importance of the American democratic example. "Our thoughts were not then of States as States, but of the States united,—of that union and oneness in which the People of the United States lived and moved and had their being." Conceding Rebel courage, Chamberlain left no doubt that advocates of Union had been right. "The cause for which we fought was higher; our thought was wider," he affirmed, before taking aim at the slaveholders' memory of the conflict: "The 'lost cause' is not lost liberty and rights of self-government. What is lost is slavery of men and supremacy of States."[13]

Citizen-soldiers who had left comfortable civilian pursuits to take up arms received extensive praise. In June 1889, Michigan governor Austin Blair spoke in the national cemetery with both Union soldiers and their cause in mind. "Our men engaged here were not mere soldiers," he commented, "they were also fellow-citizens engaged in a mighty struggle, and with a definite purpose in view. They were volunteers who had enlisted in this great war with an intelligent sense of patriotic duty." Theodore A. Dodge made a similar point in remarks at the 119th New York Infantry's monument along the line of the Eleventh Corps near the Carlisle Road. "From and after the first three days of July, 1863," said Dodge, "the tide of secession receded, until, after another two years, a million and a half soldiers melted back into the population from whence they came, and the Union was . . . pronounced one and indivisible."[14]

Many speakers gloried in the success of a democratic republic against what they characterized as an oligarchic enemy. A former officer of the Seventy-Third Ohio Infantry, who spoke in September 1887, deplored the Confederacy, with its "ambitious dream of the Southern Empire, of aristocratic government, founded upon caste and slavery as 'the chief cornerstone,' and coupled with this chivalrous ambition for the establishment of aristocratic government, that one race might be supreme at the cost of the brutal degradation of another." Arrayed against that model "was pride in the glory of the Republic and in its free institutions. . . . faith in democratic government . . . and as the outgrowth of these, there was the living and sublime purpose that freedom, and not slavery, should be the ruling power in the future government of these United States." This man opposed the idea of erecting Confederate monuments at

Gettysburg: "I do not believe there is another nation in the civilized world that would permit a rebel monument to stand upon its soil for a single day, and I can see neither wisdom not patriotism in building them here."[15]

Comparable anti-Confederate blasts appeared regularly in the regimental orations. A New Jersey colonel characterized the nascent slaveholding republic as a "military despotism born amid the throes of war, overthrown by the shock of arms, without history save four years of bloody strife, impelled by the twin furies of slavery and treason." Another speaker termed the Confederate cause one "we can never admire," while Reverend James H. Botts of the Sixth Michigan Cavalry blamed the war on "the growing power of slavery, the anticipated glory of secession and the vauntings of personal ambition." The Union cause, insisted Botts, justified the soldiers' "valor and sacrifice . . . compared with which the 'lost cause' will ultimately be lost in contempt in the impartial verdict of future generations." A former captain in the Eleventh Pennsylvania Infantry remembered comrades who thought the Confederacy so evil "they were willing to wash out the footprints of the rebel foe with their blood, and count it a joy to die."[16]

Emancipation figured in many of the speeches at Gettysburg. Colonel John Ramsey of the Eighth New Jersey Infantry, a unit that fought in the Wheatfield, spoke of "the memory of the brave men who died . . . for the safety and perpetuity of the Republic; died that four millions of human beings with their unborn generations should be free." Union victory meant that "the shackles of the slaves should be sold for old iron. That the auction block should be burned. That all men should breathe the fresh air of heaven direct, and not by inhalation from a master." Brigadier General William Hobson addressed veterans of the Seventeenth Maine Infantry in October 1888. The regiment had lost 38 percent of its men on July 2, 1863, experiencing the "thunders of artillery at Gettysburg" that proclaimed "none but free men should live in a free country, and that they all should have equal rights and power under the laws."[17]

Taken as a group, the dedicatory speeches at Gettysburg show that most Union veterans extolled the supremacy of their cause. They would welcome ex-Confederates back into the national fold—but not at the cost of forgetting what they had accomplished in saving the Union and killing slavery.

THE WAR WAS WON IN THE EAST

I was convinced by the age of twelve that military events in the Eastern Theater far exceeded in importance anything that happened west of the Appalachian Mountains. I based this conclusion on Douglas Southall Freeman's
Lee's Lieutenants: A Study in Command and *R. E Lee: A Biography,* Bruce Catton's Army of the Potomac trilogy, and biographies and memoirs devoted
to generals in the Amy of Northern Virginia and the Army of the Potomac.
However interesting the sad records of defeat forged by the Army of Tennessee and other Rebel forces in the West—or the series of triumphs crafted by
Ulysses S. Grant, William Tecumseh Sherman, George H. Thomas, and other
Union commanders—they seemed less decisive than the bloody succession
of Eastern battles that included the Seven Days, Antietam, Chancellorsville,
Gettysburg, and the Overland campaign. Forty years of additional reading
and research have brought me to a more considered, but not a different, conclusion on this much-disputed topic. In terms of political impact, effect on
morale behind the lines in the United States and the Confederacy, perceptions
in London and Paris, and many other ways, the Eastern Theater predominated.

My assessment goes against much historical writing of the past several decades, a good deal of which criticizes the degree to which Lee and his Army of
Northern Virginia, the Battle of Gettysburg, the surrender at Appomattox, and
other elements of the war in the East have shaped American understanding of
the war. Thomas L. Connelly, whose two volumes on the Army of Tennessee
remain the standard treatment, complained of what he called a "Virginia pattern" of interpretation. Begun by Lost Cause writers such as Jubal A. Early in
the 1870s and continued in the twentieth century by Freeman, that "pattern,"
Connelly asserted, helps explain "why the history of the Civil War is for many
Americans synonymous with the battlefields of Virginia."[18]

Herman Hattaway and Archer Jones reminded readers, in *How the North
Won: A Military History of the Civil War,* that Henry W. Halleck, who presided
over the first period of Union success in the Western Theater and later served
as general in chief and chief of staff, wielded great influence on the course
of the war. "Not only a western outlook but Halleck's western generals," they
wrote, "dominated the Lincoln–Halleck strategy of the war. When the war

concluded, Halleck generals commanded everywhere east of the Mississippi. Only [George G.] Meade, in the shadow of both Grant and [Philip H.] Sheridan, did not belong to Halleck's original command."[19]

Among the most effective advocates of the West's importance, Richard M. McMurry admired Lee's generalship but insisted the war was lost in the West between 1861 and 1863. By the time Lee took command of the Army of Northern Virginia on June 1, 1862, Union armies had dealt their opponents "a series of serious—arguably mortal—blows along the western rivers. Over the next twelve months, Rebel fortunes in the West continued to slide downhill, and it became less and less likely that the Confederates could avoid defeat 'by not losing' since they were, in fact, losing."[20]

I believe the war was far from decided by the summer of 1862—or the summers of 1863 or 1864. The key for the Confederacy lay in convincing a majority of the citizens in the United States that subduing the rebellion would be too costly in lives and material resources. Three times Confederate arms came close to doing so, largely because of what Lee accomplished in the Eastern Theater—in the late summer and early autumn of 1862, following southern victories in the Seven Days and Second Bull Run campaigns and the invasion of Maryland; in the late spring and early summer of 1863, after Fredericksburg, Chancellorsville, and Lee's second invasion of the United States; and, most important of all, in the summer of 1864, when the unprecedented casualties of the Overland campaign and Grant's inability to capture Richmond, together with other Union failures, sent civilian morale in the North spiraling downward.

There is ample evidence on how people on both sides thought about the Eastern Theater. Confederates focused on Lee and his soldiers because the Army of Northern Virginia supplied almost all good news from the battlefield. Such was Lee's stature that Appomattox effectively marked the end of the war. "I have looked on Genl. Lee as the rallying point for the Army of the South," wrote a Virginia woman on April 13, 1865. "I have really lived on hope for four years & now I am utterly bewildered." Eliza Frances Andrews, a young Georgian, agreed. "Fresh rumors of Lee's surrender," she noted sadly, left everyone "ready to give up hope. 'It is useless to struggle longer,' seems to be the common cry, and the poor wounded men go hobbling about the streets with despair on their faces."[21]

Frank Leslie's Illustrated Newspaper conveyed a similar attitude in its coverage of the Grand Review of Union forces in May 1865. It accorded a full measure of praise to Sherman's western forces but insisted that the Army of the Potomac, because it confronted Lee's famous command, had shouldered the greatest military burden: "Against them the power of the rebellion was mainly concentrated and consumed. Whether attacking or defending, it was the Army of the Potomac, with its mighty sledge, that battered the traitor fabric into the dust." And Lincoln famously complained, in August 1862, that a splendid record of success in the West, stretching from Forts Henry and Donelson through Shiloh and fall of New Orleans, had been offset by McClellan's retreat after the Seven Days. "Yet it seems unreasonable," the president complained to a French diplomat, "that a series of successes, extending through half-a-year, and clearing more than a hundred thousand square miles of county, should help us so little, while a single half-defeat should hurt us so much."[22]

I mean none of this to suggest that western battles and generals were unimportant—Vicksburg, for example, loomed far larger in 1863 than did Gettysburg. But whatever we may think, people at the time most often gazed eastward to gauge how the war progressed. Their perception was crucial, and we should take it seriously.

THE DESPERATE GAMBLE

Following the carnage of the failed frontal assault against the Union center at Gettysburg on July 3, 1863, General Robert E. Lee rode among survivors of Major General George E. Pickett's division as they returned to the sheltering slopes of Seminary Ridge. Luckily for future students of the battle, Lieutenant Colonel Arthur James Lyon Fremantle, the British observer and diarist temporarily attached to James Longstreet's headquarters, was on the scene to record Lee "engaged in rallying and in encouraging the broken troops." When Brigadier General Cadmus M. Wilcox approached the commanding general, "almost crying" in Fremantle's judgment, "Lee immediately shook hands with him and said, cheerfully, 'Never mind, General, *all this has been* MY *fault*—it is *I* that have lost this fight, and you must help me out of it in the best way you can.'"[23] This example of Lee's willingness to take responsibility for his own decisions—it *was* his fault, of course—provides powerful evidence of his aggressive generalship's gruesome cost.

As friendly a witness as Edward Porter Alexander, who considered Lee a supremely gifted officer, judged his old chief's tactical offensive on the third day at Gettysburg harshly: "Perhaps in taking the aggressive at all at Gettysburg in 1863 & certainly in the place & dispositions for the assault on the 3rd day, I think, it will undoubtedly be held that he unnecessarily took the most desperate chances & the bloodiest road." Confederate cavalry general Wade Hampton, while recovering from wounds incurred at Gettysburg, wrote that the Pennsylvania campaign was a "complete failure" during which Lee resorted to unimaginative offensive tactics. "The position of the Yankees there," the South Carolinian insisted, "was the strongest I ever saw & it was in vain to attack it."[24]

Why did Lee choose that bloody, and ultimately unsuccessful, course? The prudent decision, as Alexander pointed out, would have been to shift to the defensive following the Confederate tactical victory on July 1. But Lee overlooked the Federals' superior ground, waved off objections from James Longstreet, and, frustrated by what he considered substandard performances from J. E. B. Stuart, Richard S. Ewell, and A. P. Hill, decided to risk a great deal on the afternoon of July 3. In the end, a breathtaking confidence in his infantry likely proved the decisive factor in guiding Lee's actions.

A memorable episode at Chancellorsville two months earlier helps to explain Lee's behavior at Gettysburg. Heavy fighting forced a Federal withdrawal on the morning of May 3, and Lee rode northward from Hazel Grove to the Plank Road, then turned east toward Chancellorsville crossroads. A mile's ride carried him to a scene that no artist could improve. Confederate artillery south of the Plank Road sent deadly missiles into the ranks of retreating Federals. Smoke from woods set afire by musketry and shells drifted skyward. Just north of the Plank Road, in a clearing that had been the center of Hooker's line, stood the Chancellor House, itself ablaze with flames licking at its sides. Lee guided Traveller through thousands of Confederate infantrymen, general and mount dominating a remarkable tableau of victory. Emotions flowed freely as the soldiers, who had lost nearly nine thousand comrades in the morning's fighting, shouted their devotion to Lee, who acknowledged their cheers by removing his hat.

Seldom has the bond between a successful commander and his troops achieved more dramatic display. Colonel Charles Marshall of Lee's staff captured the moment: "The fierce soldiers with their faces blackened with the smoke of battle, the wounded crawling with feeble limbs from the fury of the devouring flames, all seemed possessed with a common impulse. One long, unbroken cheer, in which the feeble cry of those who lay helpless on the earth blended with the strong voices of those who still fought, rose high above the roar of battle, and hailed the presence of the victorious chief." Lee basked in "the full realization of all that soldiers dream of—triumph."[25] Chancellorsville marked the apogee of Lee's career as a general and cemented the reciprocal trust between him and his men that helped make the Army of Northern Virginia a formidable military instrument.

That trust impressed many observers as the Confederates entered Pennsylvania in June. Ample testimony about soaring confidence in the Army of Northern Virginia lends credence to the idea that Lee believed his infantry could do anything he asked. Fremantle addressed morale in his diary. Over supper on the evening of July 1, Longstreet discussed the reasons attacks might fail; however, added Fremantle, in the ranks, "the universal feeling in the army was one of profound contempt for an enemy whom they have beaten so constantly, and under so many disadvantages." The men's attitude, together with Lee's great faith in them, implied a degree of scorn for the Federals noted by Fremantle's fellow foreign observer, Captain Justus Scheibert of the Prussian army: "Excessive disdain for the enemy . . . caused the simplest plan of a direct attack upon the position at Gettysburg to prevail and deprived the army of victory."[26]

Two of Lee's statements at the time suggest the centrality of his unbridled confidence in the army's rank and file. He wrote to his wife on July 26 that the army had "accomplished all that could reasonably be expected. It ought not to have been expected to have performed impossibilities," he admitted, in a sentence that could be taken as self-criticism, "or to have fulfilled the anticipations of the thoughtless & unreasonable." Five days later, Lee expressed similar thoughts to Jefferson Davis: "No blame can be attached to the army for its failure to accomplish what was projected by me. . . . I am alone to blame, in perhaps expecting too much of its prowess & valour."[27]

On July 3, Lee concluded that his infantry could overcome the recalcitrance of his lieutenants, difficulties of terrain, and everything else to achieve great results. Fourteen years after the battle, former division commander

Henry Heth succinctly summed up what had happened in Pennsylvania: "The fact is, General Lee believed the Army of Northern Virginia, as it then existed, could accomplish anything."[28]

THE WAR'S OVERLOOKED
TURNING POINTS

The Civil War witnessed dramatic shifts of military momentum. As armies contended for supremacy on the battlefield, their successes and failures dramatically influenced politics and civilian morale on the home fronts. For nearly 150 years, those who have written about the conflict—from members of the wartime generation to recent historians—have argued about when and where the war turned decisively toward United States triumph. These debates, in turn, have sparked lively discussion in a reading public eager to identify the war's most important military operations.

Candidates put forward as decisive moments in at least one book include U. S. Grant's capture of Forts Henry and Donelson; the battle of Shiloh; the Confederate loss of New Orleans; George B. McClellan's victory at Antietam; George G. Meade's repulse of Robert E. Lee at Gettysburg; Grant's success at Chattanooga; Grant's cornering of Lee in Richmond and Petersburg as a result of the Overland campaign; William Tecumseh Sherman's capture of Atlanta; Philip H. Sheridan's multiple triumphs in the 1864 Shenandoah Valley campaign; and George H. Thomas's rout of the Army of Tennessee at Nashville. Titles of books such as Larry J. Daniel's *Shiloh: The Battle That Changed the Civil War*, Stanley F. Horn's *The Decisive Battle of Nashville*, and James M. McPherson's *Crossroads of Freedom: Antietam* (with a tagline on the cover describing the contest as "the battle that changed the course of the Civil War") reflect a widespread affinity for turning points.

Gettysburg looms largest in the public imagination as the war's grand turning point, the "high-water mark of the Confederacy" that ended any realistic hope for southern independence and pointed inexorably toward Appomattox. Yet Gettysburg affected the long-term shape of the war relatively little. Lee correctly predicted that, in its aftermath, the Army of the Potomac would be "as quiet as a sucking dove" for six months (in fact, ten months elapsed before the next big battle in the Eastern Theater), and Abraham Lincoln expressed bitter disappointment with what he considered an incomplete victory that would allow the war to "be prolonged indefinitely."[29]

Neither did the other much-trumpeted Union win of July 1863 make much of a difference. Vicksburg's surrender on the eighty-seventh anniversary of the Declaration of Independence sent joyful tremors through the loyal states, and in conjunction with the capture of Port Hudson a few days later, opened the entire Mississippi River to Union naval power. As the title of Michael B. Ballard's excellent study of the campaign indicates, Vicksburg stood as "the campaign that opened the Mississippi."[30] The key to the river's importance lay not in opening it to northern control, however, but in closing it as a great artery of Confederate commerce—and that had been accomplished in April 1862, when Union forces took control of New Orleans. Grant's famous success at Vicksburg, which undoubtedly surpassed Gettysburg in effect at the time, generated a greater emotional than military result.

What about Antietam? It rivals Gettysburg on most rosters of vital turning points, heralded as the moment when emancipation came to the fore as a central issue of the conflict and Great Britain and France backed away from some type of intervention. No one can gainsay Antietam's importance, but it neither guaranteed that the war would end slavery nor settled the question of European involvement. As late as the summer of 1864, with Union forces bogged down outside Richmond and Atlanta and the loyal citizenry reeling from the Overland campaign's grisly casualties, Republican prospects in the looming elections looked dim. George B. McClellan in the White House and a Democratic Congress might have pushed on to Union victory, but they would have expended no effort to make certain the peace settlement included freedom for enslaved African Americans. Similarly, a series of Confederate victories after Antietam probably would have rekindled British interest in brokering an end to the war.

I believe the Seven Days did more to shape the future direction of the war than any of the more commonly discussed turning points. The climactic battles of McClellan's Peninsula campaign occurred when Confederate national morale had reached a crisis because of dazzling Union successes in the Western Theater between February and early June 1862. From Forts Henry and Donelson through Shiloh and the capture of the vital rail crossroads of Corinth, Mississippi, Confederates had suffered repeated disasters. Jefferson Davis and his government struggled with the loss of New Orleans, Nashville, Memphis, most of the Tennessee heartland, and any chance of maintaining a serious presence in Kentucky. Opposed by Joseph E. Johnston, whose retreat prompted widespread criticism among Confederates, McClellan reached the outskirts of Richmond by the end of May. It is difficult to imagine how the Confederacy could have survived the loss of its capital, which seemed imminent, on top of all the bad news from the Western Theater. The war would have ended with slavery almost completely intact and with McClellan, a staunch critic of forced emancipation, as the preeminent Union war hero.

Unfortunately for Little Mac, Johnston suffered a grievous wound at Seven Pines on May 31, and he was replaced by Robert E. Lee the next day. Within a month, the armies fought five bloody battles that culminated at Malvern Hill, McClellan abandoned offensive thoughts, Richmond remained defiantly in Confederate hands, and southern civilians took heart. Lee's ascension to command of the Army of Northern Virginia prolonged the war for almost three years. As time passed, he and the Army of Northern Virginia became the most important national institution in the Confederacy. Their campaigns sustained among the Confederate people a belief in the possibility of independence and more than once spread despair across the loyal states.

Because of its striking reorientation of the strategic situation in the summer of 1862, as well as the long-term consequences of Lee's generalship with regard to morale, the possibility of emancipation, and the duration of the war, the Seven Days campaign belongs in the front rank of Civil War turning points.

DID THE FALL OF VICKSBURG REALLY MATTER?

U. S. Grant's capture of the Rebel stronghold at Vicksburg, Mississippi, in July 1863 ranks as one of the great military achievements of the Civil War. The culmination of many months' activities, which included frustrating setbacks for Union forces, the victory underscored Grant's determination, willingness to take risks, and clarity of purpose when others—including his friend and subordinate, William Tecumseh Sherman, as well as Abraham Lincoln—had expressed doubts about the final result. After John C. Pemberton surrendered the thirty-thousand-man army defending Vicksburg, Lincoln famously observed that the "Father of Waters again goes unvexed to the sea," a sentiment that spoke to the importance of Vicksburg and the river in the national imagination. As for the impact of the operation on Grant's standing at the executive mansion, the president remarked, two days before getting word of Vicksburg's fall, that if the Confederate army defending the citadel capitulated, "Grant is my man and I am his the rest of the war."[31]

General in Chief Winfield Scott had helped convince Lincoln that the Mississippi River should figure prominently in Union military planning. On May 3, 1861, in a letter to George B. McClellan, Scott stated that a successful strategy against the Confederacy would "rely greatly on the sure operation of a complete blockade of the Atlantic and Gulf ports to commerce." In tandem with the blockade, the venerable general also proposed "a powerful movement down the Mississippi to the ocean, . . . the object being to clear out and keep open this great line of communication in connection with the strict blockade of the sea-board, so as to envelop the insurgent States and bring them to terms."[32] Although never formally codified as a strategic blueprint, these ideas became part of what during the war and ever since has been labeled the Anaconda Plan, whereby Scott proposed to squeeze the life out of the Confederacy by seizing control of the waters that surrounded and bisected it.

Generations of historians have treated Vicksburg as a major event that helped shape ultimate Union victory. Many also have complained that proportionately too much attention has been accorded Gettysburg, news of which reached most loyal citizens just before that of Vicksburg. The latter charge surely is correct. Richard A. Sauers's *The Gettysburg Campaign, June 3–August 1, 1863: A Comprehensive, Selectively Annotated Bibliography* (2nd edition, 2004) contains 6,193 entries; a compendium relating to the Vicksburg campaign, should anyone be inspired to produce one, would muster only a fraction as many titles.

Despite this imbalance in the literature, Vicksburg looms very large in many modern historical accounts. James M. McPherson's *Battle Cry of Free-*

dom, for more than a quarter century the most widely read one-volume history of the war, notes that because of Grant's efforts, the "Confederacy was
cut in twain." Terry L. Jones's more recent *The American Civil War*, a detailed
treatment with a military focus, expands on McPherson's point: "The rebel-
ling states were now split in two, and the war in the west had permanently
turned in the Union's favor. The key to the Confederacy was finally in Lincoln's
pocket." David Goldfield's *America Aflame: How the Civil War Created a Nation*
deploys a more spacious geographic framework. "Vicksburg was essential to
Confederate fortunes in the West," writes Goldfield. "Holding on to Vicksburg
kept the Federals out of a major stretch of the river and the Gulf of Mexico
and shut off the Old Northwest from using the river as a commercial outlet."[33]

How should we assess the importance of Vicksburg? It doubtless represented a military debacle for the Confederacy in terms of lost manpower
and matériel, dealt a major short-term blow to southern civilian morale, and
boosted spirits on the Union home front. Unlike Gettysburg, which left Abraham Lincoln deeply dissatisfied and did not impress most Confederates as a
catastrophic defeat, Vicksburg offered an uncomplicated story line of Union
triumph. Even the most optimistic Confederate could find nothing positive
in the campaign.

Yet Vicksburg did not deliver a fatal blow to Confederate chances for independence. The war continued for nearly two more years, escalating in fury
and marked by major shifts in military momentum. In August 1864, more than
thirteen months after Pemberton's force capitulated, Lincoln predicted Republican defeat in the upcoming elections and expressed deep concern about the
war's outcome. During that bloody summer, events at Vicksburg in the first half
of 1863, like the battle of Gettysburg, were largely irrelevant. Only William Tecumseh Sherman's and Philip H. Sheridan's victories in September and October 1864 retrieved the political situation, placing United States military forces
and the Union cause on the clear path to Appomattox and Durham Station.

Neither should Vicksburg's fall be labeled the decisive moment in the
struggle to control the Mississippi. That palm should go to Union operations
against New Orleans in the spring of 1862. David G. Farragut's naval maneuvering allowed Benjamin F. Butler to take formal control of the city on May 1,
closing the river as a great economic artery for the Confederacy. Never again
could Rebels move goods into or out of their largest city and most important

port. Catherine Ann Devereux Edmondston, who followed the war closely from her home in eastern North Carolina, voiced a common reaction among Confederates. "This terrible fall of New Orleans," she wrote in her diary, "what a blow it is to us, Sugar gone, Texas Beef & wool for the food & clothing of the Army, leather, Horses! All lost to us." In her postwar memoirs, Varina Davis echoed Edmondston's language and probably spoke what both she and President Davis had thought in May 1862: "The loss of New Orleans was a terrible disaster."[34]

Although it wielded less influence than many believe, Vicksburg also represented a "terrible disaster" for the Confederacy, rendering it a compelling and consequential military operation.

WHAT IF?

What if Stonewall Jackson had been with the Army of Northern Virginia at Gettysburg? What if Nathan Bedford Forrest had been given command of an army in the Western Theater? What if Joseph E. Johnston had not been wounded at Seven Pines on May 31, 1862? What if Abraham Lincoln had not called for seventy-five thousand volunteers to suppress the rebellion on April 15, 1861? Such questions have spawned lively debates as long as people have been interested in the Civil War. The correct answer to all of these questions is that no one knows what would have happened in these or myriad other counterfactual situations. Individuals determined to discuss only what actually occurred often dismiss any speculative foray into "What if?" territory as a foolish waste of time. I believe some of the questions have more substantive potential than others, but no harm can result from addressing any of them.

The one I hear most often relates to Jackson at Gettysburg. A sarcastic answer might go something like this: "Because he had been dead for almost two months, Jackson's presence at Gettysburg as a decaying corpse would have made no difference at all." This question usually arises from a belief that the mighty Stonewall would not have behaved as Richard S. Ewell did late on the afternoon of July 1. Instead of deciding not to continue the offensive, he would have ordered attacks against Cemetery Hill and perhaps Culp's Hill, swept Union units off that critical high ground, and completed the day's tactical triumph against the Army of the Potomac's First and Eleventh Corps. It is safe to suppose that Jackson probably would have been more aggressive than Ewell, but whether that would have yielded greater success is much more problematic. Even a Federal retreat on the night of July 1 simply would have shifted the action southward, to Pipe Creek or some other position that George G. Meade would have defended.

Forrest's supporters also have an answer in mind when posing their question. Many of them second Shelby Foote's extravagant assessment of Forrest as one of the war's "two authentic geniuses," proclaiming that his ferocious audacity at the head of an army could have salvaged Confederate prospects in the Western Theater. Forrest certainly posed problems for Union commanders throughout the war and demonstrated genuine gifts for raiding and harassment of enemy forces. Yet absolutely nothing in his record reveals the type of administrative and political skills necessary to oversee an army, and his hair-trigger temper and sometimes erratic behavior almost certainly would have produced problems at any level above that at which he operated.

Joseph E. Johnston's wounding raises more intriguing possibilities. He had retreated to the outskirts of Richmond during the Peninsula campaign, mounted a breathtakingly inept series of assaults at Seven Pines, and likely would have found himself besieged in the capital within a few weeks. A siege would have played to George B. McClellan's strengths. Little Mac could have taken his time to bring superior Union strength to bear; placed powerful artillery along his positions, as he had at Yorktown in April; relied on the United States Navy to control the James River; found time to ride around his lines, receiving the adulation of his soldiers;[35] and closed the campaign with one of two likely scenarios: surrender of the Rebel army or Johnston's abandonment of Richmond.

Either of those two denouements would have made continued Confederate resistance very difficult. A relentless tide of defeat had plagued the Confederacy in the Western Theater during the previous six months, including defeats at Forts Henry and Donelson, Shiloh, and Pea Ridge; the surrender of New Orleans, Nashville, and Memphis; and the loss of the Mississippi River as a commercial artery, along with most of Tennessee's rich logistical heartland. Richmond's fall in July or August, on the heels of so much bad news from the

West, almost certainly would have undone the Confederacy and restored the Union, with McClellan as the preeminent northern military idol and emancipation unsecured.

Huge consequences also could have flowed from a decision by Lincoln to take a more conciliatory course after Fort Sumter's fall. Debates relating to the handling of Sumter within the high political and military counsels of the United States during March and early April are well known. The Confederate bombardment of the fort surely changed the equation, but an earlier instance of such aggression, when South Carolina batteries fired on the *Star of the West* on January 9, 1861, had not precipitated a major federal reaction. Lincoln could have waited, though the negative political consequences might have been great.

The actions of the Upper South hinged on Lincoln's response to Fort Sumter. Most significantly, the call for volunteers immediately changed the political situation in Virginia, where the secession convention had voted against leaving the Union but performed an abrupt about-face two days after Lincoln's call. Virginia's action virtually guaranteed a much longer and bloodier war to suppress the rebellion. It was birthplace to 91 of the 425 men who became Confederate generals, contributed more soldiers to southern armies than any other state (North Carolina's long-standing but unsupportable claim to that distinction notwithstanding), and possessed one-fifth of the Confederacy's railroad mileage and assessed value of farmland and buildings and a much higher percentage of its industrial capacity. Virginia also carried with it the immense prestige of unequaled ties to the revolutionary era's founding generation. More than all of those things, it supplied the man who would become the Confederacy's equivalent of George Washington. R. E. Lee posed the greatest obstacle to Union victory after 1862, vexing Federal military opponents and influencing civilian morale on both sides of the Potomac. Other Virginians, including Stonewall Jackson and Jeb Stuart, also played crucial roles at high levels of command. In sum, without Virginia's participation as a Confederate state, it is difficult to imagine a four-year war that extracted a massive toll in human and material resources.

What if all speculation about might-have-beens ceased immediately? Our knowledge about the conflict would not be affected . . . but some of the enjoyment of exploring its leading figures and dramatic events would be lost.

DID THE WAR END IN 1865?

On April 10, 1865, Secretary of the Navy Gideon Welles mused about news regarding U. S. Grant's "capture of Lee and his army" the previous day. "The tidings were spread over the country during the night," noted Welles, "and the nation seems delirious with joy. . . . This surrender of the great rebel Captain and the most formidable and reliable army of the secessionists virtually terminates the rebellion." Welles predicted that there would be some continued "marauding, and robbing & murder . . . but no great battle, no conflict of armies, after the news of yesterday reaches the different sections." One day later, a lawyer in New York City suggested in clipped sentences that the demise of Lee's army carried decisive weight: "People hold the war virtually ended. It looks so. Lee is out of the game." Acerbic Richmond editor Edward A. Pollard, whose massive *Southern History of the War* chronicled the stormy life of the Confederacy as it unfolded, echoed Welles and the New Yorker. In the final volume of *Southern History*, completed in 1865, Pollard remarked, "The surrender of General Lee drew after it important and rapid consequences, and, in effect, terminated the war."[36]

Although these three witnesses anticipated how most Americans would understand the end of the Civil War, an increasing number of scholars have questioned whether Lee's surrender should be reckoned the decisive indicator of Confederate national failure and the effective end of the war. The onset of the sesquicentennial of Reconstruction has inspired a good deal of attention to what some historians have labeled the "long Civil War." This builds on a phenomenon that has been present for a number of years and seeks to emphasize postwar violence in the former Confederacy and the conflict's other enduring consequences. Within this chronological reframing, the war did not end at Appomattox but rather extended through Reconstruction, or through the Jim Crow era, or down to the present—the "war that never ended" syndrome.

For far too long, argue those who embrace the analytical lens of a long Civil War, a disproportionate number of authors and readers have burrowed ever more deeply into the period between Fort Sumter and Appomattox, treating those four bloody years largely in isolation and thereby robbing the conflict of

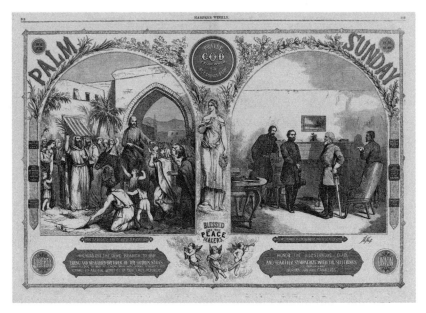

"Palm Sunday." Thomas Nast's two-page illustration, which juxtaposes Jesus entering Jerusalem with Grant meeting Lee at Appomattox, treats the war as essentially over. Text along the right side reads: "The Armies of the Republic Have by the Blessing of God Triumphed over the Foes of the Union the Constitution and the Laws." For Nast, as for so many others in the United States and the Confederacy, Appomattox essentially ended the conflict. (*Harper's Weekly*, May 20, 1865, pp. 312–13.)

needed context. A longer perspective works against a focus on Appomattox, which stood alongside Gettysburg as one of the two events that received the most popular attention during the sesquicentennial. Too much attention to Appomattox, in this view, creates a misleading impression that Grant and Lee fashioned an agreement that ended fighting and opened the way for reunion and reconciliation.

No serious person can dispute the necessity of placing the Civil War within a spacious nineteenth-century landscape. More specifically, any attempt to grasp the centrality of the war to the larger story of American history must engage with its long-term racial, constitutional, social, and commemorative effects. Many of the profound questions with which the Civil War generation grappled remain present, in some form, as we move through the second decade of the twenty-first century. Continuing debates about state versus central authority, the difficulty of ordering a biracial (now multiracial) society in a fair manner, the challenges of a military occupation, the friction between military and political imperatives in a war, and the messy aftermaths of armed confrontations all bring Civil War examples to mind.

But constructions of a long Civil War should not obscure the fact that the conflict, which placed more than three million men under arms and killed perhaps a quarter of them, *did end* in 1865. Clear indications of this fact include the surrender of all Confederate military forces, the dismantling of the Confederate state, the restoration of the Union, the destruction of slavery, and the rapid demobilization of a million citizen-soldiers of the United States. These are huge outcomes that underscore the unequivocal termination of a war that, had the verdict on the battlefield been otherwise, would have established a powerful republic devoted to the perpetuation of slavery.

The political and social conflict that followed Appomattox should not be considered an extension of the war by other means. Postwar violence, however grotesque at times, did not approach in scale or fury the seismic military carnage of the war years. The bloodiest incidents during Reconstruction, among them the New Orleans and Memphis riots of 1866 and the Colfax massacre of 1873, scarcely would have qualified as skirmishes during the actual war. Moreover, former Confederates perpetrating much of the postwar violence had vastly scaled back their goals, from establishing a proslavery nation-state to regaining local political power and maintaining white supremacy.

Ex-Confederates mounted a determined effort to salvage what they could from a shattering defeat. Most almost certainly would have preferred to reinstitute slavery, but they settled for a watered-down version of what the Confederacy had provided: a social structure within which white people exerted economic, legal, and social control over millions of black people. The Jim Crow South, a reality by the late nineteenth century, lasted for many decades and should be viewed as the most obvious expression of the Confederate generation's response to defeat and emancipation.

To describe postwar events as a violent continuation of the military action of 1861 to 1865, however, robs the most all-encompassing war in American history of much of its singularity and meaning. Too great an emphasis on the long Civil War, in fact, can reduce the war itself to just one episode or event among many—and strip Appomattox of any claim to signaling the conclusion of the nightmarish conflict. U. S. Grant, it is worth mentioning, immediately accepted the centrality of what transpired on April 9, 1865. In his *Memoirs*, he averred that Lee's surrender essentially closed the rebellion. "I determined to return to Washington at once," he explained, "with a view to putting a stop to the purchase of supplies, and what I now deemed other useless outlay of money."[37] For the general in chief, managing the transition to peace already had begun.

OCCUPATION AND THE UNION MILITARY EFFORT

Scholarship on Civil War soldiers has explored in detail the immediate experience and long-term impact of combat. Disease, hard marching, and exposure to the elements all took a toll during the conflict, but above all, as one scholar put it, "the major psychological trauma that Civil War soldiers encountered related to the terror of battle." Another historian noted that "even victory had a price" for Union veterans because the "terror of this unprecedented war long outlived the stacking of arms at Appomattox."[38]

This rich literature raises an obvious question: What about soldiers who never really "saw the elephant"? What did it mean to have little or no chance of engagement with the enemy's regular forces? On the Union side, William F. Fox's classic *Regimental Losses in the American Civil War, 1861–1865* highlights strikingly different types of service. The Army of the Potomac's Second Corps anchored one end of the spectrum in terms of combat. It included individual regiments that suffered the largest percentage and numerical loss in any battle, the regiments that sustained the largest numerical loss for the whole war, and, quite remarkably, thirty-five of the one hundred Union regiments that lost the most men in battle. On the other hand, the United States fielded "over 300 regiments which were not in action, with as many more which were under fire but a few times. A large part of the Union Armies was used in protecting communications, guarding lines of supply, in garrison duty, and as armies of occupation."[39]

An emerging body of work examines the many thousands of men, in both white regiments and United States Colored Troops units, who rendered their principal duty as occupying forces. Gregory P. Downs's *After Appomattox: Military Occupation and the Ends of War* (2015) and Andrew F. Lang's *In the Wake of War: Military Occupation, Emancipation, and Civil War America* (2017) expose the futility of seeking to understand Civil War soldiering—and its impact over time—through the creation of a universal template featuring combat.

Union troops occupied approximately one hundred cities, towns, and hamlets across various parts of the Confederacy as well as in the loyal slave states of Missouri, Kentucky, and Maryland. They dealt extensively with Confederate civilians, often had sustained contact with African Americans as refugees or residents of the occupied areas, protected railroads and lines of communication, and mounted forays to deal with local guerrillas. In large cities such as New Orleans and Nashville, they acted as police and represented a crucial component of the effort to implement the process of Reconstruction.

White and black soldiers often reacted differently to occupation duty. Much like soldiers deployed to deal with Indian threats in remote areas, a significant number of officers and enlisted men in white units resented their situation. They looked to the great national armies as most responsible for saving the Union and lamented having to deal with politics, counterinsurgency, boring garrison duty, and the complex process of emancipation. As citizen-soldiers carrying out a civic responsibility, they had enlisted to crush armies of Rebels who would destroy the work of the revolutionary generation. But as occupiers, they resembled British regulars who had menaced republican liberty during the revolutionary era.

Charles O. Musser of the Twenty-Ninth Iowa Infantry, stationed in Little Rock, Arkansas, groused in June 1864 of exile to a backwater. Reading about U. S. Grant's confrontation with Robert E. Lee in Virginia, he expressed a "wish we could be transferred to the 'Army of the Potomac.' I would rather go there and run the chances of being Shot than Stay here all Summer." Most comrades in the regiment also wanted "a change of Department," he added, and if the Virginia campaign "is to be the decisive one of the war, we would like to participate in it."[40]

Another Iowan wrote from near Brownsville, Texas, in April 1864, about unpleasant elements of occupation. "Upon our arrival [at] Santiago," his regiment realized "there was daily labor for hundreds of men and which of necessity must have been performed by soldiers. . . . Forts and fortifications were to

"Pickets of the First Louisiana 'Native Guard' Guarding the New Orleans, Opelousas and Great Western Railroad." The accompanying text, which betrays common racial prejudice from the era, pronounced black soldiers "impervious to miasma" and thus well qualified for occupation duty in the Deep South. "Among the cypress swamps of Louisiana negro soldiers are invaluable" because conditions "unendurable to our soldiers of the North" hold "no horrors to them." (*Frank Leslie's Illustrated Newspaper*, March 7, 1863, front cover.)

be made requiring the labor of hundreds of men for months. Streets were to be swept and cleaned daily and this is work of a very disagreeable character." In this instance, African American soldiers—"the laborers of the Army"—would be assigned most of this tedious work. "I thank the originators of the Corps d' Afrique," stated Benjamin F. McIntyre coldly, "for taking from us such labor as belongs to menials."[41]

Black soldiers, who after 1863 composed a significant percentage of the occupying forces, often displayed attitudes antithetical to those of white counterparts. Well aware that combat against Confederate military forces represented the ideal for citizen-soldiers, most USCT men nonetheless considered occupation a valuable dimension of the war effort. It placed them on the slaveholders' ground, allowed them to provide a measure of protection for black refugees, and directly undermined governmental and social structures that sustained slavery. Whereas many white occupiers questioned the use of military forces to control Confederate civilians, USCT soldiers typically welcomed the opportunity to impose a harsh regime on their enemy's home front.

The diary of William Woodlin of the Eighth USCT describes an operation in Florida typical of innumerable others. A "three days tramp" in early June 1864 "brought in quite a large quantity of cattle & two prisoners who were taken to Jacksonville on the whole it was quite a successful foraging expedition. two adult Contrabands with their children were brought in, as well as a goodly No. of white trash whom we did not keep long . . ."[42]

In May 1865, most U.S. soldiers believed their military obligation ceased with the reestablishment of the Union and emancipation. The loyal citizenry agreed. Congress reduced the size of the volunteer army from a million to only eleven thousand within eighteen months. The regular army, by 1869, mustered just thirty-seven thousand, many of them deployed in the West. These figures underscore how little support existed to approve—and fund—a large army of occupation in the South. This reality lessened the possibility of equality across racial lines during Reconstruction and highlighted an ideology that limited the army's peacetime role in a constitutional republic.

~ IV ~
HISTORIANS AND BOOKS

Time consigns almost all historians and their work to obscurity. Each generation produces a new crop of authors whose books build on earlier literature, garner reviews and attention, and reshape the field. In many instances, older books feature discredited assumptions about race or thoroughly debunked interpretive conventions that render them unworthy of notice except as historiographical relics or curiosities. One epoch's influential phenomenon can become another's embarrassment, as demonstrated by Claude G. Bowers's *The Tragic Era: The Revolution after Lincoln* (1929). Other historians and books merit continuing attention because of their superior analysis, depth of research, or success in taking historical literature on the Civil War era in important new directions. The thirteen essays in this section gave free rein to my bibliophilic tendencies and provided a great deal of enjoyment. I chose historians active from the 1920s until the early twenty-first century (some academic and some popular), a few specific titles, and genres that have interested or impressed me across many years. David Donald, Benjamin Quarles, Kenneth M. Stampp, and T. Harry Williams, among others, easily could have joined this roster, as could a very large number of superior books. I finish with a discussion of bibliographic tools that can help modern readers find past gems while navigating through the intimidating mass of publications in the field.

LESSONS FROM DAVID M. POTTER

David M. Potter's work has influenced me throughout my professional career. While in graduate school, I read *Lincoln and His Party in the Secession Crisis; The South and the Sectional Conflict*, which included a version of Potter's brilliant essay "The Historian's Use of Nationalism and Vice Versa"; and *The Impending Crisis, 1848–1861*, a volume in the prestigious New American Nation series. All three revealed Potter's gifts for writing analytical narratives, explaining complex issues clearly, and demonstrating the need to engage historical actors within the circumstances of their eras.

Lincoln and His Party alerted me to what Potter calls "the fallacy of reading history backward."[1] I refer to it as the "Appomattox syndrome," the phenomenon of beginning with the end of a historical story firmly in mind and then searching back in the evidence to understand what happened. This approach almost always obscures at least as much as it reveals and promotes a sense of historical inevitability historians should try to avoid.

In *Lincoln and His Party,* Potter cautions about assuming that Republican leaders, as they debated how to deal with threats of secession in 1860, must have known war was possible. "Inasmuch as they had been the first to foresee an 'Irrepressible Conflict,'" he remarks, regarding a common perception about Republicans, "it seems implausible that they should have been the last to recognize that the conflict was on the eve of materializing." Historians and lay readers who knew battles such as Shiloh and Gettysburg followed secession and establishment of the Confederacy found it "scarcely credible that the Republicans should have been so oblivious to the impending tragedy."[2]

But Potter's discussion of evidence reveals how Republicans could have misjudged the likelihood of secession and war. Sources from the time indicate "that the only reliable indices of the future were the warnings of secession which came from Southern politicians, editors, and legislators"—and

Republicans, as well as Democrats, had "long experience of Southern threats which had never led to action. For thirty years the Republic had flourished and expanded under constant threats of dissolution." President James Buchanan remarked in 1856 that southern members of his Democratic Party "have so often cried 'wolf' . . . that it is difficult to make people believe it." Three years later, a Republican congressman from Indiana somewhat humorously alluded to how "our Southern friends have dissolved the Union forty or fifty times."[3]

First to last, judges Potter, Republicans sought to find a nonmilitary solution to the sectional crisis. At first doubtful that secession would come, and subsequently convinced that unionism among southerners "would restore their states to the Union," Lincoln and the Republicans refused to compromise on slavery's extension into western territories. "Tactically," states Potter, "the policy was executed with great skill. Strategically, it was defective in that it overestimated the extent of Southern Unionism in some measure, and misconceived the character of Southern Unionism entirely."[4]

Potter also taught me to assume complexity beyond any simplistic—and often beguiling—formulation when dealing with such things as human motivation. He applied this insight to his exploration of the topic of loyalty in "The Historian's Use of Nationalism and Vice Versa." Rather than frame the issue as forcing individuals to choose between the Union and their native state (Robert E. Lee's example often is presented in these terms), Potter reminds us that every human being possesses numerous overlapping and often mutually reinforcing loyalties, with different ones emerging as most important at various times. He mentions, among other things, cultural factors, "the invigorating effect which war had had upon national spirit," and "community of interest, not in the narrow sense of economic advantage only, but in the broad sense of welfare and security through membership in the society." Within the South during the Civil War era, the last of these applied most obviously to white insistence on maintaining supremacy in a society that included millions of enslaved black people.[5]

The Impending Crisis, 1861–1865 served as a capstone to much of Potter's earlier work. His death at age sixty in 1971 left the manuscript just short of completion, and Don E. Fehrenbacher, a colleague at Stanford University, wrote the last two chapters in a way that maintained Potter's interpretive cast. After more than forty years, this six-hundred-page study remains the best narrative on the coming of the Civil War. Brimming with perceptive analysis of characters and events, it instructs readers about history's vexing complications. The war with Mexico establishes the starting point for Potter's narrative. A moment when U.S. victory and "acquisition of the Southwest had sealed the triumph of national expansion, . . . it had also triggered the release of forces of sectional dissension." How best to develop the vast western areas fueled escalating political warfare over the ensuing quarter century. "Perhaps it may even be said," ventures Potter, "that the developments which gave American nationalism the strength to survive also generated a supreme threat to its survival."[6]

Fehrenbacher's two closing chapters revisit consistent themes throughout Potter's work. They call for rejecting "an illusion produced by scholarly logic infused with scholarly hindsight" and for viewing the secession winter "as contemporaries did, in all its disorderly and changing variety of options and potential consequences." The political crisis, replete with contingent twists and turns, was "over secession and not, in any direct way, over slavery. Yet all of the efforts at compromise in Congress dealt with the issue of slavery and only obliquely with the problem of secession." In other words, the crisis had everything to do with slavery's powerful influence over American political affairs, but the increasingly heated rhetoric did not focus on whether the nation would keep or jettison the institution. Four years of war settled "the issues that inflamed the antebellum years. . . . Slavery was dead; secession was dead; and six hundred thousand men were dead. That was the basic balance sheet of the sectional conflict."[7]

Anyone interested in antebellum sectionalism or the conduct and meaning of the Civil War should explore David M. Potter's writings. He belongs on any short list of the most perceptive interpreters of mid-nineteenth-century United States history.

TWO GIFTED WRITERS

The Civil War era has attracted more than its share of talented writers. Unexcelled political drama, compelling individuals in and out of uniform, and storied battles provide rich material for anyone seeking to tell a gripping story. Each generation since Appomattox has produced splendid authors, beginning with participants such as U. S. Grant and Edward Porter Alexander. Winston Churchill explored the conflict in *A History of the English-Speaking Peoples,* the last volume of which, completed in the 1950s, devoted considerable attention to military events and personalities. Readers interested in the coming of the war have turned with profit for more than forty years to David M. Potter's *The Impending Crisis: 1848–1861.* In our own time, Shelby Foote and James M. McPherson, whose appealing prose styles differ markedly, are probably read more widely than any other historians in the field.

Bruce Catton and Douglas Southall Freeman command far less attention now than when they drew me into the world of Civil War history more than fifty years ago. This is much to be lamented, for few authors have written so movingly and perceptively about the war. Between the mid-1930s and the mid-1960s, the pair produced a number of classic titles and achieved wide recognition. Freeman appeared on the cover of *Time* in 1948, and Catton received a Presidential Medal of Freedom in 1977.

A native of Michigan, Catton (1899–1978) cast the wider net in selecting subjects. He wrote a trilogy on the Army of the Potomac—*Mr. Lincoln's Army, Glory Road,* and *A Stillness at Appomattox*—that heralded his appearance as a major author and won a Pulitzer Prize in 1954. Catton's other books include a second trilogy, *The Centennial History of the Civil War,* comprising *The Coming Fury, Terrible Swift Sword,* and *Never Call Retreat,* published between 1961 and 1965; three volumes on U. S. Grant; a one-volume history of the North during the war titled *This Hallowed Ground;* and *The American Heritage Picture History of the Civil War,* which earned a Pulitzer Prize special citation in 1961. The last of these, with Catton's graceful text and well-chosen illustrations, remains unexcelled as an enjoyable introduction to the Civil War.

Catton's narratives abound with memorable passages. In *Glory Road,* for example, he dramatically brings the Iron Brigade's five Midwestern regiments onto the first day's field at Gettysburg, where they would lose roughly two-thirds of their 1,800 men. "The Westerners fell into step and came swinging up the road," writes Catton, in setting the stage for a bloody day's work on McPherson's Ridge and Seminary Ridge, "their black hats tilted down over their eyes, rifle barrels sparkling in the morning sun. . . . On the ridge to the west there was a crackle of small-arms fire and a steady crashing of cannon, with a long soiled cloud of smoke drifting up in the still morning air, and at the head of the column the drums and the fifes were loud—playing 'The Girl I Left Behind Me,' probably, that perennial theme song of the Army of the Potomac, playing the Iron Brigade into its last great fight."[8]

Catton's description, in *A Stillness at Appomattox*, of the explosion of the mine at Petersburg on July 30, 1864, is equally superb. "First a long, deep rumble, like summer thunder rolling along a faraway horizon," caught the attention of waiting Union attackers, "then a swaying and swelling of the ground up ahead, with the solid earth rising to form a rounded hill, everything seeming very gradual and leisurely. Then the rounded hill broke apart, and a prodigious spout of flame and black smoke went up toward the sky, and the air was full of enormous clods of earth as big as houses, of brass cannon and detached artillery wheels, of wrecked caissons and fluttering tents and weirdly tumbling human bodies; . . . the landscape along the firing line had turned into dust and smoke and flying debris, choking and blinding men and threatening to engulf Burnside's whole army corps."[9]

Freeman (1886–1953) focused more narrowly on Robert E. Lee and the Army of Northern Virginia. The son of a Confederate veteran from Virginia and longtime editor of the *Richmond News Leader,* he published *R. E. Lee: A Biography,* a four-volume Pulitzer Prize winner that remains the most detailed life of Lee, and the trilogy *Lee's Lieutenants: A Study in Command,* a combination of battle narrative and biographical portraits of key officers in the Confederacy's most important army. Freeman's last project, a multivolume biography of George Washington, garnered a posthumous Pulitzer Prize in 1958.

Modern readers should keep in mind that Freeman embraced Lost Cause interpretive conventions—scarcely surprising, considering his background. His biography of Lee, though a bonanza of carefully mined factual detail, often veers toward hero worship. "Because he was calm when others were frenzied," reads one passage, "loving when they hated, and silent when they spoke with bitter tongue, they shook their heads and said he was a superman or a mysterious man."[10]

Yet Freeman's descriptive prose and character sketches remain engaging and informative, as when, in *Lee's Lieutenants,* he deals with the artillery fighting on May 3, 1863, at Chancellorsville. "At Hazel Grove, in short, the finest artillerists of the Army of Northern Virginia were having their greatest day," he observes of cannoneers conditioned to face a more powerful foe. "They had improved guns, better ammunition, and superior organization. Officers and men were conscious of this and of the destruction they were working. For once they were fighting on equal terms against an adversary who on fields unnumbered had enjoyed indisputable superiority in weapons and in ammunition. With the fire of battle shining through his spectacles, William Pegram rejoiced. 'A glorious day, Colonel,' he said to Porter Alexander, 'a glorious day!'"[11]

Catton and Freeman stand up very well alongside more recent narrative specialists. Their literary gifts evoke events and individuals in ways that justify more than one reading and place them among the distinguished chroniclers of the Civil War.

"THE PLAIN FOLK'S PIONEER"
REFRAMED HISTORY

Bell Irvin Wiley (1906–1980) created an influential body of scholarship that marked him as a pioneer in exploring the lives of common people during the Civil War. Born in Tennessee and trained in history at Yale University, he spent most of his teaching career at Louisiana State University and Emory University. Long before such topics had gained wide favor, he examined men in the ranks of both Confederate and United States armies, the yeomanry and poorer white southerners, and the experiences of free and enslaved black people in the Confederacy. Few historians of his or any other era can claim a greater corpus of pathbreaking work.

Publication of Wiley's *The Life of Johnny Reb: The Common Soldier of the Confederacy*, in 1943, and *The Life of Billy Yank: The Common Soldier of the Union*, nine years later, marked a watershed in scholarship relating to the military history of the Civil War. It is no exaggeration to say that Wiley invented the genre of soldier studies that, many decades later, featured works by historians such as James M. McPherson, Reid Mitchell, James I. Robertson Jr. (a student of Wiley's), and Chandra Manning. The overwhelming focus of earlier publications in the field had been on generals and the strategic and tactical details of famous campaigns. Before the appearance of Wiley's two volumes, anyone seeking information about the war's citizen-soldiers looked most obviously to John D. Billings's *Hardtack and Coffee, Or, The Unwritten Story of Army Life* (1887) or Carlton McCarthy's *Detailed Minutiae of Soldier Life in the Army of Northern Virginia, 1861–1865* (1882), a pair of titles by veterans who sought to capture the flavor of enlisted men's daily experiences.

Wiley based his conclusions about common soldiers on a close reading of thousands of letters. He dealt with the process of enlistment, motivations to serve and remain in the ranks, what the men ate and wore, how they amused themselves, how they were armed, how they reacted to combat, why and in what numbers they deserted, how they related to people on the home front, the plague of disease, attitudes toward the enemy, and religious practices. Influenced by what he knew of American soldiers in World War II, he found relatively little evidence of strong ideological commitment—an aspect of his work that has undergone significant revision by later scholars.

Though rigorous in handling evidence, and far from a romantic, Wiley nonetheless allowed his admiration of Civil War soldiers to show. He closes *The Life of Billy Yank* with an appreciative look at the rival combatants, concluding that "the similarities of Billy Yank and Johnny Reb far outweighed their differences. They were both Americans, by birth or by adoption, and they both had the weaknesses and the virtues of the people of their nation and time. For the most part they were of humble origin, but their conduct in crisis compared favorably with that of more privileged groups and revealed undeveloped resources of strength and character that spelled hope for the country's future." He evinced a strong element of reconciliationist sympathy in lamenting "that people so similar and basically so well-meaning found it necessary to resort to arms in settling their differences . . . Their descendants can point with justifiable pride to the part played in the struggle by both the Blue and the Gray."[12]

Every scholar who has written a word about common soldiers owes a debt to Wiley, whose books retain great value as repositories of compelling wartime testimony, storehouses of factual material, and reminders of how historians can breathe new life into a field as extensively studied as the Civil War. Reprinted numerous times, the two volumes are available in a handsome paperback edition from Louisiana State University Press.

The Confederate home front also attracted Wiley's attention in *The Plain People of the Confederacy*, a slight volume published the same year as *The Life of Johnny Reb*. Originating as the Fleming Lectures at LSU, it comprises three chapters, "The Common Soldiers," "The Folk at Home," and "The Colored Folk." Wiley's chapter on white civilians contradicts the Lost Cause portrait of a united and gallant struggle against hopeless odds and anticipates much recent literature that emphasizes disaffection and demoralization on the home front. Many civilians, both men and women, remained steadfast in the face of great hardship, but "Long before the finale at Appomattox, the doom of the Confederacy had been firmly sealed by the widespread defection of her humblest subjects."[13] Although I find greater evidence of Confederate national sentiment and give more weight to Union military operations as a contributor to southern defeat, I believe Wiley's opinions merit continued attention and respect.

The same is true of his handling of the black experience in the Confederacy—both in the final chapter of *Plain People of the Confederacy* and in *Southern Negroes, 1861–1865*, the latter first published in 1938 and subsequently reprinted at least three times. In examining black people, Wiley once again placed himself far ahead of most white scholars of the 1930s and 1940s. His prose betrays attitudes and phraseology that offend modern sensibilities, but his analysis also counters the then-prevalent image of loyal slaves most dramatically evident in the 1939 cinematic version of *Gone with the Wind*. "Long after hostilities had ended," observes Wiley in *Plain People of the Confederacy,* "writers and speakers were wont to descant upon the perfect confidence that masters reposed in their slaves during the dark days of conflict, but these testimonials do not square with repressive measures enacted at the time."[14]

A volume of essays dedicated to Wiley in 1976 by former doctoral students rendered a fair judgment regarding his overall contribution to Civil War studies. "Wiley is—and will remain for years to come—the premier authority on the heretofore faceless masses of the 1860s. . . . [He] gave new life to the Civil War's common folk."[15] A substantial literature now exists, and continues to grow exponentially, on topics Wiley engaged long before they were popular—a testament to his prescience and scholarly imagination.

RECOVERING ALLAN NEVINS

Authors who imagine they write for the ages should look to the chastening example of Allan Nevins (1890–1971). Once a giant in the field, whose name often appeared alongside earlier luminaries such as James Ford Rhodes, Nevins worked almost literally to the end of his long life. A prolific historian and twice winner of the Pulitzer Prize who spent much of his academic career at Columbia University, Nevins produced a body of work that reached a broad popular as well as a scholarly audience. His masterwork, titled *Ordeal of the Union* and published between 1947 and 1971, covered the origins of the Civil War and the conflict itself in eight large volumes (he died before writing two proposed volumes on Reconstruction). The four volumes on the war, which carry the general title *The War for the Union*, total 1,972 pages and reflect engagement with a daunting range of historical sources. Written with verve and attentive to military, political, economic, social, and diplomatic aspects of the conflict, *The War for the Union* makes a powerful case for the modernizing impact of the conflict on the loyal states.

The final two volumes, subtitled *The Organized War, 1863–1864* and *The Organized War to Victory, 1864–1865*, detail how the United States marshaled and applied resources to suppress the rebellion. "That the Civil War brought a systematic shift in American society from an unorganized society to a well-organized nation is undoubtedly much too strong a statement," suggests Nevins. "But that the Civil War accentuated and acted as a catalyst to already developing local tendencies toward organization, there can be no doubt. . . . That such a pragmatic trend would have occurred without wartime demands is unquestionable, but it certainly would have been different and perhaps slower."[16]

Nevins's close examination of how the United States mounted a powerful war effort does not convey a sense of inevitable Confederate defeat. For example, a chapter on the "Balance Sheet at Mid-War" reminds readers of "a fundamental difference" between the task each side faced in the spring of 1863. "The North had to fight for a decisive victory in the field," notes Nevins, "for the destruction or hopeless crippling of the Confederate armies, and the subjugation of the rebellious areas and their inhabitants." The Confederacy, in contrast, "could pursue a less difficult objective, well short of an elimination of the main Union forces." A draw was as good as a win for the Confederacy because "Northern war-weariness would compel acquiescence in Confederate independence."[17] In other words, Nevins exposes the shallowness of the notion that Confederates strove against impossible odds—a notion made most popular, perhaps, by Shelby Foote's observation in Ken Burns's PBS series that the Union fought the war "with one hand tied behind its back" and always could have deployed the other hand if necessary.

Although Nevins meticulously avoids demonizing the Confederacy's people and leaders, his sentiment clearly lies with the soldiers in blue uniforms who saved the Union and gave force to the Emancipation Proclamation. For him, the war marked a milestone of national advancement and improvement, a hard but worthwhile test for a republic that had wrestled with issues relating to slavery for many decades. His handling of the war's devastation in much of the Confederacy illuminates this theme. "Yet the dragon of desolation that ravaged the South in the last year of war," he observes, "carried, like Shakespeare's ugly and venomous toad, a precious jewel in its head. It cleared a field for new tillage; it did a work of transformation that, however brutal, had to be done. . . . Much was being destroyed in the South, but much had to be destroyed if a better land, with better institutions and ideas, was to be born."[18]

Like many citizens of the loyal states at the close of the war, Nevins finds purpose in the struggle to save the Union beyond its meaning for Americans. "The republic emerged from the struggle," he argues, "as men enjoying a little perspective of time later realized, in the grip of some heady new impulses of vast extent and irresistible force." The western world recognized, after the verdict of Appomattox, "the permanence of American institutions" and watched as the United States extended its economic and, in time, political and military reach.[19]

Nevins wrote toward the end of a time when historians took on projects that sometimes extended across a decade or two and yielded sweeping narratives of grand events or detailed biographies of leading figures. Reviewers generally recognized the scale of effort involved in *The Ordeal of the Union*, predicting that it would stand the test of time. "It can be safely asserted," suggested one reviewer in 1972, "that *The War for the Union* and the other volumes in *Ordeal of the Union* will outlast the carpings of their critics. The historical world can ill afford to lose an Allan Nevins whose dedication to scholarship, good writing, and diligent labor have served as an unattainable ideal to his students and countless others both professionals and amateurs. Fortunately his multitudinous works . . . remain as an inspiration to those writers who would try to recreate the past."[20]

A leading bibliography of the war echoes the reviewer in predicting long-term influence for Nevins. "This incomparable work," reads the annotation, "delivers a massive, heavily documented, and detailed story of the secession crisis and the Civil War written by one of the master historians of the modern era. . . . the great accomplishment of this narrative will remain valuable for decades to come."[21]

In fact, Nevins's four volumes on the war remain valuable but almost never consulted. They have disappeared from the literary landscape of the Civil War almost completely, like some vibrant commercial center relegated to obscurity because railroad planners chose a route that went through another town. Such a fate is as undeserved as it is unfortunate. Nevins wrote before social, gender, and cultural history hit their strides and substantially expanded what we know about the era, but the descriptive and analytical strengths of *The War for the Union* guarantee continuing value.

ACKNOWLEDGING ELLA LONN

During the first third of the twentieth century, women produced a body of work that anticipated directions Civil War–era scholarship would take many decades later. Annie Heloise Abel's trilogy *The Slaveholding Indians* (1915–1925) offered a detailed examination of Native Americans between the late-antebellum years and the early phase of Reconstruction. Bessie Martin's *Desertion of Alabama Troops from the Confederate Army* (1932) and Georgia Lee Tatum's *Disloyalty in the Confederacy* (1934) agreed that disaffection on the military and civilian fronts, often fueled by class conflict, undercut the southern war effort. Louise B. Hill's *State Socialism in the Confederate States of America* (1936) presented the Confederacy as "the most successful demonstration of State Socialism to be found up to the time in modern civilization."[22] Although they are all in some respects dated, these titles reflect their authors' rigorous academic training, retain value, and, except for Hill's, are available in paperback editions.

Ella Lonn's career overlapped with the other four historians, and her publications, in both quantity and topical reach, made her the most important woman in the field between the 1920s and the 1950s. Educated at the University of Chicago and the University of Pennsylvania, Lonn wrote six books, five of them devoted to the war or Reconstruction. Very few men during the same period, though in many instances better known, matched, never mind exceeded, her accomplishment.

Lonn's first book, *Reconstruction in Louisiana After 1868,* appeared during the era when a series of state studies, many produced by students of John H. Dunning at Columbia University, brought the postwar years to scholarly prominence. As with the volumes produced by what came to be called the Dunning School, Lonn's book reflects the racial prejudice of the era and treats Reconstruction as a dark time of great travail for the white South. Lonn argues that social conflict during Reconstruction "was largely a race question, though the bitterness of feeling toward . . . [the South's] conquerors and contempt of carper-bagger and scalawag enter to complicate the matter."[23] Despite its flaws, the book reflects considerable research and remained the standard title on the subject for half a century.

Desertion During the Civil War, Lonn's second book, addresses a controversial element of the conflict and remains, after almost ninety years, the only general treatment of the subject. "To the casual reader the knowledge of any desertion in the brave ranks of the armies engaged in the Civil War . . ." wrote Lonn, at a time when thousands of Civil War veterans remained very visible, "will come as a distinct shock; even by the historical scholar the full extent of the evil . . . and the enormous numbers implicated on both sides may not be fully grasped."[24] In a text divided evenly between the United States and the Confederacy, Lonn explores the causes and extent of desertion, the behavior of men after they left their units, and efforts to control the problem. She estimates that 8,600 of 12,000 deserters from Virginia and nearly 9,000 of 24,000 from North Carolina rejoined the army, while also emphasizing that the presence of thousands of deserters greatly demoralized civilians in parts of North Carolina, Georgia, Florida, and Mississippi.

Recognizing that many Confederate "offenders had little conception of the gravity of their offense in military law," she nevertheless concludes that the Richmond government and military authorities "were unduly lenient" in handling their crime. Lonn judges desertion a contributing factor to Confederate defeats after 1862 and "a prime factor in precipitating catastrophe in 1865," but she pronounces northern desertion "the more to be deplored" because it lengthened a war that Union resources otherwise might have ended sooner.[25]

Lonn next turned her attention to a mineral critical to the Confederate war effort. *Salt as a Factor in the Confederacy* documented the centrality of salt to mid-nineteenth-century society and war making. Lonn examines Confederate efforts to produce enough salt, U.S. targeting of salt-making facilities, and the direct and ancillary military, as well as economic and social, consequences related to shortages of salt. In the end, insists Lonn, the "fact that salt could become a major problem to the confederacy reveals strikingly the industrial backwardness of the south, its complete dependence on outside sources for primary needs and emphasizes that fact as the most serious of its disadvantages in the unequal struggle."[26]

Seven years passed before Lonn produced *Foreigners in the Confederacy*, a pathbreaking five-hundred-page work that reviewers praised for its comprehensive research and originality. Lonn seeks to counter the Lost Cause idea that hordes of foreigners helped fill Union ranks while Confederates lacked access to such manpower. Comparatively, she demonstrates, foreigners were overrepresented in Confederate armies, and she underscores the presence of significant foreign-born populations in major southern cities. Although Lonn exhibits prejudices common to the time in generalizing about the Irish, Hispanics, and other groups, the book, which contains a mass of useful information, places her far ahead of the scholarly curve in reminding readers that the conflict played out within a context that included Europe, Mexico, and other parts of the world.

Foreigners in the Union Army and Navy provided a companion to Lonn's earlier study. Its more than seven hundred pages dealt with units composed wholly or primarily of foreign-born soldiers as well as with a number of prominent officers (the navy gets relatively little attention). Lonn estimates that one-quarter of all Union soldiers—more than five hundred thousand—were born outside the United States, with Germans and Irish placing first and second in terms of numbers. As in her book on foreigners in the Confederacy, she links common characteristics, both positive and negative, to ethnicity. Describing her research as "the most laborious of the writer's entire experience," she apologizes for not mastering Polish, Russian, and Italian sufficiently to engage with sources in those languages. In the end, she states, "men from all parts of the world" created "a truly American army, composed of native sons and adopted sons. . . . all animated by a genuine devotion to the ideals for which the Union stood and hence constituting from its divergent parts a unity."[27]

Ella Lonn wrote and taught at a time when Civil War scholarship was thoroughly dominated by men, who studied military operations, great captains, and political events and leaders. An outlier in many respects, she merits serious attention from modern students of the conflict.

SHELBY FOOTE, POPULAR HISTORIAN

Shelby Foote's appearance as the principal talking head on Ken Burns's influential PBS documentary made him one of the most widely read Civil War historians of the past twenty-five years. His *The Civil War: A Narrative,* published by Random House in three volumes between 1958 and 1974 and later repackaged in many forms, has earned a large audience of readers seeking a general treatment of the conflict. Foote's prominence invites a few thoughts about *The Civil War: A Narrative* and the nature of his legacy in the field of Civil War history.

Foote's narrative gifts and comprehensive geographic approach stand out. As one who admired Bruce Catton's Army of the Potomac trilogy and Douglas Southall Freeman's *Lee's Lieutenants: A Study in Command,* I was not overly impressed when I initially encountered *The Civil War* in the mid-1960s. I subsequently formed a greater appreciation for Foote's style. "It was a Monday in Washington, January 21; Jefferson Davis rose from his seat in the Senate," begins volume one. After briefly narrating how seven states had left the Union, Foote returns to Davis to complete the opening paragraph: "The senator from

Mississippi rose. It was high noon. The occasion was momentous and expected; the galleries were crowded, hoop-skirted ladies and men in broadcloth come to hear him say farewell. He was going home."[28] This passage, which reflects Foote's admiration for Ernest Hemingway, draws the reader into an epic narrative of 2,934 pages that effectively conjoins literary merit and absorbing subject matter.

The three volumes reveal what a gifted stylist can do with even well-known episodes. The description of Spotsylvania's Bloody Angle on May 12, 1864, exemplifies this attribute: "The Bloody Angle. The term had been used before, in other battles elsewhere in the war, but there was no doubt forever after, at least on the part of those who fought there, that here was where the appellation best applied. . . . These were the red hours of the conflict, hours no man who survived them would forget, even in his sleep, forever after. Fighting thus at arm's length across that parapet, they were caught up in a waking nightmare, although they were mercifully spared the knowledge, at the outset, that it was to last for another sixteen unrelenting hours."[29]

Foote relied almost entirely on published primary materials—especially memoirs and the 128 thick volumes of the *Official Records of the Union and Confederate Armies*—and on secondary works, many of which would be described as quite dated today. His research did not approach what most contemporary scholars, who spend a great deal of time combing through unpublished manuscripts, consider an acceptable standard. Yet I believe Foote was careful, did his best to write evocatively and accurately—and succeeded to an impressive degree.

The three volumes' subtitles pair eastern and western events that reveal Foote's geographic palette. Fort Sumter, Fredericksburg, and Appomattox join Perryville, Meridian, and Red River—and Meridian, which for novices probably would conjure images of imaginary lines that circle the globe but nothing associated with the Civil War, most forcefully expands traditional geographic boundaries. At the end of volume three, Foote explains his desire to combat the notion "that the War was fought in Virginia. . . . It was my hope to provide what I considered a more fitting balance, East and West, in the course of attempting my . . . purpose of re-creating that war and making it live again in the world around us."[30] He succeeds very well indeed in this effort, and untold readers have been the beneficiaries.

However pleasurable to read and admirable in embracing the war's geographic whole, much of Foote's narrative fits a bit too comfortably within the Lost Cause tradition developed by former Confederates. Although he includes U. S. Grant and William Tecumseh Sherman as well as R. E. Lee and Nathan Bedford Forrest among his favorite characters, he cannot accept slavery's centrality to the coming of the war, attributes United States triumph to overwhelming numbers and matériel, portrays the Confederacy battling gallantly and with no loss of honor against hopeless odds, and imagines Reconstruction as a horror inflicted on the white South by victorious Yankees. He reiterated themes from the books in his contribution to Burns's series. "I think the North fought that war with one hand behind its back" he remarked, regarding inevitable Union victory. "I don't think the South ever had a chance to win that war."

Foote flies his sectional flag honestly in volume one. "One word more perhaps will not be out of place," he notes. "I am a Mississippian." He remembered Confederate veterans—all dead by the time he wrote. "I hope I have recovered the respect they had for their opponents until Reconstruction lessened and finally killed it. . . . I yield to no one in my admiration for heroism and ability, no matter which side of the line a man was born or fought on. . . . If pride in the resistance my forebears made against the odds has leaned me to any degree in their direction, I hope it will be seen to amount to no more, in the end, than the average American's normal sympathy for the underdog in a fight."[31]

What about Foote's legacy? Most important and lasting, I believe, is that his memorable performance on Burns's series prompted thousands of people to buy and read his trilogy and then go on to other authors and titles. He also anticipated scholarly arguments that the Western Theater was at least as important as the Eastern Theater, but academic historians did not go down this interpretive path because of Foote's work. I believe the trilogy has had almost no impact in terms of shaping scholarship—just as Bruce Catton's has not. Even the best popular writers face a formidable task in crossing the chasm between the academic and nonacademic worlds of Civil War history. Foote often compared the Civil War for Americans to the Trojan War for Greeks, characterizing it as our *Iliad*. He never would have equated himself with Homer, I suspect, but many of his readers might.

GETTYSBURG'S GREAT HISTORIAN

The sad news of Harry Pfanz's death in 2015 evoked fond memories of working with him in the early period of developing a Civil War list at the University of North Carolina Press. In the fall of 1985, I learned that Harry had a big manuscript devoted to part of the battle of Gettysburg. I raised the possibility of soliciting the manuscript with Matthew Hodgson, who served as director of the press and had spoken with me about publishing some studies of Civil War military campaigns. Impressed that Harry was chief historian of the National Park Service and had spent many years at Gettysburg National Military Park earlier in his career, Matt asked to see a sample chapter. Harry sent him one. "I have read your chapter with considerable interest," Matt wrote Harry in December 1985, "and would very much like to read your manuscript in its entirety."[32]

Harry soon delivered a narrative of more than one thousand manuscript pages that examined fighting on the southern end of the battlefield on July 2. After going through the text, I reported to Matt that it was a model of the genre and predicted that it "should take its place among the classic Civil War tactical studies." I made the same point to Harry a bit later. He responded with his usual quiet modesty, expressing the hope that his manuscript would please Matt and UNC Press. "It covers well-known ground that has been scratched but not plowed," he observed. Then, with understatement, he added, "The subject ought to have considerable appeal."

Gettysburg—The Second Day was published in December 1987 and became an instant success. It met a standard for tactical studies that few other books, before or after, have equaled. The History Book Club made it a selection in March 1988, and reviewers praised the quality of Harry's research, the clarity of his prose, and the soundness of his judgment. Pfanz knew Gettysburg's terrain "about as well as it is possible to know it" and displayed "meticulous research and a vigorous, lucid sense of narrative" in the book, wrote one reviewer, and another praised "the most complete account of the main fighting on July 2 that will ever be written."[33] *Gettysburg—The Second Day*—which Harry called "the orange covered book" in reference to its original dust jacket—quickly went through five printings, quite a remarkable achievement for a six-hundred-page study that assesses the performances of scores of officers and tracks the movements of a huge number of regiments, batteries, and larger units. I have a note Harry sent me in early 1987, which I laid in my copy of the book's first edition. "I've been thinking of the help that you gave me in making contact with the University of North Carolina Press," he wrote graciously, "and continue to be grateful for it."

UNC Press was equally grateful to Harry, as was I, for sending his impressive work to Chapel Hill. That gratitude grew over the next several years, as Harry delivered two more superior manuscripts. *Gettysburg—Culp's Hill and Cemetery Hill* and *Gettysburg—The First Day* appeared in January 1994 and July 2001, respectively. The three titles total 1,642 pages and remain foundational for anyone interested in the most famous battle of the Civil War. No one else approaches Harry in terms of contributions to our understanding of the tactical story of Gettysburg. As one prominent historian put it, Harry's volumes on Gettysburg "comprise a great classic, and the best Gettysburg material ever published."[34]

On a more personal note, I grew to treasure my friendship with Harry and learned an immense amount from him. In our extensive walks around the Gettysburg battlefield in the 1980s and early 1990s, he helped me understand many complicated episodes of the fighting. His amazing command of the battle's ebb and flow allowed me, for example, to grasp the incredibly complex action in the Wheatfield, the often-slighted struggles along the slopes of Culp's Hill, Jubal Early's two-brigade assault against East Cemetery Hill and Cemetery Hill on the evening of July 2, and James Longstreet's convoluted flank march on July 2. Those walks and my other time with Harry convinced me that, without question, Edwin C. Bearss had it right in his blurb for *Gettysburg—The First Day*: "No one knows and understands the battle of Gettysburg better than Harry W. Pfanz."

One golden afternoon when Harry and I had the Wheatfield to ourselves stands out especially vividly. As we traversed every part of what had been brutally contested ground on July 2, Harry explained successive phases of the fighting that brought units from the Union Third, Fifth, and Second Corps into action against Confederates from John Bell Hood's and Lafayette McLaws's divisions. We finished our walk by following the advance of John R. Brooke's brigade through the field and up to the ridge opposite the Rose farm (Harry and his family lived in the Rose house at one time), stopping for a few minutes just south of the knoll where George B. Winslow deployed his New York battery. Harry urged me to take in the array of Union regimental monuments visible from that spot, and we talked about how the sculptors incorporated into their designs the different Union corps badges—the diamond of the Third, the Maltese Cross of the Fifth, and the trefoil of the Second. Contemplating how all those units went into action within two or three hundred yards of our position underscored just how effectively the Federals had exploited their advantage of interior lines. Ever since my walk with Harry that day, I have used the monuments, with their corps symbols, to make that point about interior lines with groups I take to the Wheatfield.

I always was struck by how lightly Harry carried his knowledge, how his service as a combat soldier in World War II informed his analysis of the Civil War, and how he almost never claimed to have definitive answers to historical questions. I consider myself very lucky, as an editor and a historian, to have worked with Harry. More than that, I am fortunate to have known such a fine and generous man.

BRITISH WRITERS VIEW THE CONFEDERACY

In November 1865, Robert E. Lee informed Jubal A. Early that he intended to write a history of the Army of Northern Virginia. "My only object," he explained, regarding the soon-abandoned project, "is to transmit, if possible, the truth to posterity, and do justice to our brave Soldiers." Early provided Lee with a number of documents and agreed that the story of the conflict should not be entrusted to the pens of the winners. In their search for vindication, Early observed later, in a letter to the editor of the London *Standard,* ex-Confederates would have to rely on an appeal to "foreign nations and to the next age."[35] Early could not have known that between 1861 and 1961 no European nation would accord more attention to Civil War history than Great Britain—or that its writers often would express admiration for what Lee and his army had accomplished.

The first British accounts appeared while the war still raged. Arthur James Lyon Fremantle's *Three Months in the Southern States, April–June 1863*, published in Edinburgh in 1863 and the following year in New York and Mobile, gave readers on both sides of the Atlantic a heroic portrait of the Army of Northern Virginia. Some famous incidents of the battle of Gettysburg come to us from this account, including Lee's comments to Fremantle in the aftermath of the Pickett-Pettigrew assault. "He spoke to all the wounded men that passed him," wrote the Britisher, "and the slightly wounded he exhorted 'to bind up their hurts and take up a musket' in this emergency. . . . He said to me, 'This has been a sad day for us, Colonel—a sad day; but we can't expect always to gain victories.'"[36]

Field Marshal Viscount Garnet Wolseley's writings on the war, published between 1863 and 1890 and later collected by James A. Rawley in *The American Civil War: An English View*, mirrored Fremantle's in their profound admiration for the Confederate nation. Like Fremantle, Wolseley spent time with Lee, "the renowned soldier, whom I believe to have been the greatest of his age, . . . [and] whom I have always considered the most perfect man I ever met." In language Jubal Early would have approved, Wolseley, following a visit to the Confederacy in 1862, castigated the Union's war against the Confederacy as "merely the military despotism of a portion of the States striving under the dictatorship of an insignificant lawyer to crush out the freedom of the rest."[37]

Perhaps most widely read of the early British authors was George Francis Robert Henderson, an officer who published *Stonewall Jackson and the American Civil War* in 1898. This two-volume military biography marked the apogee of admiring British writing on the Confederate war effort. "Almost immediately it was acclaimed the greatest of all works on the Confederacy," noted Douglas Southall Freeman in 1939. "For a Southerner to confess, after 1900, that he had not read Henderson," added Freeman, "was for him to put himself under suspicion of treason to his inheritance."[38]

Three British officers publishing in the 1920s and 1930s broke with the tradition of pro-Confederate writings emanating from England. B. H. Liddell Hart's *Sherman: Soldier, Realist, American* and Alfred H. Burne's *Lee, Grant, and Sherman: A Study of Leadership in the 1864–65 Campaign* praised the two most important Union officers. Liddell Hart described Sherman as "not a typical man of his age, but the prototype of the most modern age" and called on readers to "fully appreciate Sherman's outlook on war and peace." Burne located things to admire in all three of the commanders he studied, shunning the Lost Cause pattern of lauding Lee while deprecating Grant as a butcher and reducing Sherman to nothing but a brutal practitioner of total war. Burne found "no substance" in the criticism of Grant as "a butcher, regardless of the lives of his men." As for Sherman, he "displayed imagination, resource, versatility, broadness of conception, and genuine powers of leadership" during the 1864 campaigns.[39]

In *The Generalship of Ulysses S. Grant* and *Grant & Lee: A Study in Personality and Generalship,* Major General J. F. C. Fuller rehearsed arguments present in the work of Thomas L. Connelly and Alan T. Nolan in the 1970s and 1990s. Fuller insisted that Lee's strategic vision was limited to his home state and that he too often indulged in frontal assaults that cost the Confederacy priceless manpower. Lee was "so obsessed by Virginia that he considered it the most important area of the Confederacy. . . . To him the Confederacy was but the base of Virginia." Moreover, the Confederate chieftain repeatedly "rushed forth to find a battlefield" and "by his restless audacity, he ruined such strategy as his government created." On balance, concluded Fuller, Grant easily outstripped Lee as a strategist.[40]

The most famous British author to write seriously about the Civil War was Winston Churchill, whose assessments echoed earlier pro-Confederate writers. In volume four of *A History of the English-Speaking Peoples,* Churchill said of Lee, "His noble presence and gentle, kindly manner were sustained by religious faith and an exalted character." Churchill compared Stonewall Jackson to the Calvinist Oliver Cromwell and cast him and Lee as gifted soldiers holding back a Union tide: "Against Lee and his great lieutenant, united for a year of intense action . . . were now to be marshalled the overwhelming forces of the Union."

Such language would have delighted Lost Cause writers who pronounced northern numbers the key to victory in a war the Confederates never could have won. Churchill's portrait of Grant echoed intemperate attacks by former Confederates. Pronouncing Grant's plan during the Overland campaign as "brutal and simple," Churchill singled out the Federal attacks at Cold Harbor: "In that comparatively civilised and refined epoch in America Cold Harbour was deemed a horror almost beyond words." Grant's strategy and tactics at Petersburg "eventually gained their purpose" but "must be regarded as the negation of generalship." Churchill also applauded the resilience of the Confederate people. "By the end of 1863 all illusions had vanished," he contended. "The South knew they had lost the war, and would be conquered and flattened. It is one of the enduring glories of the American nation that this made no difference to the Confederate resistance."[41]

A modern reading of Churchill and other influential British authors confirms what Lee and Early hoped would be the case—that winners do not always control the public memory of historic events.

BIOGRAPHERS AND GENERALS

Biographies of Civil War generals have appealed to generations of Americans. Famous commanders often attract readers who end up pursuing a lifelong interest in the conflict. Jeb Stuart played that role for me. As an eleven-year-old, I was drawn to him as a romantic and gifted cavalry officer. I began with Burke Davis's *Jeb Stuart: The Last Cavalier* (1957), which featured a colorful dust jacket based on Charles Hoffbauer's mural *Autumn* at the Virginia Historical Society. I turned next to Indiana University Press's edition of H. B. McClellan's *The Life and Campaigns of Major-General J. E. B. Stuart* (1885), reprinted in 1958 as *I Rode with Jeb Stuart*. I was most taken with John W. Thomason Jr.'s *Jeb Stuart* (1929), a gripping narrative enhanced by the author's unforgettable sketches. "Jeb Stuart was a symbol," observes Thomason, "a gonfalon that went before the swift, lean columns of the Confederacy. He served as the eyes and ears of Lee: his hands touched the springs of vast events."[42] I had never before encountered the word "gonfalon" (a "battle standard . . . usually ending in streamers; especially such a standard used by any of the medieval republics of Italy"), and when I looked it up I thought Thomason captured much of what appealed to me about Stuart.

Early exposure to military biographies spurred an interest that has led me to track the genre since the 1960s. Several trends stand out. Not surprisingly, biographers often choose figures such as Robert E. Lee, U. S. Grant, Stonewall Jackson, and William Tecumseh Sherman. For example, eight large volumes on Sherman have appeared since 1991. Charles Royster's *The Destructive War: William Tecumseh Sherman, Stonewall Jackson, and the Americans* (1991) emphasized how Sherman shaped the conflict's massively disruptive violence. In short order, John F. Marszalek's measured *Sherman: A Soldier's Passion for Order* (1993), Michael Fellman's unabashedly psychological *Citizen Sherman: A Life of William Tecumseh Sherman* (1995), and Stanley P. Hirshson's workmanlike *White Tecumseh: A Biography of General William T. Sherman* (1997) joined Royster's study on bookstore shelves. Lee Kennett's *Sherman: A Soldier's Life* (2001), which raised questions about Sherman's attitude toward Grant, completed an interpretive smorgasbord. These books presented conflicting explanations for Sherman's actions: a search for order after a rootless childhood of uncertainty (Marszalek), a tendency to act from barely suppressed rage (Fellman), or envy arising from a belief that Grant received too much credit (Kennett). After a decade's pause, a three-year spasm brought Robert P. Broadwater's *William T. Sherman: A Biography* (2013), Robert L. O'Connell's *Fierce Patriot: The Tangled Lives of William Tecumseh Sherman* (2014), and James Lee McDonough's *William Tecumseh Sherman: In the Service of My Country, A Life* (2016).[43]

A second trend confirms that authors and publishers embrace generals in the Army of Northern Virginia. Apart from Lee and Jackson, each corps commander has been the subject of at least one biography since the mid-1980s: James Longstreet (1987, 1993); A. P. Hill (1987); Richard S. Ewell (1998, 2004); Jubal A. Early (1992, 2014); Jeb Stuart (1987, 2008); John B. Gordon (1989); Wade Hampton (2003, 2007, 2008); Richard H. Anderson (1985); and Fitzhugh Lee (1989, 2005). Division commanders also have received attention, among them George E. Pickett (two biographies in 1998); Robert E. Rodes (2000, 2008); Stephen Dodson Ramseur (1985); William Dorsey Pender (2001, 2013); Isaac Ridgeway Trimble (2005); Cadmus M. Wilcox (2001); Benjamin Huger (1985); and John Bankhead Magruder (1996, 2009). Other biographers have looked to the brigade and regimental levels, producing works on such figures as South Carolinian Micah Jenkins, a relatively unimportant brigadier (two titles in 1996); William C. Oates of the Fifteenth Alabama (2006); and Henry King Burgwyn Jr. of the Twenty-Sixth North Carolina (1985).

In contrast to the coverage of generals in Lee's army, a number of Union army commanders await modern scholarly biographies. Three examples will illustrate this phenomenon. It has been almost half a century since William M. Lamers published *The Edge of Glory: A Biography of General William S. Rosecrans,* a lengthy but lightly documented life of one of the most important officers in the Western Theater. As head of the Army of the Cumberland, Rosecrans fought the battles of Stones River and Chickamauga, directed the impressive Tullahoma campaign, and presided over the defense of Chattanooga in September and October 1863. One of the few high-ranking Catholic officers in the Union army, he pursued a postwar career that included stints as minister to Mexico, congressman from California, and register of the United States Treasury (though Lamers devoted only twenty-three pages to Rosecrans's non–Civil War activities). A huge collection of Rosecrans's papers at the University of California, Los Angeles, awaits any future biographer.

Joseph Hooker similarly deserves fresh treatment. The Army of the Potomac's third commander has been the subject of just one biography—Walter H. Hebert's *Fighting Joe Hooker,* published in 1944. Central to the Chancellorsville campaign and the opening moves that led to Gettysburg, Hooker was later assigned to the Western Theater and played a role at Chattanooga and in operations against Atlanta. Intensely political, he proved willing to change parties in order to advance his career. Well outside the inner circle of army notables after the war, he pronounced Sherman "crazy" and said that Grant possessed "no more moral sense than a dog."[44] Hooker's life offers excellent material to explore the intersection between military and political affairs—as well as behavior that lends itself to psychological speculation.

Irvin McDowell has been more neglected than Rosecrans and Hooker. The preeminent Union field commander early in the war, he suffered defeat at First Bull Run but remained important during the Shenandoah Valley, Peninsula, and Second Bull Run campaigns of 1862. Secretary of the Treasury Salmon P. Chase staunchly supported McDowell, praising him as "a loyal, brave, truthful, capable officer" who rightly believed "this war sprung from the influence of slavery."[45] Exiled to the Department of the Pacific, McDowell never regained the limelight after 1862. A careful exploration of his life and career would make a valuable contribution to understanding the Union's military effort.

I look forward to the time when I can place the first biography of McDowell—or a new one of Hooker or Rosecrans—in my library, where they will join many shelves of volumes on Grant, Sherman, and Lee.

A TACTICAL HISTORY MASTERPIECE

Tactical and operational studies occupy a prominent place in the literature devoted to the Civil War. Admirable examples of well-researched, analytical military narratives published over the past several decades include Edwin B. Coddington's pioneering *The Gettysburg Campaign: A Study in Command* (1968), Richard J. Sommers's detailed *Richmond Redeemed: The Siege at Petersburg* (1981), John J. Hennessy's graceful *Return to Bull Run: The Campaign and Battle of Second Manassas* (1993), Albert Castel's revisionist *Decision in the West: The Atlanta Campaign of 1864* (1992), and Timothy B. Smith's gripping *Shiloh: Conquer or Perish* (2014). Multiple volumes by authors such as Stephen W. Sears, Peter Cozzens, Earl J. Hess, and Gordon C. Rhea underscore the vitality of this genre of Civil War studies.

Coddington's book, which raised the bar for all subsequent campaign treatments, reached readers more than half a century after John Bigelow Jr.'s *The Campaign of Chancellorsville: A Strategic and Tactical Study* set a standard so high it retains a place among the very best works of its kind. Published in 1910 by Yale University Press, Bigelow's 528-page masterpiece was reissued by Morningside Press in a first-rate reprint in the 1990s. (All other reprints, which lack the original's superlative maps, should be avoided.)

Bigelow brought firsthand military experience to his project. A West Pointer who ranked forty-sixth in the class of 1877, he served with the Ninth and Tenth U.S. Cavalry in the 1870s and 1880s and received multiple wounds and won a Silver Star at San Juan Hill during the war with Spain. During an assignment to teach military science and tactics at the Massachusetts Institute of Technology in 1894, Bigelow chose Chancellorsville as the "theme for a course of lectures . . . because that campaign presented a greater variety of military problems and experiences than any other in which an army of the United States had taken part." In addition, he added, no other battle approaching Chancellorsville "in importance, has been so imperfectly apprehended and described."[46]

Bigelow consulted a range of sources, including regimental histories, memoirs, congressional reports, newspapers, and, most important by far, the *Official Records of the Union and Confederate Armies*. The recent availability of a mass of reports and correspondence in the *Official Records,* he observed, allowed him to offer "a certain minuteness of detail" about the campaign. Because of these published documents, he noted approvingly, "no war that has been fought admits of such thorough investigation as our Civil War." The phenomenon of historians across many generations immersing themselves in the rich bounty of the *Official Records* really began with *The Campaign of Chancellorsville.*

Bigelow sought to evaluate commanders in light of what they knew when making decisions. Appreciating what is often termed the "fog of war," he pronounced it "a common fault of military narration to fail to give the mental point of view and field vision of the opposing commanders." He sought "to keep the reader informed as to how much or how little each commander knew about the tactical or strategic situation." Scrupulously fair in assessing leaders on both sides and meticulous in charting the ebb and flow of the action, Bigelow fully met his stated goals "to tell what was done, but also to show how it was done, to present a characteristic, or typical, view of the conditions and methods of troop-leading that obtained during our Civil War."

Anyone who reads tactical history knows the value of good maps. "I have tried to provide the reader with such maps as he will need," Bigelow stated, with a striking degree of understatement as well as somewhat obscure phrasing, "but am aware that I have not made his way a royal road."[47] In fact, the forty-seven three-color maps in *The Campaign of Chancellorsville* constitute one of the book's great strengths, often depicting the tactical situation in thirty-minute increments and permitting readers to follow the action very closely. Bigelow credited the maps of Jedediah Hotchkiss, who had been Stonewall Jackson's cartographer, as especially useful in the preparation of his own.

Bigelow's summary judgments indict Joseph Hooker for fumbling an opportunity to punish Lee and the Army of Northern Virginia. Hooker repeatedly displayed a lack of aggressiveness and strong purpose. The Federal commander's "irresolution in this campaign was only partially due to the injury he received at the Chancellor House" on the morning of May 4, insisted Bigelow. "It was exhibited . . . long before he sustained that injury, and would in all probability have lasted through the campaign had he not been injured at all." To the end, Hooker might have crafted a victory. "No greater mistake was made during the campaign than Hooker's final one of recrossing the Rappahannock," asserted Bigelow. "Lee was about to play into his hands by attacking him on his own ground; the condition on which his plan of operation was based was at last to be realized, when he weakly retired from the contest."[48]

Hooker's post-battle criticism of Sixth Corps chief John Sedgwick for not, in effect, saving the larger part of the Army of the Potomac on May 4 rankled Bigelow. "But if Hooker, with the mass of the army, could not safely undertake to join Sedgwick when Sedgwick was moving to join him," Bigelow commented sharply, "it was hardly to be expected that Sedgwick, with a single corps, would succeed in joining Hooker."[49]

As for R. E. Lee, Bigelow praised his "brilliant use of interior lines" and pronounced his strategic decisions generally sound and "in accordance with the fundamental principles of war." Yet the magnitude of the Confederate victory yielded a mixed result. The two months following Lee's victory marked "the brightest period of the Civil War" for Confederates. "But its brightness," cautioned Bigelow, "was that of a false and treacherous light. The overconfidence born of the victory of Chancellorsville carried the Army of Northern Virginia against the impregnable front of the Federal lines at Gettysburg."[50]

Very few scholarly books written a century ago stand up against more modern scholarship. Bigelow's impressive treatment of Chancellorsville meets that test. Anyone seriously interested in the compelling action that unfolded along the Rappahannock River frontier in late April and early May 1863 should consult *The Campaign of Chancellorsville*.

OFF THE TRACKS

On April 12, 1864, Robert E. Lee implored Secretary of War James A. Seddon to address the management of railroads in the Confederacy. Problems of supply plagued the Army of Northern Virginia, and Lee wanted all obstacles to deliveries removed. "I earnestly recommend that no private interests be allowed to interfere with the use of all the facilities for transportation that we possess," he wrote, "until the wants of the army are provided for. The railroads should be at once devoted exclusively to this purpose, even should it be found necessary to suspend all private travel for business or pleasure upon them for the present."[51]

More than half a century later, historian Charles W. Ramsdell emphasized that the Confederacy never overcame the railroad-related troubles Lee had mentioned to Seddon. "It would be claiming too much to say that the failure to solve its railroad problem was the cause of the Confederacy's downfall," stated Ramsdell's pioneering article, "yet it is impossible not to conclude that the solution of that problem was one of the important conditions of success." Ramsdell's piece inspired no other scholar to produce a full-scale treatment of the subject, and in 1939, Douglas Southall Freeman's *The South to Posterity* listed "a study of the Southern railroads" as one of the topics most deserving of book-length attention.[52]

Robert C. Black III's *The Railroads of the Confederacy* filled this glaring gap in the literature. Published by the University of North Carolina Press in 1952, it remains, after more than sixty-five years, a superior overview that has been augmented but never superseded. Modern readers will find a few anachronistic elements of the book. For example, Black subscribes in significant measure to Frank L. Owsley's thesis in *State Rights in the Confederacy* (1925); namely, that John C. Calhoun's "glorification of the individual state" carried over into the war and proved inimical to waging a successful defense against a powerful opponent. A self-described "northerner by birth, background, and education" who became a "converted Yankee," Black also consistently uses the term "War between the States," which Lost Cause writers had embraced in the years after Appomattox, to describe the conflict. Yet he largely succeeds in his determination "not to bring any preconceived notions to bear and to allow the politicians and soldiers and railroaders of the Confederacy to speak for themselves."[53]

Black's well-researched, comprehensive book expands on many of the themes in Ramsdell's article and cites substantial evidence to reach similar conclusions. Did southern railroads figure prominently in the Confederacy's failure to secure independence? "To this question the author can only answer—yes," insists Black. "Railroad transportation in the Confederacy suffered from a number of defects, all of which played a recognizable part in the southern defeat." Black explores how insufficient mileage, gaps between key lines, inability to repair and maintain tracks and rolling stock, differences of gauge, and failure to build badly needed new lines all hurt the Confederacy. Beyond such physical difficulties, he argues, *"the Confederates by no means made the best use of what they had. It is men who are most at fault when a war is lost—not locomotives, or cars, or even economic geography."*[54] The publisher's decision to provide numerous maps, including one in foldout format locating all the railroads and their gauges in June 1861, greatly enhanced the value of the text.

In terms of railroad-related logistics, Black isolates two principal shortcomings that yielded pernicious results for the Confederacy. First, national needs went unmet because the railroads' "owners, managers, and even employees were unwilling to make serious sacrifice of their personal interests." In terms of the railroading sector, at least, Black finds an absence of overriding national sentiment. Second, Jefferson Davis's administration and the congress in Richmond proved "loath to enforce the kind of transportation policy the war effort demanded"—the kind Lee, a committed Confederate nationalist, urged upon Seddon in April 1864. Although undoubtedly a nationalist himself, Davis "was not to acquiesce in the enforcement of really rigid transportation regulations until Appomattox was hardly a month off." Overall, concludes Black, the Confederacy lacked the "wholehearted public cooperation" and the "government coercion" necessary "to wage a modern war."[55]

During the decades following its publication, *The Railroads of the Confederacy* enjoyed a high reputation. A standard bibliography published during the mid-1960s described it as an "able and detailed treatment of the management, difficulties, and significance of Southern railways, with emphasis on the railways themselves." Noted bibliographer Richard B. Harwell placed it among his two hundred essential titles on the Confederacy, calling it "a major contribution to Confederate economic history" that demonstrated how the "collapse of the Confederate railroad service was of immense importance in hastening the breakdown of the Confederacy." In 1981, the editors of *Civil War Times Illustrated* included it on a roster of essential books, compiled on the basis of suggestions from "over thirty consultants." More recently, a major annotated bibliography termed it "a soundly documented study" that details how "Confederate military authorities failed to use effectively the valuable interior railroad lines scattered throughout the South that were available to support numerous campaigns."[56]

Anyone who consults Black's book will better appreciate accounts by participants on both sides that discuss the Confederate rail system. Typical is artillerist Edward Porter Alexander's handling of the frustrations James Longstreet's First Corps experienced in traveling from Virginia to reinforce Braxton Bragg's army in northern Georgia in September 1863. "In those days the

Southern railroads were but lightly built & equipped," explained Alexander, who became a railroad executive after the war, "&, now, for two years they had been cut off from all sorts of supplies of railroad material but what their own small shops could produce. Naturally, therefore, the movement of our corps . . . was very slow." The meticulous Alexander reckoned the "entire journey by rail had been about 852 miles in about 182 hours"—an average of just more than four and one half miles an hour. Such a poor performance mattered in a conflict that, according to Black, "to its last weeks, remained a railroad war."[57]

THE "OTHER" CONFEDERATE ARMY

The Army of Tennessee always has lived in the shadow of the Army of Northern Virginia. During the war, it labored under a succession of flawed commanders, lost battles that claimed a huge toll in casualties, and watched the fruits of a great tactical triumph at Chickamauga (its single undisputed success) slip away through the mismanagement of its leaders. Because their principal western army almost never presented them with victories, the people of the Confederacy increasingly looked to R. E. Lee and his soldiers for good news from the battlefield. Blessed with gifted subordinates such as Stonewall Jackson, James Longstreet, and Jeb Stuart—and fortunate to face a group of modestly talented opponents in 1862 and 1863—Lee won celebrated victories beginning with the Seven Days and extending through Chancellorsville. These achievements helped make the Army of Northern Virginia synonymous with the Confederacy in the minds of many white southerners and much of the loyal citizenry of the United States; in contrast, the Army of Tennessee seemed a force capable of stalwart service that nonetheless gave up huge chunks of territory to advancing Union armies in Tennessee, Mississippi, Georgia, and the Carolinas.

A canvass of military literature on the Confederacy reinforces the image of the Army of Tennessee as a junior partner to the Army of Northern Virginia. Far more authors have written about Lee, his lieutenants, and their campaigns

in the Eastern Theater than about Confederate operations in the Western Theater. In the decades after the war, Jubal A. Early and other Lost Cause writers
used a variety of forums, most notably the pages of the Southern Historical
Society's *Papers*, to portray Lee and his army as the backbone of Confederate
resistance. Apart from the efforts of men such as Early, the exploits of Lee and
Jackson understandably generated more interest among nineteenth-century
southern white readers than the failures of Albert Sidney Johnston, Braxton
Bragg, John Bell Hood, and others who led the Army of Tennessee. Former
Confederates seeking to give meaning to a war that had ended in catastrophic
defeat took solace in the impressive achievements of the Army of Northern
Virginia. The writings of Douglas Southall Freeman, easily the most influential twentieth-century historian of Confederate military affairs, solidified the
reputation of Lee and his army as one of the most impressive field forces in
history. In *R. E. Lee: A Biography* and *Lee's Lieutenants: A Study in Command*,
Freeman supplied portraits of Lee and his principal subordinates that shaped
the thinking of generations of readers.

A year before the appearance of the initial volume of *Lee's Lieutenants*, the
Bobbs-Merrill Company published Stanley F. Horn's *The Army of Tennessee*.
Horn brought writing skills honed by experience as a reporter and editor, as
well as a Tennessean's frank admiration for the Confederacy's western soldiers,
to the first modern treatment of the subject. Contrary to popular perceptions,
notes Horn, in phrasing that betrays his southern perspective, "all of the War
Between the States was not fought in Virginia." The Army of Tennessee "carried the fortunes of the Confederacy on its bayonets no less valiantly than
its more famous sister army in Virginia. With stubborn bravery it faced the
armies of stout Midwesterners under such leaders as Grant and Sherman and
Thomas, and it matched them blow for blow."[58]

Horn sketches a resilient army that suffered chronic failures of command
during "its Via Dolorosa, stretching from Shiloh's bloody field to the final
furling of its ragged flags at Durham Station in North Carolina." He presents
Albert Sidney Johnston as a general who disappointed early southern expectations, emphasizes Braxton Bragg's shortcomings as a field commander and
military politician, and dismisses the notion that Joseph E. Johnston could
have saved Atlanta if left in charge of the army after mid-July 1864. Not surprisingly, John Bell Hood receives some of Horn's sharpest criticism. At Frank-

lin, claims the author bitterly, "Hood was consumed with a burning impetuosity. He could not wait even long enough to make proper preparations." Horn marvels that even Franklin and Nashville failed to break the spirit of the army, the remnants of which traveled east to fight on in North Carolina. When the end came at Durham Station, concludes Horn, the survivors knew they "had fought a good fight, they had finished their course, they had kept the faith."[59]

Much excellent work on the Army of Tennessee has appeared since Horn wrote his narrative. This literature includes Thomas L. Connelly's *Army of the Heartland: The Army of Tennessee, 1861–1862* (1967) and *Autumn of Glory: The Army of Tennessee, 1862–1865* (1971) and Richard M. McMurry's *Two Great Rebel Armies: An Essay in Confederate Military History* (1989), as well as campaign histories, biographies, and soldier studies by, among many others, Albert Castel, Peter Cozzens, Larry J. Daniel, Earl J. Hess, Grady McWhiney, Charles P. Roland, Craig L. Symonds, and Steven Woodworth. Horn's research fell considerably short of the standard attained by these later historians, and his emotional attachment to the Army of Tennessee too often colored his analysis. Still, his pioneering book remains a good introduction to the army that protected the vast midsection of the Confederacy.

Even the steady accretion of solid books on the leaders, soldiers, and campaigns of the Army of Tennessee has failed to change popular perceptions. Braxton Bragg and Joseph E. Johnston have received their share of excellent scholarly attention of late, yet they remain—and likely always will—a tough sell compared to R. E. Lee. How many Americans know at least something about Appomattox? And how many at least something about Joseph Johnston's surrender of a larger number of troops to William Tecumseh Sherman at Durham Station just less than three weeks later? No novel on the western army rivals Michael Shaara's *The Killer Angels*, Stephen Crane's *The Red Badge of Courage*, or John W. Thomason's *Lone Star Preacher*, and no film does for the Army of Tennessee what *Gettysburg* and *Gods and Generals* do for its more celebrated eastern counterpart. Similarly, viewers introduced to the conflict by Ken Burns's widely praised *The Civil War*, still widely aired after more than a quarter century, find in that documentary far more detailed coverage of Lee's army than of Braxton Bragg's. In these and other ways, the Army of Tennessee serves as the steady character actor overshadowed by the Army of Northern Virginia, which continues in the glamorous leading role.

DECIDING WHAT TO READ

The deluge of Civil War–related publications during the sesquicentennial complicates the problem of separating the wheat from the chaff in a literature that runs to scores of thousands of titles. Attempting to keep abreast of new work can be confusing and frustrating, and the process of trying to find the best of the enormous older literature poses even greater challenges. A look at the catalog of John Page Nicholson's famous library suggests how quickly the literature grew. Privately printed in 1914, this 1,022-page tome includes thousands of items Nicholson collected during the half century following the war. Had Nicholson not excluded titles on the naval war and on Lincoln, as well as what he termed "scurrilous books," the number would have been far larger.[60] In the century since Nicholson's catalog appeared, many thousands of additional books have rendered even more perilous the shoals of Civil War historiography.

The best way to lay out a program of reading or collecting is to explore some of the better bibliographies. I would start with David J. Eicher's *The Civil War in Books: An Analytical Bibliography*. Though more than twenty years old, this volume usefully evaluates 1,100 titles, providing bibliographic information about original editions and reprints and up to a full two-column page of annotation. Although he is most interested in the military side of the conflict, Eicher includes hundreds of nonmilitary titles. The commentary is perceptive and sometimes quite critical. Describing John B. Gordon's *Reminiscences of the Civil War*, for example, Eicher notes its "many lively anecdotes" but alerts readers that a number "are the product of the general's fertile imagination." Overall, Gordon's "outstanding career, keen military insight, and enjoyable style make this a highly important work."[61]

Thirty years before Eicher published his work, Allan Nevins, James I. Robertson Jr., and Bell I. Wiley edited *Civil War Books: A Critical Bibliography*. I spent countless pleasant hours leafing through these books as a young student of the war and still keep them close at hand. A cooperative venture for which eminent scholars succinctly annotated entries grouped under fifteen categories, this bibliography covered nearly six thousand books published before the mid-1960s. Unlike Eicher's book, which omits titles of little value, *Civil War Books* casts a much wider net. Within a page of one another in the section on military campaigns, readers will find John Gross Barnard's *The C.S.A. and the Battle of Bull Run. (A Letter to an English Friend.)*, dismissed as "an untrustworthy and pretentious revamping of published reports and accounts by a chief engineer of the Army of the Potomac," and John Bigelow's *The Campaign of Chancellorsville: A Strategic and Tactical Study,* accurately described as "a masterful study—one of the very finest ever written on an American campaign; thoroughly documented and notably impartial."[62]

A two-volume set guides readers to four hundred titles relating to the Confederacy, supplying a great deal of information and some engaging commentary along the way. Richard B. Harwell's *In Tall Cotton: The 200 Most Important Confederate Books for the Reader, Researcher and Collector* took as its inspiration Douglas Southall Freeman's *The South to Posterity: An Introduction to the Writing of Confederate History.* "I cannot presume to bring his work up to date," observes Harwell of Freeman. "I have tried to bring the coverage of the same topic up to date in my own way."[63] Harwell's annotation ranges from a single terse sentence in some cases to more than two dozen lines in others. Although some of his choices are unusual, Hervey Allen's forgettable novel *Action at Aquilla* being a prime example, Harwell lists many titles of great importance.

In Taller Cotton: 200 More Important Confederate Books for the Reader, Researcher, and Collector, cowritten by Nathaniel Cheairs Hughes Jr., Robert K. Krick, and me, adds many books published since Harwell's compilation as well as important ones left out of the earlier volume. Krick's brief prefatory note addresses the fact that each compiler brought different sensibilities to the task: "Professors Hughes and Gallagher are interested in things about which I care not at all, as will be obvious from the listings, and a couple of Professor Gallagher's choices seem to me to be ineffably dreadful books."[64] Some of Krick's selections, in turn, might impress an impartial referee as idiosyncratic. Therein lies the attraction of anointing certain books from an enormous pool of candidates.

For Union topics with a heavy emphasis on military affairs, readers can consult *The Union Bookshelf: A Selected Civil War Bibliography.* Michael Mullins and Rowena Reed selected 246 titles, "including several superior regimental histories and participant accounts," annotated 114 of the entries, and gave bibliographic information about both original and reprint editions of all the titles. The authors acknowledge a degree of "subjectivity in making choices" and sometimes indulge in excessive praise, as when they describe William M. Lamers's *The Edge of Glory: A Biography of General William S. Rosecrans*, a pedestrian effort at best, as a "fully documented" work giving "the complete story" of its subject.[65]

Firsthand accounts published during the second half of the twentieth century inspired Garold L. Cole's *Civil War Eyewitnesses: An Annotated Bibliography of Books and Articles, 1955–1986* and *Civil War Eyewitnesses: An Annotated Bibliography of Books and Articles, 1986–1996*. In volume one, Cole explains, "Diaries, journals, letters, and memoirs constitute the majority of the 1,395 items. Anthologies and special studies that utilize personal narratives exclusively and discuss the genre of Civil War eyewitness writings are also included."[66] The second volume adds 596 items, grouped, as in the first volume, under headings such as "The North," "The South," and "Anthologies and Studies." Soldiers, civilians, and foreign travelers are well represented, and Cole's annotation tends to be descriptive rather than analytical.

These bibliographies form the basis for a sound reading list or basic library of titles published through the early twenty-first century. Reviews in magazines, newspapers, scholarly journals, and online sites are the best options to track more recent publications in a literature that long ago assumed unmanageable size.

V

TESTIMONY FROM PARTICIPANTS

Studying the Civil War affords great pleasure in discovering superior testimony written by the generation that experienced it. Very high literacy rates in both the United States and the Confederacy, together with the fact that millions of Americans suffered family separations in the midst of gripping events, contributed to the creation of a vast corpus of letters and diaries. Because the war represented the dramatic high point of their lives, many participants also recorded their actions and opinions in memoirs. This section samples the war's published primary record in thirteen essays that, as with those in part 4, emerged from a delightful process of revisiting books and authors central to my life's work. I begin with an essay on soldiers' letters, a large and continuously growing category of testimony. The next five essays deal with Union sources, including one of the best diaries in all of American history, testimony given before the war's most famous congressional committee, and an assortment of letters, memoirs, and campaign accounts. Confederates receive their turn in six essays that explore the frequently quoted diary of a Rebel war clerk, letters and diaries written by women and staff officers, a massive history of the war composed while fighting still raged, and a postwar magazine that helped define the Confederate memory of the war. The final piece presents two talented British sketch artists whose images depicted action, people, and places in ways beyond the capacity of mid-nineteenth-century photography.

SEEING THE WAR THROUGH
SOLDIERS' LETTERS

Few ways of exploring the Civil War yield greater satisfaction than reading letters written by soldiers. The conflict produced a staggering volume of such correspondence. In the single month of April 1863, for example, the Sixtieth New York Infantry—which mustered fewer than four hundred men—mailed 3,855 letters. The United States Army counted roughly seven hundred thousand men present for duty during that same period. Untold thousands of letters have been preserved in repositories or gathered in books or articles. Although any list of the best published letters is open to debate, I will discuss three volumes worthy of anyone's attention.

The first is *Intrepid Warrior: Clement Anselm Evans, Confederate General from Georgia—Life, Letters and Diaries of the War Years*, edited by Robert Grier Stephens Jr. Readers will find engrossing testimony from an officer who served in the Army of Northern Virginia throughout the war, rose to the rank of brigadier general, and led a division in 1864 and 1865. A combination of letters and diary entries, the text includes excellent descriptions of battles, observations about the physical impact of the war, assessments of various commanders, and remarks about the state of morale inside Robert E. Lee's army and on the home front. Some of the passages will surprise readers, as when Evans described Gettysburg as a hard but not disastrous battle. "The last fight at Gettysburg was a very fearful affair," he informed his wife on July 8, 1863. "At some points the Yankees fought pretty stubborn but where ever we had a fair field we whipped & slaughtered them in great numbers. Both armies are now maneuvering & preparing for another battle. It will soon come. I do hope that these fights may be decisive." Two days later, the Georgian termed the enemy "uneasy—not confident of their ability to whip us."[1]

Some of Evans's best letters deal with the 1864 Shenandoah Valley campaign, which ended ignominiously for Jubal A. Early's Army of the Valley at Cedar Creek on October 19. Confederates later argued about who should be blamed for that defeat, with supporters of Early and of John B. Gordon often squaring off against one another. Evans fought under Gordon and recorded his opinion on October 21. "I can hardly see how anyone could describe a victory so glowingly as to exaggerate ours in the morning of the 19th," he wrote, "for on my word I never saw anything equal to it in all this war. The victory is due to the plan & management of Gen. Gordon, the defeat is due to Gen. Early." Then, bitterly, he posed a question regarding Old Jube: "When shall we be relieved of this heavy incubus?"[2]

Alpheus S. Williams operated at a higher level of responsibility than Evans, commanding a division and a corps in both the Eastern and Western theaters. *From the Cannon's Mouth: The Civil War Letters of General Alpheus S. Williams,* edited by Milo M. Quaife, illuminates myriad aspects of the war through descriptions of battles and places, unvarnished assessments of various Union generals, and revealing material about important political and social issues. Whether interested in details of military operations, daily life in the Army of the Potomac or among William Tecumseh Sherman's forces in Georgia and the Carolinas, morale among Union officers, or the war's impact on the Confederate home front, readers will learn much from this correspondence. They also will discover that Williams, who seemed incapable of dull writing, invariably holds their attention.

Two passages convey the tenor of Williams's letters. He called Major General J. K. F. Mansfield, his commander in the Twelfth Corps, "an officer of acknowledged gallantry" but also noted that, at Antietam, Mansfield was "greatly excited," exhibited "a very nervous temperament and a very impatient manner," and brought his corps onto the field in a formation that invited significant casualties. "Feeling that our heavy masses of raw troops were sadly exposed," recorded Williams, "I begged him to let me deploy them in line of battle, in which the men present but *two* ranks or rows instead of *twenty*, as we were marching, but I could not move him."[3]

Opposed to destroying Confederate civilian property early in the war, Williams almost cheerfully recounted the harsh treatment of white South Carolinians during Sherman's march across their state. "South Carolina will not soon forget us," he claimed. "A blackened swath seventy miles wide marks the path over which we traveled right through her center and sweeping in the march her capital and her chief commercial city. The first gun on Sumter was well avenged." The departing Union army left South Carolina's houses "comfortless and shabby, and the people at home rusty, ignorant, and forlorn." Williams concluded of South Carolina's Confederates that "the tornado of war may do them good in the end."[4]

Edwin H. Fay played a less important role than Evans or Williams, enlisting in a cavalry unit in Louisiana in April 1862 and spending most of the war in backwater duties in Mississippi, Arkansas, and Louisiana. His letters, edited by Bell I. Wiley in *This Infernal War: The Confederate Letters of Sgt. Edwin H. Fay,* reveal a man who chafed at military service and sought repeatedly to get out of uniform—yet developed a profound hatred of Yankees. Within a month of enlisting, Fay commented that "the patriotism of our Co[mpany] at least is about consumed. If they were at home I don't know a man who would volunteer with his present knowledge, unless I did." Despite constant complaining about tyrannical officers and other aspects of army life, he could not envision living under Union rule. In the wake of Vicksburg's surrender, he angrily wrote his wife, "I expect to murder every Yankee I ever meet when I can do so with impunity if I live a hundred years and peace is made in six months. . . . There can be no fellowship between us forever." He wondered about "the fate of the Confederacy," conceding that it might be conquered "as a power of the Earth" even if he did "not near believe the people are subjugated. I have little hope for the future." Removal to a foreign country, he stated more than once, would be preferable to living in a United States controlled by the North.[5]

Taken together, these three soldiers' letters transport readers to several military theaters, shed light on an array of experiences, and supply an ample store of memorable vignettes. They exemplify the interpretive and descriptive riches of this genre of evidence.

FATHER NEPTUNE'S WAR

Gideon Welles was fifty-nine years old when he arrived in Washington to become Abraham Lincoln's secretary of the navy. With a long white beard and full wig that covered his bald pate, Welles stood out as a memorable figure who soon won Lincoln's admiration and the affectionate nickname "Father Neptune." Over the course of the war, Welles oversaw the navy's growth from fewer than nine thousand sailors and officers and fifty vessels on active duty to more than fifty thousand men and 650 ships (dozens of them ironclads). He took an active role in Union strategic planning, which included important naval and combined operations along the 3,500-mile-long Confederate coast, on rivers from the Mississippi to the James, and on the oceans. The president paid tribute to the navy's role in fashioning victory when he wrote, "Nor must Uncle Sam's Web-feet be forgotten. At all the watery margins they have been present. Not only on the deep sea, the broad bay, and the rapid river, but also up the narrow muddy bayou, and wherever the ground was a little damp, they have been, and made their tracks."[6] Welles put his imprint on virtually every aspect of the naval operations Lincoln applauded and must be reckoned among the best secretaries of the navy in United States history.

He also ranks among the most important American diarists. He began making entries in August 1862 and continued through the early summer of 1869. For the years of the Civil War, he observed events from the center of power, where he participated in crucial cabinet meetings, knew and interacted with innumerable influential people, and developed a strong relationship with Lincoln. His voluminous comments about fellow members of the cabinet, military and naval commanders, political events, and a wide range of other topics carry special weight because he usually recorded them almost immediately rather than waiting and trying to recall what had happened. Welles's diary is essential to a full understanding of the Lincoln administration and the Union war effort, more revealing than Salmon P. Chase's wartime journals or Edward Bates's diary (both of which also have been published)

Two unsatisfactory three-volume editions of Welles's entire diary appeared in 1911 and 1960. The first is profoundly flawed because of how sloppily—and silently—the editors assembled the text from wartime entries and later revisions and additions (it is not clear precisely who did the editing); the second, prepared by academic historian Howard K. Beale, superimposes editorial symbols and proofreader's marks on the text of the 1911 edition and is confusing and hard to use. I have consulted Beale's version extensively in my own work and been frustrated every time.

Happily for all students of the Civil War, a new edition of Welles's wartime diary appeared in 2014. Edited by William E. Gienapp and Erica L. Gienapp under the title *The Civil War Diary of Gideon Welles, Lincoln's Secretary of the Navy*, it marks a milestone in the published primary literature on the conflict.[7] Meticulously faithful to the original document, it renders the sections devoted to the war in both earlier editions entirely irrelevant except, perhaps, to specialists charting changes between the original manuscript and the 1911 and 1960 versions.

How good is Welles as a witness? I will offer several examples of why his diary demands our attention. On September 22, 1862, the president raised the topic of his preliminary proclamation of emancipation with the cabinet. "It is momentous both in its immediate and remote results," commented Welles, "and an exercise of extraordinary power which cannot be justified on mere humanitarian principles, and would never have been attempted but to preserve the national existence. These were my convictions and this the drift of the discussion. . . . For myself the subject has from its magnitude and its consequence oppressed me, aside from the ethical features of the question. . . . There is, in the free states a very general impression that this measure will insure a speedy peace. I cannot say that I so view it."[8]

On July 14, 1863, Welles and Lincoln discussed George G. Meade's failure to strike the Army of Northern Virginia before it retreated safely across the Potomac after Gettysburg. Leaving a cabinet meeting, "we walked together across the lawn and stopped and conversed a few minutes at the gate. He said with a voice and countenance which I shall never forget, he had feared yet expected this—that there has seemed to him for a full week, a determination that Lee should escape with his force and plunder,—and that, my God, is the last of this Army of the Potomac. There is bad faith somewhere. . . . What does it mean, Mr Welles—Great God what does it mean?"[9]

In the bloody summer of 1864, Welles wrestled with the question of how harshly the war should be prosecuted. "I have often thought that greater severity might well be exercised," he observed, "and yet it would tend to barbarism. No traitor has been hung—I doubt if there will be, but an example should be made of some of the leaders, for present and for future good. . . . Were the leaders to be stripped of their possessions, and their property confiscated—their families impoverished the result would be salutary in the future. But I apprehend there will be very gentle measures in closing up the rebellion. The authors of the enormous evils that have been inflicted will go unpunished—or will be but slightly punished."[10]

On April 10, 1865, Welles joined most other loyal citizens in celebrating news from Appomattox: "This surrender of the great rebel Captain and the most formidable and reliable army of the Secessionists virtually terminates the rebellion." "Called on the President," Welles added, "who returned last evening, looking well and feeling well." On April 14, Lincoln told the cabinet that reconstructing the Union "was the great question now before us, and we must soon begin to act. Was glad Congress was not in session."[11] Welles next saw Lincoln, slipping toward death, at the Petersen House across from Ford's Theatre.

ABNER DOUBLEDAY'S REVENGE

The battle of Gettysburg stood supreme in its ability to spark postwar controversies among officers in both the Confederate and Union high commands. Infighting among former generals of the Army of Northern Virginia has garnered the most attention from historians, resulting in a sizeable literature that features James Longstreet playing villain to Jubal A. Early and other Lost Cause warriors who sought to absolve Lee of all responsibility for defeat. Jeb Stuart, Richard S. Ewell, and A. P. Hill held supporting roles in these long-running debates that filled many pages in the Southern Historical Society's *Papers*, personal memoirs, and other publications. On the United States side, Daniel E. Sickles's decision, on July 2, to abandon his position on Cemetery Ridge and occupy a line stretching from the Klingel farm along the Emmitsburg Road to Devil's Den generated the most acrimony. Congress helped fuel the fires among Union generals because the Joint Committee on the Conduct of the War solicited and published testimony from many of the key actors.

Few officers on either side nursed a deeper sense of grievance than Abner Doubleday. New York born and a graduate of West Point in 1842, he fought as an artillerist during the war with Mexico and during the secession crisis served under Major Robert Anderson as a captain in the First U.S. Artillery stationed at Fort Sumter. He commanded the Second Division in John F. Reynolds's First Corps at Fredericksburg and, in the spring of 1863, took charge of the Third Division in that corps and led it at Chancellorsville (his troops played insignificant roles in both battles). Still head of the Third Division on July 1 at Gettysburg, he assumed corps command after Reynolds's wounding early in the action and led it for the rest of the day. That evening, based largely on Oliver Otis Howard's reporting to Winfield Scott Hancock that "Doubleday's command gave way" during the chaotic late afternoon fighting,[12] George G. Meade placed the First Corps under John Newton. Seething at what he considered unfair treatment (Newton was junior to him in rank), Doubleday returned to the Third Division for the rest of the battle but soon left the Army of the Potomac. He never held another field command during the war, spending much of his time on courts-martial in Washington, D.C.

Howard and Meade had incurred the New Yorker's enduring wrath, a fact made evident in Doubleday's *Chancellorsville and Gettysburg*. Written as part of Scribner's Campaigns of the Civil War series and published in 1882, the book bristled with criticism of the pair. Especially upset with Howard's unfair insinuation that the First Corps collapsed prior to the retreat of the Eleventh Corps on July 1, Doubleday observed, "General Howard hastened to send a special messenger to General Meade with the baleful intelligence that the First Corps had fled from the field at the first contact with the enemy. . . . It is unnecessary to say that this astounding news created the greatest feeling against the corps, who were loudly cursed for their supposed lack of spirit and patriotism."[13] Doubleday also averred that Reynolds, rather than Howard, deserved credit for selecting Cemetery Hill as a position of great strength.

As for Meade, Doubleday portrayed him as timid and eager to abandon the field after the second day's action. "At night a council of war was held," he wrote with clear malice, "in which it was unanimously voted to stay and fight it out. Meade was displeased with the result, and although he acquiesced in the decision, he said angrily, 'Have it your own way, gentlemen, but Gettysburg is no place to fight a battle in.'" The army's new chief, added Doubleday, had been rattled by the fierce Confederate attacks on July 2 and "thought it better to retreat with what he had, than run the risk of losing all." Doubleday buttressed his version of events with a long footnote that acknowledged a public discussion about Meade's intensions on the night of July 2. "There is no question in my mind," he reiterated in the note, "that, at the council referred to, General Meade did desire to retreat." The aftermath of Pickett's Charge, suggested Doubleday, similarly showed Meade's indecisiveness. At the critical moment at Waterloo, the Duke of Wellington had ordered, "*Up, guards, and at them!*" In contrast, "General Meade had made no arrangements to give a return thrust."[14]

Howard surely knew about Doubleday's vituperative comments, but he chose not to respond in his own memoirs. Published in two hefty volumes in 1907 as *Autobiography of Oliver Otis Howard, Major General United States Army,* they mentioned Doubleday's actions at Gettysburg in purely descriptive passages. After chronicling hard pressure on both the First and the Eleventh Corps after 3:30 p.m. on July 1, Howard stated simply that, with firing "growing worse and worse," he determined that the "front lines could not hold out much longer. I will not attempt to describe the action further. . . . The order that I sent to Doubleday then was this: 'If you cannot hold out longer, you must fall back to the cemetery and take position on the left of the Baltimore pike.'"[15]

Meade reacted with more emotion. Doubleday's testimony before the joint committee, which anticipated criticisms he leveled in *Chancellorsville and Gettysburg,* spurred Meade to complain to his wife in early March 1864 about "the explosion of the conspiracy to have me relieved . . . in which the Committee on the Conduct of the War, with Generals Doubleday and Sickles, are the agents." The two-volume edition of Meade's letters, compiled by his son and published by his grandson in 1913, included as an appendix a newspaper article by Sickles, printed in the *New York Times* on April 1, 1883, that detailed Meade's "proposed retreat on the night of the 2nd of July." Another appendix offered a stinging reply to Doubleday's version of events, pronouncing General Meade's actions "utterly inconsistent . . . with any such intention as that ascribed to him by General Doubleday."[16]

Impartial observers can find admirable and self-interested behavior and statements from Doubleday, Meade, and Howard regarding Gettysburg. Modern visitors to the battlefield will find statues to all three men that face resolutely toward the enemy.

CONGRESSIONAL OVERSIGHT
WITH A PUNCH

Report of the Joint Committee on the Conduct of the War stands among the indispensable sources on the Union war effort. Published in eight volumes between 1863 and 1866 and reprinted and indexed by Broadfoot Publishing in 1998, this set consists of more than five thousand pages of testimony, official reports, and other documents relating to military campaigns as well as to such topics as alleged misconduct in the area of supply. Virtually every senior Union general gave testimony before the committee, addressing Gettysburg and Antietam, the campaigns in Tennessee and along Louisiana's Red River, First and Second Bull Run, Ball's Bluff, and many other operations. Witnesses appearing before the committee often sought to justify their own actions or to damage the reputations of others. Their testimony consequently reveals a good deal about factions within the Union high command, but it also contains a vast amount of useful detail about the planning, execution, and contemporary analysis of Union military affairs.

The Joint Committee on the Conduct of the War (JCCW) emerged out of the intensely fractious political atmosphere of late 1861. Ignominious defeat at First Bull Run on July 21 and the galling debacle at Ball's Bluff on October 21 shook loyal citizens. The removal of John Charles Frémont from command in Missouri, where he had tried to strike at slavery and slaveholders, alienated Radical Republicans and abolitionists. Perhaps most important, George B. McClellan's failure to mount an offensive during the late summer and autumn prompted some congressional Republicans to question the ability and even the allegiance of many Democratic generals. The death at Ball's Bluff of Colonel Edward D. Baker, a Republican senator from Oregon and close friend of Abraham Lincoln (the Lincolns named their second son after him), prompted a group of politicians to train an accusatory spotlight on Brigadier General Charles P. Stone. Although Baker's rashness and lack of military ability had brought disaster at Ball's Bluff, he became a martyr, and Stone, a Democrat and Baker's military superior, became a convenient scapegoat for Republicans unhappy with the war's progress.

A group of Republican senators and congressmen feared that professional soldiers of McClellan's and Stone's stripe would not wage hard war against the Rebels. Especially unhappy were Radical Republicans, who hoped the conflict would kill slavery as well as restore the Union. On December 5, Senator Zachariah Chandler of Michigan called for creation of a joint congressional committee to examine events at First Bull Run and Ball's Bluff. Established on December 10, the seven-man committee consisted of senators Chandler, Benjamin F. Wade of Ohio, and Andrew Johnson of Tennessee, together with congressmen George W. Julian of Indiana, John Covode of Pennsylvania, Daniel W. Gooch of Massachusetts, and Moses Fowler Odell of New York. All were Republicans except Johnson and Odell, and Wade (the chairman), Chandler, Julian, Gooch, and Covode were Radicals. Although composition of the committee changed as the war progressed, Radicals remained a powerful force in its activities.

Members of the committee considered it part of their role to provide congressional oversight of the Lincoln administration's military policies. They consistently called for offensive campaigns and demanded the removal of George B. McClellan; several also sought to drive George G. Meade from command of the Army of the Potomac, attacked other commanders deemed too timid or too Democratic, and championed officers such as Joseph Hooker and John Pope, whose politics they found more congenial.

Lincoln struggled to forge policy amid cacophonous demands put forward by constituencies extending from the Radicals on one end of the spectrum to conservative Democrats on the other. As early as the fall of 1861, before the committee was formed, Lincoln's secretary John Hay noted in his diary that Chandler, Wade, and others in the "Jacobin club," as Hay called the Radical Republicans, had been criticizing McClellan's lack of action and trying to "worry the administration into a battle." In their postwar history of the Lincoln administration, Hay and John G. Nicolay described the committee as "often hasty and unjust in its judgments, but always earnest, patriotic, and honest."[17]

The committee inspired heated reactions from supporters and critics. Democratic officers called to testify typically expressed a mixture of anger and concern. On February 28, 1863, for example, McClellan, removed from command of the Army of the Potomac the preceding November, described a difficult day to his wife. "I have just got back from that confounded Committee & have to appear before them again on Monday morning," he wrote. "I have been under their hands for several hours & you may imagine that my brain is *rather* tired out." Just more than a year later, Meade confided to his wife that he detected "nothing less than a conspiracy" among members of the committee and some fellow officers to remove him from command of the army: "I intend to await the action of the committee, give them a chance to do me justice, failing which I will publish a pamphlet giving my side of the question."[18] Unlike McClellan, Meade retained his military position but nevertheless nursed a grudge against the politicians he saw as partisan tormentors. Democrats in general came to characterize the committee as a grotesquely biased body that hounded honest officers and tried to transform a war to restore the old Union into a crusade to kill slavery.

On the Republican side, Radicals and their allies believed the JCCW served a necessary purpose in striving to make the United States muster and apply its full resources against the Confederacy. Many moderate Republicans, in contrast, viewed the committee's actions with more mixed feelings.

Students of the Civil War should be thankful for the JCCW's *Report*. Here is much of the story of how the North struggled to define its objectives, find its leaders, and construct a winning strategy. The *Report* reveals details about debates over the fate of slaves who made their way to Union lines, about whether to add emancipation to the nation's war aims, and about how harshly to treat rebel civilians and their property. Indeed, a full understanding of the political and military history of the Army of the Potomac is impossible without reference to the committee's evidentiary record, as is a proper appreciation of the degree to which George B. McClellan dominated much of the early-war period. It is no exaggeration to state that few published sources so clearly illuminate the often chaotic process by which the United States struggled to manage an event of cataclysmic proportions.

VOICES FROM THE ARMY OF THE POTOMAC

Indispensable published primary materials relating to the Army of the Potomac represent a category of evidence that yields both enjoyment and enlightenment. Letters and diaries from officers account for a significant portion of this testimony and have been cited frequently over many decades of historical investigation. Any list of the best such titles should include an important artillerist's journal and sets of correspondence from a staff officer and a division chief.

Charles S. Wainwright commanded a brigade of guns in the First Corps, and later in the Fifth Corps, and saw significant action in most of the battles from Fredericksburg through Appomattox. A well-educated New Yorker, he kept a journal that Allan Nevins edited as *A Diary of Battle: The Personal Journals of Colonel Charles S. Wainwright, 1861–1865*. The journal offers a wealth of material about military affairs, political leaders and events, and the most famous Union army's "long arm." A Democrat and staunch supporter of George B. McClellan, Wainwright frequently criticized the Lincoln administration and, most harshly, the Radical Republicans in Congress. For Wainwright, the war was a struggle to preserve the Union, in which emancipation figured only tangentially. Put off by the attention the New York press paid to a newly raised black regiment in March 1864, for example, Wainwright remarked, "For my part, I wish all the negroes in the country were safely back in Africa."[19]

In the aftermath of Chancellorsville, Wainwright listened while Joseph Hooker unburdened himself to a group of officers, blaming John Sedgwick, among others, for his failure to defeat Lee. "I said nothing in reply to his statements," he noted, "but my feelings were divided between shame for my commanding general, and indignation at the attack on so true, brave, and modest a man as Sedgwick." On July 14, 1863, Wainwright addressed the fact that Lee's army had recrossed the Potomac into Virginia: "People at home of course will now pitch into Meade, as they did McClellan after Antietam, for letting him escape. My own opinion is that under the circumstances and with the knowledge General Meade then had he was justified in putting off his attack."[20]

For testimony regarding General Meade and the rest of the army's high command during the last eighteen months of the war, few accounts rival Theodore Lyman's *Meade's Headquarters, 1863–1865: Letters of Colonel Theodore Lyman from the Wilderness to Appomattox*. Acquainted with Meade since the mid-1850s, the Harvard-educated Lyman joined the general's staff in September 1863 and soon began writing richly descriptive and analytical letters home. (Lyman's equally valuable wartime journals were edited by David W. Lowe and published in 2007 as *Meade's Army: The Private Notebooks of Lt. Col. Theodore Lyman.*)

Two passages suggest the irresistible appeal of Lyman's correspondence. On April 12, 1864, after a group of staff officers first saw Ulysses S. Grant in Culpeper, Virginia, Lyman wrote what became a widely quoted comment about the new general in chief. "Grant is a man of a good deal of rough dignity; rather taciturn; quick and decided in speech," observed Lyman perceptively. "He habitually wears an expression as if he had determined to drive his head through a brick wall, and was about to do it. I have much confidence in him." Several weeks later, after the bloodlettings at the Wilderness and Spotsylvania, Lyman recorded Meade's reaction to a letter from William Tecumseh Sherman to Grant. The letter conveyed Sherman's hope that Grant could make the Army of the Potomac fight as well as the Union's western armies. In a voice Lyman likened to "cutting an iron bar with a handsaw," Meade raged, "Sir! I consider that despatch an insult to the army I command and to me personally. The Army of the Potomac does not require General Grant's inspiration or anybody's else inspiration to make it fight!" As for Sherman's men, Meade dismissed them as "an armed rabble."[21]

Politics are far less obvious in Lyman's letters than in Wainwright's, though his unhappiness with waning resolution behind the lines in the North emerges clearly. A conservative Boston Brahmin, he joined Wainwright in expressing little enthusiasm for black soldiers, as when, on May 7, 1864, he revealed his thoughts about the United States Colored Troops division in Ambrose E. Burnside's Ninth Corps: "As I looked at them, my soul was troubled and I would gladly have seen them marched back to Washington. Can we not fight our own battles, without calling on these humble hewers of wood and drawers of water, to be bayonetted by the unsparing Southerners?"[22]

The Civil War Letters of General Robert McAllister, edited by James I. Robertson Jr., takes readers into the campaigns of the Army of the Potomac from the perspective of a fighting regiment's colonel. Forty-seven years old when war broke out, Robert McAllister, a native Pennsylvanian, served with the First New Jersey Infantry through the Seven Days campaign and then, promoted to colonel, took charge of the Eleventh New Jersey and led it through the rest of the war. The regiment suffered heavily at Chancellorsville and Gettysburg, and McAllister, wounded in the Peach Orchard on July 2, won a brevet to brigadier general for his actions during the Petersburg campaign.

McAllister supported George B. McClellan as a military leader and embraced the cautious culture Little Mac promoted in the Army of the Potomac. "I feel for Genl. McClellan," he informed his wife, shortly after Lincoln removed the general from command in November 1862. "He was a safe man; and if he got into difficulties, he could get us out." But McAllister opposed McClellan as the Democratic candidate for president in 1864 and cheered Lincoln's reelection. During the late summer of 1864, when civilian morale in the United States sank to its wartime low and Republican prospects looked bleak, McAllister stood by U. S. Grant as "a good General and a great man. I am satisfied that if the Rebels come against us here, we will, by the help of God, whip them."[23]

Saving the Union always stood paramount for McAllister as the war's purpose. He took a hard line toward Confederates. "I must confess I have very little sympathy for these people," he wrote shortly after the Overland campaign, and he thought "women are by far the worst secessionists." Because he held them responsible for hundreds of thousands of deaths, McAllister looked "*with contempt* on those that have helped to mould Southern sentiment and arouse their demon-like passions to prepare these people to destroy this fair fabric, our Union." McAllister fought to safeguard "civil and religious liberty" and prove to the world "that Republican Government can be sustained."[24]

As a group, the writings of Wainwright, Lyman, and McAllister rival in perception and descriptive value any of the myriad firsthand accounts that illuminate the history of the greatest Union army.

HARVARD MEN AT WAR

Men who attended Harvard left all students of the Army of the Potomac deeply in their debt. Published letters and diaries include those by Theodore Lyman, a member of George G. Meade's staff, whose astute observations I have discussed in the preceding essay. Robert Gould Shaw's correspondence during his time with the Second Massachusetts Infantry, gathered by editor Russell Duncan in *Blue-Eyed Child of Fortune: The Civil War Letters of Colonel*

Robert Gould Shaw, describes his service at Cedar Mountain, Antietam, and elsewhere, while *Touched with Fire: Civil War Letters and Diary of Oliver Wendell Holmes, Jr.,* edited by Mark De Wolfe Howe, covers the first three years of the war, with especially rich material on the Overland campaign. Two officers in the First Massachusetts Cavalry, Henry Lee Higginson and Charles Francis Adams Jr., provide valuable testimony about operations in the spring and summer of 1863 in Bliss Perry, *Life and Letters of Henry Lee Higginson,* and Worthington Chauncey Ford, ed., *A Cycle of Adams Letters, 1861–1865.*

Charles Russell Lowell Jr., whose time at Harvard overlapped with Higginson's, served on George B. McClellan's staff in 1862. Just fifteen when he entered Harvard, he graduated as valedictorian in the class of 1854 and later married Robert Gould Shaw's sister Josephine. Among his letters (edited by Ralph Waldo Emerson's son Edward, in *Life and Letters of Charles Russell Lowell*) is one that recounts Antietam's toll among Harvard officers: "Frank Palfrey is wounded, not seriously,—Paul Revere, slightly wounded,—Wendell Holmes shot through the neck, a narrow escape, but not dangerous now,—[Norwood P.] Hallowell badly hit in the arm, but he will save the limb,—Dr. Revere is killed,—also poor Wilder Dwight, . . . Bob Shaw was struck in the neck by a spent ball, not hurt *at all,*—Bill Sedgwick very badly wounded. This is not a pleasant letter . . . ," admitted Lowell to his mother. "We have gained a victory—a *complete* one, but not so *decisive* as could have been wished."[25]

Connections among Harvard officers also appear in Higginson's letters, including one from July 1864 that mentions a dinner at City Point, Virginia, with "Barlow, Channing Clapp, and Charles Adams."[26] "Barlow" was Francis Channing Barlow, who commanded the First Division in Winfield Scott Hancock's Second Corps and, like Charles Russell Lowell, graduated first in his class at Harvard (1855) and married one of Rob Shaw's sisters (though, unlike Lowell and Shaw, he would survive the war). Known as one of the army's fighting generals, Barlow suffered terrible wounds at Antietam and Gettysburg. *"Fear Was Not in Him": The Civil War Letters of Major General Francis C. Barlow, U.S.A.,* edited by Christian G. Samito, illuminates elements of a complicated personality as well as important military events.

Barlow's letters reveal a somewhat dark worldview, scant admiration for many leading officers in the army, and open contempt for some of the soldiers who served under him. In January 1862, he pronounced his army routine "a damned stupid life," adding, "I hardly think this disgusting country is worth fighting for." In the wake of the Seven Days, he observed "that McClellan has little military genius & . . . he is not a proper man to command this Army." Heading a brigade in Oliver Otis Howard's Eleventh Corps at Chancellorsville, Barlow was deployed east of the position where Stonewall Jackson's flank attack crushed the Federal line on the evening of May 2. "Howard is full of mortification & disgust," he wrote home six days later about the humiliating rout, "& I really pity him." As for the part of Howard's command that collapsed, Barlow thought his family could "imagine my indignation & disgust at the miserable behavior of the 11th Corps."[27]

During the Overland campaign, Barlow experienced a partial mental breakdown, aggravated by lingering effects of his wounds. On July 15, deep pessimism dominated a letter that responded, in part, to news of Jubal A. Early's raid across the Potomac River and to the outskirts of Washington. "I am utterly disgusted with the craven spirit of our people," wrote Barlow. "I wish the enemy had burned Baltimore & Washington & hope they will yet." As for operations at Petersburg and Richmond, "I do not believe we shall starve out the rebel Army by cutting the railroads even if we could keep them cut." The enemy, he predicted, "have enough rations there to subsist their Army all summer."[28]

War Diary and Letters of Stephen Minot Weld, 1861–1865, privately published in 1912, rivals the finest sets of letters by any officer in the Army of the Potomac. Weld manifested negativity similar to Barlow's in the aftermath of the Overland campaign. Commander of the Fifty-Sixth Massachusetts Infantry, part of the First Division of the Ninth Corps, Weld gave his father a summary of the previous six weeks' action on June 21, 1864. "The feeling here in the army," stated an embittered Weld, "is that we have been absolutely butchered, that our lines have been periled to no purpose, and wasted. In the Second Corps the feeling is so strong that the men say they will not charge any more works."[29]

Weld's wartime career included stints as a staff officer as well as in regimental and brigade command, and his letters address politics, military affairs, and many other aspects of the war. A conservative, he hoped slavery would end but had no patience with abolitionists and cared little about black people. He thought Lincoln's Emancipation Proclamation unnecessary and predicted that the Union army would prove decisive in killing slavery. "Leave the whole thing alone," he recommended, "and as our armies advance, slavery must go under." Lincoln's actions, feared Weld, buttressed "all this abolition talk" that would provide "a great handle for Jeff. Davis and Co." to drum up support for the Confederate war effort. A supporter of George B. McClellan, Weld told his father in late June 1863 that the "more I see of this war, the stronger and firmer is my belief in McClellan." But he drew the line when his former army commander ran for president in 1864. On September 2, he accurately predicted that "McClellan's nomination on a peace platform . . . will kill him." Weld joined the majority of Union soldiers, who cheered Lincoln's reelection, happy that the president would push through to military victory over the Rebels.[30]

Unlike Weld, Henry Livermore Abbott did not live to see the Confederate surrender. An officer in the Twentieth Massachusetts Infantry, popularly known as the "Harvard Regiment," he experienced a great deal of combat before being mortally wounded on May 6, 1864, in the Wilderness. *Fallen Leaves: The Civil War Letters of Major Henry Livermore Abbott*, edited by Robert Garth Scott, presents readers with additional evidence of George B. McClellan's powerful hold on the Army of the Potomac. Devoted to the Union, Abbott mirrored McClellan in preferring that emancipation remain far from center stage. "The president's proclamation is of course received with universal disgust," he reported to an aunt on January 10, 1863, "particularly the part which enjoins officers to see that it is carried out." Not surprisingly, Abbott hoped for Little Mac's return after Ambrose E. Burnside's failure at the battle of Fredericksburg: "The enthusiasm of the soldiers has been all gone for a long time. They only fight from discipline & old associations. McClellan is the only man who could revive it."[31]

Abbott expected success as the armies prepared to engage in the spring of 1864. Meade and U. S. Grant seemed a good combination, the former "quick witted, skilful, a good combiner & maneuverer" and the latter an officer of "force, decision &c, the character which isn't afraid to take the responsibility to the utmost." Yet Abbott's admiration for McClellan remained undiminished. On March 6, he praised his old chief's "sagacity & foresight, both political & military, wonderful comprehensiveness, energy, tenacity & directness of purpose, & above all his *pluck*."[32]

The literary record of Harvard's Civil War soldiers lends support to the claim of Thomas Wentworth Higginson (a distant cousin of Henry Lee Higginson), who edited a collection of biographical tributes published in 1867. "There is no class of men in this republic," affirmed Higginson, "from whom the response of patriotism comes more promptly and surely than from its most highly educated class."[33]

JOHN B. JONES'S WAR

A deep divide between military and nonmilitary topics runs through the literature on the Civil War. Historians interested in the home front too often have explored politics, society, civilian morale, and economics, with scarcely a nod toward the campaigning of massive armies. In many such works it is possible to lose track of the fact that the largest war in American history was in progress. Similarly, historians primarily interested in strategic and tactical movements often have ignored the broader political and social context within which armies maneuvered and fought. Both approaches deny readers an appreciation of the innumerable ways in which the home front and the battlefield intersected. These intersections were especially crucial in a conflict between two democracies, wherein the respective peoples let their political and military leaders know what they expected.

Letters and diaries written by participants highlight the reciprocal impact of events on the home front and the battlefield—how civilian morale rose and fell in response to victories and defeats, for example, and how political imperatives shaped strategic planning. No published primary source offers better insights into this phenomenon than John Beauchamp Jones's *A Rebel War Clerk's Diary at the Confederate States Capital*. Published in Philadelphia in 1866, its two substantial volumes comprise nearly nine hundred pages of reporting and commentary on the war as seen through the eyes of a man well positioned near the seat of Confederate government. Although frequently quoted over the years, Jones's diary never has been fully exploited, in part, no doubt, because the absence of an index in the original edition militated against easy access to its many riches. Unsatisfactory two-volume reprints in 1938 and 1982 failed to provide careful annotation and a full index, and a one-volume abridged version in 1958 deleted so much useful material as to seriously compromise the diary's integrity. Fortunately, James I. Robertson Jr. undertook the task of preparing an annotated, indexed edition of Jones's diary, the 2015 publication of which marked a milestone in Confederate historiography.

Jones's discussion of civilian attitudes toward Confederate military strategy illustrates the diary's value. Historians have expended great effort debating whether the Confederacy should have pursued a more rigorously defensive strategy in order to conserve precious manpower. Robert E. Lee has come in for particularly harsh criticism from scholars such as J. F. C. Fuller, Thomas L. Connelly, and Alan T. Nolan (and later writers who parroted those three men's arguments) because his offensive tactics resulted in horrendous casualties. Too often ignored in this debate are civilian expectations in the Confederacy. What kind of military action did the people want? What effect did offensive and defensive operations have on civilian morale?

Jones's diary should give pause to those who argue that Confederate generals too often took the offensive. It makes clear how popular morale often sagged when the people perceived that their armies stood on the defensive everywhere. In late June 1862, to name a crucial instance, Jones described widespread concern that Richmond would be besieged (every major siege of the war, it is worth noting, ended in Confederate disaster—though this was not apparent in the early summer of 1862): "Our people are beginning to *fear* there will be no more fighting around Richmond until McClellan *digs* his way to it. The moment fighting ceases, our people have fits of gloom and despondency; but when they snuff battle in the breeze, they are animated with confidence." Even Lee's aggressive, and exceedingly bloody, triumph during the Seven Days failed to satisfy many Confederates. "Lee does not follow up his blows on the whipped enemy," observed Jones, three days after the battle of Malvern Hill, "and some sage critics censure him for it."[34]

Jones included in his diary a vast amount of useful information and opinion about an astonishing range of events and issues. In early April 1863, he wrote about the famous bread riots in Richmond. When the commotion began, one young woman in the mob—"seemingly emaciated, but yet with a smile"—told Jones the rioters sought only "to find something to eat." "I could not, for the life of me," noted Jones, "refrain from expressing the hope that they might be successful." Just two days later, however, his last entry on the topic repeated a rumor "that the riot was a premeditated affair, stimulated from the North, and executed through the instrumentality of emissaries. Some of the women, and others, have been arrested."[35]

Jones accorded a good deal of attention to the war's impact on slavery—and especially to how Union military forces threatened to disrupt Confederate control over black people. In late March 1863, for example, he wrote, "A very large number of slaves, said to be nearly 40,000, have been collected by the enemy on the Peninsula and at adjacent points, for the purpose, it is supposed, of co-operating with Hooker's army in the next campaign to capture Richmond." In January 1865, as Confederates debated whether to arm some slaves in the face of increasing Federal pressure, Jones reacted strongly to a comment that General Lee "was always a thorough emancipationist." Were that true about Lee, thought Jones (it was *not* true, I hasten to add), "and if it were generally known, . . . how soon would his great popularity vanish like the mist of the morning!" This passage appears in the diary just more than three weeks after Jones commented that most Confederates, having concluded that Jefferson Davis was inadequate to the task of winning independence, "desire to see Gen. Lee at the head of affairs."[36] Even Lee's towering reputation, the diary thus reveals, was subject to damage from the rip currents generated by discussions relating to slavery.

On April 17, 1865, Jones and his family prepared to leave Federal-occupied Richmond. "I never swore allegiance to the Confederate States Government," he wrote in his penultimate entry, "but was true to it."[37] The pages of *A Rebel War Clerk's Diary* highlight that loyalty, and its pages introduce modern readers to a very perceptive witness.

RIGHT-HAND MEN

Students of the Army of Northern Virginia know that staff officers left a great deal of wonderful testimony about prominent generals, less famous officers, and the campaigns and battles in which they participated. Any bibliography of essential works on the army would include Jedediah Hotchkiss's *Make Me A Map of the Valley: The Civil War Journal of Stonewall Jackson's Topographer* (edited by Archie P. McDonald), which features indispensable material on the Second Corps; Thomas J. Goree's *Longstreet's Aide: The Civil War Letters of Major*

Thomas J. Goree (edited by Thomas W. Cutrer), a collection of wartime and post-war letters relating to Goree's Confederate service; and Walter H. Taylor's *Lee's Adjutant: The Wartime Letters of Colonel Walter Herron Taylor, 1862–1865* (edited by R. Lockwood Tower), a prime title on Lee and the army's headquarters.

The best memoirs include G. Moxley Sorrel's *Recollections of a Confederate Staff Officer,* an unusually literate and revealing volume on James Longstreet and the First Corps; Henry B. McClellan's *The Life and Campaigns of Major-General J. E. B. Stuart,* which remains the best published source on the cavalry and its colorful commander; and Walter H. Taylor's *Four Years with General Lee* and *General Lee: His Campaigns in Virginia, 1861–1865,* two titles that supplement Taylor's letters. Other frequently cited postwar accounts by staff officers include Henry Kyd Douglas's dramatic but often unreliable *I Rode with Stonewall;* Heros von Borcke's equally exaggerated account of cavalry affairs, titled *Memoirs of the Confederate War for Independence;* and William Willis Blackford's highly engaging *War Years with Jeb Stuart.*

A number of less well-known staff officers also wrote valuable reminiscences, including George Campbell Brown, Francis W. Dawson, and Joseph Lancaster Brent. Brown's memoir, edited by Terry L. Jones as *Campbell Brown's Civil War: With Ewell and the Army of Northern Virginia,* pulls readers into the company of Richard Stoddert Ewell, one of the army's great characters. The son of Ewell's wife, Lizinka (the Ewells were married in May 1863), Campbell, as he was known, chronicled his stepfather's operations from First Bull Run through Sailor's Creek. Brown's memoir does much to humanize Ewell, who appears in many other accounts—especially Richard Taylor's widely quoted *Destruction and Reconstruction*—as a deeply eccentric character, more comic relief than serious leader in the high command of Lee's army.

Brown served alongside Ewell at Gettysburg and during the first three weeks of the Overland campaign, a period when Robert E. Lee decided that Jubal A. Early would do a better job as head of the Second Corps. Bitter and despondent after Lee broke the news, Ewell believed that Early and perhaps others had conspired to force him out of the army. Campbell Brown, who remained at Second Corps headquarters after Early assumed command, shared the general's anger. "I intend on seeing little of Early," Brown wrote Ewell on June 13, 1864, "& will get along finely. He looks at me like a sheep-stealing dog, out of the corner of his eye & when I reported myself for duty this evening, I was astonished at this peculiarity—very different from his usual manner."[38]

Dawson's *Reminiscences of Confederate Service* was first published in an edition of one hundred copies in 1882 and then reprinted by Louisiana State University Press, with an introduction by Bell I. Wiley, in 1980. An Englishman who began his Confederate career in the navy, Dawson joined Longstreet's staff as a lieutenant of ordnance in 1862, served with Old Pete for roughly two years, and later transferred to Fitzhugh Lee's staff in the cavalry. Dawson's portrait of Longstreet combines praise with fairly strong criticism. "The reputation that Longstreet had as a fighting man was unquestionably deserved, and when in action there was no lack of energy or quickness of perception," wrote the Englishman, "but he was somewhat sluggish by nature, and I saw nothing in him at any time to make me believe that his capacity went beyond the power to conduct a square hard fight."[39]

Dawson's book boasts memorable accounts of several famous incidents— including Robert E. Lee's reaction to news that Longstreet had been grievously wounded in the Wilderness on May 6, 1864. "We lifted Longstreet from the saddle, and laid him on the side of the road," Dawson recalled of the moments after his chief was struck down. "It seemed that he had not many minutes to live." But Longstreet rallied, and as his staff accompanied the general's ambulance away from the battlefield they met Lee. "I shall not soon forget the sadness in his face," Dawson observed, "and the almost despairing movement of his hands, when he was told that Longstreet had fallen. . . . It seemed a fatality that our onslaught should have been arrested at the moment when the promise of victory was brightest."[40]

Joseph Lancaster Brent, a native of Maryland who spent much of his antebellum career in California, served as chief of ordnance on John Bankhead Magruder's staff during the Peninsula campaign and the Seven Days battles. Brent's *Memoirs of the War Between the States,* published in a limited private edition in 1940, contains invaluable material about Magruder's actions during the spring and early summer of 1862. Sympathetic to his superior, Brent nonetheless sketched him as an officer who suffered serious physical and mental lapses at crucial moments. The morning of the battle of Glendale showed Magruder at his worst. He displayed great nervous energy, galloping back and forth to no apparent purpose, reversing orders, and focusing on minor details best left to members of his staff. "I hope you will pardon me," said Brent gently to his commander, "but I have never seen your usual calmness so much lost by an extreme irritability, sometimes exhibited without any apparent cause, and hence I inferred that you must be feeling badly." Magruder admitted to "feeling horribly" and mentioned two days of indigestion, medicine he believed had triggered an allergic reaction, and loss of "so much sleep that it affects me strangely." Magruder appreciated the expression of concern, and Brent felt "greatly relieved when I saw that the General did not resent my interference, but actually strove to assume his usual deportment."[41]

Readers looking for published primary accounts on Lee's army would do well to set aside a shelf for staff officers—and to reserve space on that shelf for Brown, Dawson, and Brent as well as their more famous comrades.

CONFEDERATE WOMEN VIEW THE WAR

More than 150 Confederate women's diaries, sets of letters, and reminiscences—most of them from slaveholding households—fill the shelves of one large bookcase in my library. I often consult these volumes for information about conditions on the home front, fluctuations in morale, attitudes and opinions regarding political and military figures in both the Confederacy and the United States, and evidence of the war's profound impact on daily life. Mary Chesnut's famous diary—early editions of which were a combination of diary and reminiscence—is the most quoted, but certainly not the best, such account. Superb diaries include those of Kate Stone and Sarah Morgan from Louisiana, Emma Holmes from South Carolina, Eliza Francis Andrews from Georgia, and Judith W. McGuire and Sallie B. Putnam from Virginia. Kate Cumming's journal and Phoebe Yates Pember's memoir offer splendid accounts of nursing in the Western Theater and at Richmond's Chimborazo Hospital, respectively. All these books create a sense of immediacy that transports readers into the turbulent years of the war.

Two diaries merit special attention. My favorite is *"Journal of a Secesh Lady": The Diary of Catherine Ann Devereux Edmondston, 1860–1866*, edited by Beth Gilbert Crabtree and James W. Patton. In more than seven hundred pages of densely printed entries, Kate Edmondston provides an unrivaled look behind the scenes on the Confederate home front. Married to a planter in

Halifax County, North Carolina, she followed the war via newspapers, letters from friends and relatives, and discussions with a circle of acquaintances. As effectively as any other participant's account, her diary charts the fluctuations of morale and expectations behind the lines.

Three passages suggest the quality of the diary. As with most Confederates, Edmondston came to consider Robert E. Lee the greatest figure of the war. But in June 1862 she reacted unfavorably to reports that he had replaced Joseph E. Johnston in command of the Army of Northern Virginia. Lee was "too timid, believes too much in masterly inactivity, finds 'his strength' too much in 'sitting still,'" she wrote. "His nick name last summer was 'old-stick-in-the-mud.' There is mud enough now in and about our lines, but pray God he may not fulfil the whole of his name."[42]

An ardent Confederate, Edmondston often mentioned the importance of slavery to the southern cause. She recorded her thoughts about the debate over whether to arm slaves and place them in Confederate service as 1864 drew to a close. "We have hitherto contended that Slavery was Cuffee's normal condition," she observed, in opposition to the proposal, "the very best position he could occupy, the one of all others in which he was happiest. . . . No! freedom for whites, slavery for negroes. God has so ordained it." As the war ground toward its conclusion, she repeatedly vowed to resist to the bitter end, and after Appomattox she poured out feelings of anger and defiance: "The Vulgar Yankee nation exults over our misfortunes, places its foot upon our necks, & extols its own prowess in conquering us. They command all the R Roads & other routes of travel & they have the ability to force their detested oath down the throat of every man amongst us."[43]

The Civil War Journal of Mary Greenhow Lee (Mrs. Hugh Holmes Lee) of Winchester, Virginia, edited by Eloise C. Strader, rivals Kate Edmondston's in value. It abounds with information about myriad aspects of civilian life in a much-contested area in the Confederacy. Union and Confederate military forces regularly passed through Winchester, fought several battles within a twenty-mile radius, and sent large numbers of wounded soldiers into the city—all of which prompted comments from Mrs. Lee. She also recorded rumors from other theaters of the conflict, which reminds modern readers that morale often rose or fell on the basis of false information. The vagaries of life under Union occupation forms a theme through much of the journal, as does the effort by residents to keep up a normal routine centered around business affairs, social relations, and religious activities. A number of entries describe the ways in which the institution of slavery weakened under the stress of war. Most obviously, the journal's many references to lost friends, material and mental hardships, and debilitating uncertainty underscore the conflict's profound disruption of normal living patterns.

Like Kate Edmondston, Mary Greenhow Lee resolutely supported the Confederacy and harbored deep animosity toward the Federals. Lee's surrender in April 1865 left her stunned: "I have looked on Genl. Lee as the rallying point for the Army of the South . . . ," she observed on April 13, "but that hope is destroyed & I can only pray for strength to bear, what will be the greatest trial of all." April 15 brought an anguished moment of acceptance regarding what she termed "my country, my beloved Southern Confederacy." She never had doubted ultimate victory but conceded that "now if we fall, all has been in vain & the precious blood spilt has been that of martyrs. I shall have to drag on a weary existence, struggling with dire poverty in a country infested by Yankees, for they will pervade every section like the locusts of Egypt."[44]

Anyone who embraces the idea of easy reconciliation after the war will find no comfort in Lee's journal. On October 8, 1865, she described a stronger and more united sentiment "against the Yankees than existed a year ago. Old & young men fire with wrath at our present condition & are ready to side with any party who will chastise our tyrannical foe."[45]

Kate Edmondston and Mary Greenhow Lee, together with other Confederate women who left literary evidence, should be part of any attempt to comprehend the short-lived southern nation. Their voices, as much as those of soldiers and politicians, illuminate the story of secession, war, and defeat.

WARTIME CHRONICLE

Edward A. Pollard's *Southern History of the War* belongs in the top echelon of essential books on the Confederacy. The four-volume set, published between 1862 and 1866 under a combination of Richmond and New York imprints, totals more than 1,500 pages and offers a kaleidoscopic view of the conflict as it unfolded. A native Virginian born in 1832, Pollard joined the editorial staff of John Moncure Daniel's *Richmond Examiner* in the summer of 1861. Colorful, controversial, and sometimes violent, Pollard tried to go to Great Britain in 1864 but was captured by a U.S. warship and imprisoned. After being released in January 1865, he returned to Richmond and rejoined the *Examiner*'s staff.

He began work on *Southern History of the War* in 1861 and continued with the project sporadically for several years. His preface to the first volume disclaimed any intention of writing "a brilliant or elaborate book," promising instead "a compact . . . popular narrative." Although often critical of Jefferson Davis and other political and military figures, Pollard claimed to be "honest, fair, independent, and outspoken." He unquestionably deserved the last of those four adjectives, and his initial volume triggered outrage from many of his targets. Pollard characterized these responses as "unjust, ignorant, and contemptible criticism, emanating mainly from favorites of the government and literary slatterns in the Departments." He had made no attempt "to conciliate either these creatures or their masters" because he was "not in the habit of toadying to great men."[46]

Though opinionated, *Southern History of the War* affords a window into Confederate military, political, and social history and usefully charts fluctuating public opinion about top leaders. For example, the first volume shows how Robert E. Lee's reputation plummeted in late 1861. Lee's campaign in western Virginia that summer and fall, wrote Pollard, was "conducted by a general who had never fought a battle, who had a pious horror of guerrillas, and whose extreme tenderness of blood induced him to depend exclusively upon the resources of strategy, to essay the achievement of victories without the cost of life."[47]

Pollard directed some of his most unsparing language toward Jefferson Davis, accusing him of ignoring "the sentiment and wisdom of the people" and of making "himself the supreme master of the civil administration of the government, so far as to take the smallest details within his control, and to reduce his cabinet officers to the condition of head clerks." In the realm of martial affairs, Davis "was unfortunately possessed with the vanity that he was a great military genius, and that it was necessary for him to dictate, from his cushioned seat in Richmond, the details of every campaign, and to conform every movement in the field to the invariable formula of '*the defensive policy*.'"[48]

Some of Pollard's best analysis deals with the effects of major military operations. He reminds readers that many Confederates considered the action in the Eastern Theater between June and September 1862 to be one grand drama in three acts. The Seven Days blunted McClellan's offensive against Richmond, Second Bull Run reoriented the war to the Potomac frontier, and the Antietam campaign carried the conflict across the national frontier and into the United States. Lee's withdrawal from Maryland did not signify failure in a campaign that had shifted the spotlight from Richmond to the Potomac. "The army which rested again in Virginia had made a history that will flash down the tide of time a lustre of glory," concluded Pollard. Lee's troops "had done an amount of marching and fighting that appears almost incredible, even to those minds familiar with the records of great military exertions."[49]

Pollard recognized that the summer of 1863 did not mark a decisive turning point. "Great as were the disasters of Vicksburg and Gettysburg," he explained, "they were the occasions of no permanent depression of the public mind." In fact, the two campaigns' aftermath demonstrated that the "most remarkable quality displayed by the Southern mind in this war has been its elasticity under reverse, its quick recovery from every impression of misfortune." The summer of 1863 "taught the lesson that the spirit of the Confederacy could not be conquered unless by some extremity close to annihilation."[50]

A southern rights advocate before the war, Pollard favored arming some slaves late in the conflict. He aligned himself with Lee, who saw establishing the nation as more important than holding a firm line on slavery. "The question divided the country," Pollard remarked. "The slaveholding interest, in its usual narrow spirit—in its old character of a greedy, vulgar, insolent aristocracy—took the alarm" and argued that enrolling slaves in the army "would stultify the whole cause of the Confederacy." In the end, Congress "had not nerve enough to make a practical and persistent effort at safety."[51]

Federal armies did eventually crush Confederate military resistance—but only by means Pollard decried as beyond the pale. In this respect, he echoed most other Rebels during and after the war. The Union's embrace of emancipation, he angrily asserted, in language that reflected common racial views, "forced into military service one hundred thousand blacks" and "whetted their ignorant and savage natures with an appetite for the blood of the white man of the Confederacy." As the war grew increasingly ferocious, Pollard's bitterness deepened. The Union foe, he claimed, showed none "of that noble spirituality common to the great conflicts of civilized nations. . . . The track of his armies has been marked by the devouring flame, or by the insatiate plunder and horrid orgies of a savage and cowardly foe."[52]

When U.S. forces demonstrated they could subdue Lee's army, despair gripped the South and brought a swift end to the conflict. The "suddenness and completeness of the catastrophe" revealed "a widely spread rottenness in the affairs of the Confederacy, and that its cause went down in a general demoralization of the army and people."[53]

After the war, Pollard reconfigured the material in *Southern History of the War* to publish large single volumes titled *The Lost Cause* (1866), his most read book, and *Lee and His Lieutenants* (1867). But the fullest rewards lie in a careful perusal of the original four volumes, which unmasks a violent, partisan, and prejudiced world of military and political conflict.

A WINDOW INTO CONFEDERATE MEMORY

Former Confederates wrote accounts of their wartime experiences for various magazines and newspapers. Virtually all students of the Civil War are familiar with four of these publications. The most widely known of the quartet is the Century War Series, published in the *Century* magazine between 1884 and 1887 and later issued in four impressive, heavily illustrated volumes as *Battles and Leaders of the Civil War*. During the 1870s, a few ex-Confederates also contributed to a Civil War series in the *Philadelphia Weekly Times*, several dozen articles from which appeared in book form as *The Annals of the War*. The two most important outlets for Confederate testimony were the *Southern Historical Society Papers*, which commenced publication in January 1876 and provided a forum for the bitter "Gettysburg Controversy" of the 1870s and 1880s, and *Confederate Veteran*, the inaugural issue of which appeared in January 1893. The first three of these publications featured writings by notable military officers, and the *Southern Historical Society Papers*, the contents of which reflected the guiding hand of Jubal A. Early, focused on events in the Eastern Theater.

Although unfamiliar to most modern readers, the *Southern Bivouac* also offers a wealth of primary material on the Confederate war effort. Its relative obscurity stems from several factors: The publishers never issued a hardbound compilation of war-related articles from its pages comparable to *The Annals of the War* or the overwhelmingly successful *Battles and Leaders of the Civil War.* The *Bivouac* also enjoyed just a five-year publishing life—a very brief run compared to that of the *Southern Historical Society Papers* (1876–1959) and *Confederate Veteran* (1893–1932). It also trained its lens on events in the Western Theater rather than on the more famous battles and campaigns waged by Robert E. Lee and the Army of Northern Virginia. Perhaps most important, its roster of authors included few leading military figures of the type who regularly wrote for the Century War Series and the *Southern Historical Society Papers.*

Launched in August 1882 as the *Bivouac* (it adopted its final name in November 1882), the new magazine counted four members of Kentucky's celebrated Orphan Brigade among its five-person editorial committee and promised to publish "all kinds of articles of interest to the ex-Confederate soldier, his family, and to all friends of the South and its history."[54] The first year's issues set patterns that would continue despite later changes of editors and ownership. Articles on the Western Theater markedly outnumbered those on the East (not surprisingly, the Orphan Brigade was a favorite early topic); the common soldier rather than celebrated generals frequently held the spotlight; and miscellaneous short pieces, queries, and correspondence rounded out the war-related offerings.

Like Jubal Early and others who shaped the *Southern Historical Society Papers,* the editors of the *Southern Bivouac* consciously sought to influence future generations of readers by getting the Confederacy's version of the war down on paper. J. William Jones, editor of the *Southern Historical Society Papers,* praised the *Bivouac* in late 1882 and welcomed its founders "as our co-laborers in the great work of vindicating the truth of Confederate history." Although the *Bivouac's* editor conceded that both North and South would make contributions to the literature on the conflict, he added pointedly that "the survivors of the lost cause can least of all afford to be silent" because the "fairest history a victor may write never does justice to the cause of the conquered."[55]

The *Southern Bivouac* departed from the *Southern Historical Society Papers* in important ways. Whereas the latter featured debates among prominent Confederate officers about Gettysburg and other campaigns, the *Southern Biv-*

ouac emphasized the importance of men in the ranks. (*Confederate Veteran* would follow its lead a decade later.) "When we consider the power of ambition," stated one editorial, "the valor of high dignitaries is easily accounted for in behalf of any cause; but the motive which impels the privates and subordinate offices to suffer and bleed so long, demands the fullest explanation." The magazine actively solicited accounts from "the old soldiers or the members of their families." The *Southern Historical Society Papers* printed many official reports; the *Southern Bivouac*, in contrast, announced its intention to preserve "for history the stories and incidents of the war that never appear in army reports." In language that surely rankled Early and others associated with the *Southern Historical Society Papers*, the *Southern Bivouac* claimed to be "the only Confederate soldiers' magazine published in the United States."[56]

The *Southern Bivouac* also called for critical examination of all Confederate leaders—including Robert E. Lee. In a clear reference to efforts by Early and his followers to absolve Lee of blame for his reverses at Gettysburg and elsewhere, the *Southern Bivouac* denounced hero worship that masqueraded as history: "Really great men do not hesitate to avow their responsibilities, even of errors which prove disastrous." The time had come to put aside personal feelings and seek historical objectivity. "That in some cases this is unpleasant to the personal friends of the heroes of history is true," remarked the editors: "But this is of no consequence."[57] In a letter to Basil W. Duke, who served a stint as coeditor of the *Southern Bivouac*, Jubal Early complained that the magazine published too many articles by low-ranking officers and enlisted men, printed negative comments about Lee by untrustworthy individuals, and indulged in sensationalism. Duke defended the *Southern Bivouac's* editorial policies and stated, somewhat pointedly, that a "carefully prepared narrative of an officer of inferior rank, or of a private soldier, may be as valuable as that of a division of corps commander." Closing with a touch of humor, Duke invited Early to contribute to the magazine.[58]

The May 1887 issue announced to readers that the *Southern Bivouac* had been purchased by the Century Company and would cease publication. (A few articles on the Civil War already in hand would become part of *Battles and Leaders of the Civil War*.) In just half a decade, the editors had bequeathed to future students of the Civil War a rich store of material. Scores of articles cover major battles and campaigns as well as a number of lesser-known operations. Nearly every issue contains personal anecdotes relating to combat, camp life, and other facets of the soldier's experience. The magazine also sheds a good deal of light on the Lost Cause interpretation of the Confederate war and the reconciliation movement that developed in the 1880s. Overall, few publications provide a more useful lens through which to view how the postwar South chose to remember its failed attempt to found a slaveholding republic.

AN INDISPENSABLE CONFEDERATE AND HIS DIARY

Confederate armies never lost a battle because they lacked sufficient arms or ammunition. This achievement came despite formidable challenges and depended, to a significant extent, on the vision and efforts of Josiah Gorgas (1818–1883). "In no branch of our service," affirmed Jefferson Davis, "were our needs so great and our means to meet them relatively so small as in the matter of ordnance and ordnance stores." The chief executive looked to Gorgas, "a man remarkable for his scientific attainment, for the highest administrative capacity and . . . zeal and fidelity to his trust," to produce results, regarding arms and ammunition, "greatly disproportioned to the means at his command."[59]

The Pennsylvania-born Gorgas graduated sixth in the class of 1841 at West Point, served as an ordnance officer during the war with Mexico, and married the daughter of a former governor of Alabama in 1853. He stayed in the U.S. Army until the secession crisis, then resigned his commission and took charge of the Confederate Ordnance Department, at the rank of major, on April 8, 1861. He headed the department throughout the conflict and ended his service as a brigadier general. Among the Confederacy's logistical high command, Gorgas earned a reputation strikingly at odds with that of Lucius B. Northrop, the widely loathed commissary general, and to a lesser degree that of Quartermaster General Abraham Myers, whose place the able Alexander R. Lawton took in the fall of 1863.

Gorgas kept a journal for more than thirty years, the Civil War portion of which Frank E. Vandiver edited for publication in 1947. *The Civil War Diary of General Josiah Gorgas* contains insights into the development of Confederate ordnance as well as a wealth of commentary about events and leaders. Three years into the war, Gorgas recorded a useful summary of his work. "Since I took charge of the Ordnance Department . . . ," he wrote on April 8, 1864, "I have succeeded beyond my utmost expectations. From being the worst supplied of the Bureaus of the War Department it is now the best." He mentioned large arsenals in Richmond, Charleston, Selma, and elsewhere, a "superb powder mill . . . at Augusta, [Georgia,] the credit of which is due to Col. G. W. Rains," as well as smelting works, cannon foundries, armories, leather works, laboratories, and other installations. "Where three years ago we were not making a gun, a pistol nor a sabre, no shot nor shell (except at the Tredegar Works)—a pound of powder—we now make all these in quantities to meet the demands of our large armies." His tireless labors, concluded Gorgas with understatement, "have not been passed in vain." General Joseph E. Johnston would have agreed with this sentiment. In the spring of 1864, he observed, "The efficient head of the Ordnance Department has never permitted us to want any thing that could reasonably be expected from him."[60]

Interacting regularly with the top Rebel leaders, Gorgas commented about them frequently. His diary shows the growing importance of Lee and his army as national rallying points across the Confederacy. By the last winter of the conflict, even members of Congress seemed willing to convey great power to Lee. "There is deep feeling in Congress at the conduct of our military affairs," Gorgas wrote, with William T. Sherman's capture of Savannah and John Bell Hood's fiasco in Tennessee fresh in mind. "They demand that Gen. Lee shall be made Generalissimo to command all our armies—not constructively and 'under the President'—but shall have full control of all military operations and be held responsible for them." Gorgas thought Hood's campaign "completely upset the little confidence left in the President's ability to conduct campaigns—a criticism I fear I have made long ago."[61]

Gorgas retained expectations of possible victory until the final stage of the conflict. Although Lincoln's reelection "by overwhelming majorities" in November 1864 proved the folly "of disguising the fact that our subjugation is popular at the North," Gorgas envisioned continued resistance. The Confederacy should apply military pressure until hope for victory among the northern populace "is crushed out and replaced by desire for peace at any cost." In late January 1865, he confessed to having fallen into a "momentary depression." But his attitude changed "when I think of the brave army in front of us, sixty thousand strong. As long as Lee's army remains intact there is no cause for despondency. . . . We must sustain and strengthen this army, that is the business before us."[62]

The possible effects of emancipation drew Gorgas's attention in 1862 and 1864. News of Lincoln's preliminary proclamation in the aftermath of Antietam elicited three brief sentences. "Lincoln has issued his proclamation liberating the slaves in all rebellious states after the 1st of January next," noted Gorgas matter-of-factly. "It is a document only to be noticed as showing the drift of opinion in the northern Government. It is opposed by many there." Two years later, with large numbers of black men in United States Colored Troops units, Confederates discussed the possibility of freeing and arming some slaves. The absence of sufficient white manpower, insisted Gorgas, demanded enrollment of African Americans in the Confederate army. It came down to a question of priorities for him—protecting slavery as it existed or accepting change in pursuit of Confederate nationhood. "The time is coming now," he predicted on September 25, 1864, "when it will be necessary to put our Slaves into the field and let them fight *for their freedom,* in other words give up a part of *the institution* to save the country, *or the whole* if necessary to win independence."[63]

Gorgas remained close to the center of government until the end. He moved southward with Jefferson Davis's party after the fall of Richmond, learning late in April of Johnston's surrender to Sherman at Durham Station. On May 4, he unburdened himself: "The calamity which has fallen upon us in the total destruction of our government is of a character so overwhelming that I am as yet unable to comprehend it. I am as one walking in a dream, and expecting to awake." Eight days later, in Washington, Georgia, Gorgas's war closed. "We got *paroles* for ourselves," began the last sentence of the wartime diary.[64]

EVERY SKETCH TELLS A STORY

Because technological limits prevented Civil War–era photographers from capturing subjects in motion, sketch artists provided the most dramatic images of many memorable incidents. London-born Alfred R. Waud stood out among a talented group whose work found a large audience in the loyal states and included, among many others, Winslow Homer; Waud's brother, William; and Edwin Forbes. The relative absence of major illustrated weeklies in the Confederacy (the *Southern Illustrated News* paled in comparison to *Harper's Weekly* or *Frank Leslie's Illustrated Newspaper*), among other factors, made for a much less dynamic market for sketch artists in the Rebel states. Another Englishman, named Frank Vizetelly, sent in 1861 by the *Illustrated London News* to cover the American conflict from the Union side, decided, in mid-1862, to change his base to the Confederacy. During the remainder of the conflict, he produced a large body of firsthand illustrative evidence relating to the southern nation at war.

Alfred Waud's sketches, many of which were published as engravings in *Harper's Weekly*, include some of the best-known Civil War images. His rendering of Union soldiers carrying comrades away from menacing fires during the second day of the battle of the Wilderness brilliantly conveys the horror of combat. One soldiers crawls toward safety, another raises his arm in hopes of securing help, and two of the four principals, with a wounded man slung in a blanket held by two muskets, look over their shoulders toward the encroaching flames. Equally effective is Waud's spare drawing of the moment when Confederate infantry overran a Union battery at Gaines's Mill on June 27, 1862. Attackers emerge from dark woods in the background, approaching open ground littered with dead and dying horses, while artillery shells burst to the top right and rear. The Confederates appear as an indistinct mass, with only a few figures well defined, yet the drawing pulses with a sense of movement and power.

Two memorable sketches of the battle of Fredericksburg display Waud's artistic gifts. For the charge of Andrew A. Humphreys's division against Confederates situated along the base of Marye's Heights on the afternoon of December 13, 1862, Waud left figures in the main body of the division indistinct while highlighting Humphreys, astride his horse and waving his hat, against a cloud of smoke from the Rebel infantry line behind the famous stone wall. An engraving of the sketch appeared in *Harper's Weekly* on January 10, 1863, and, though engraver Henry L. Stephens did an admirable job, a comparison of sketch and engraving shows how published versions often lost much of the drama and immediacy of the originals. The second sketch, frequently reproduced over succeeding decades, depicts soldiers of the Fiftieth New York

"Genl. Humphreys charging at the head of his division after sunset of the 13th Dec." Waud's drawing captures the drama of Humphreys's assault, with the general at the front of his division waving his hat and smoke from Confederate artillery and infantry fire blanketing Marye's Heights. (Library of Congress, Prints and Photographs Division, LC-DIG-ppmsca-19522.)

Engineers building the upper pontoon bridge across the Rappahannock River under Confederate fire from William Barksdale's Mississippians on December 11. The men's vulnerability and purpose seem equally evident in Waud's gripping treatment.

Away from the battlefield, Waud sketched many prominent figures and famous episodes of the war. On the afternoon of April 9, 1865, he waited in the yard of Wilmer McLean's house at Appomattox Court House, Virginia. Inside the substantial red brick structure, Ulysses S. Grant and Robert E. Lee labored over details regarding the surrender of the Army of Northern Virginia. Lee appeared on the front porch between 3:30 and 4:00 p.m., called for an orderly to bring him his horse, and within a few minutes had mounted Traveller. Waud watched the scene intently. Of the many famous episodes he had witnessed, none exceeded in importance or interest this final scene of the war in Virginia. Waud rapidly captured the action as Lee departed. Two figures dominated his study—a grim-visaged Lee on Traveller and, trailing slightly behind, Colonel Charles Marshall of the general's staff. Waud's eyewitness sketch would grace numerous books about the war, and a more polished version appeared as an engraving in the Century Company's *Battles and Leaders of the Civil War.* Because of Waud's presence at Appomattox, generations of readers formed a visual impression of the most important Confederate shortly after he signed a document that essentially ended the four-year conflict.

Although Vizetelly's sketches match Waud's in neither artistic quality nor historical impact, they provide invaluable glimpses of the war. Some deal with combat—perhaps most famously, a sketch of the heavy Federal bombardment of Fort Fisher on January 13, 1865. Amid shell bursts above and inside the fort, Confederate gunners work their guns. Vizetelly's notes on the sketch describe "an officer + two men killed by fragments of shell" in the left foreground and "a few dead" in the middle of the fort. "The exposed position of the men," he wrote of the day's action, in the *Illustrated London News,* "with shells of the largest size falling and exploding in the midst of them, is terribly apparent in our illustration." Present to witness the attack on Fort Wagner on July 18, 1863, Vizetelly prepared a drawing and described the burial of Union dead in language that aligns well with the final scene in the film *Glory:* "In the ditch they lay piled, negroes and whites, four and five deep on each other."[65]

"The War in America: Interior of Fort Fisher, Near Wilmington, during the Second Bombardment," by Frank Vizetelly. (*Illustrated London News,* March 18, 1865, p. 249.)

Vizetelly also sketched disparate scenes unrelated to battles. These include a vignette of Jeb Stuart and some of his staff and subordinates in the autumn of 1862; the prisoner of war camp on Belle Isle in the James River at Richmond; white refugees in the woods near Vicksburg in 1863 ("The country for forty miles round Vicksburg is covered with small encampments of women and children who have been driven from their homes by predatory bands of Northern soldiers," he wrote); and a Federal shell exploding in the streets of Charleston in 1863. Vizetelly accompanied Jefferson Davis's small party as it made its way southward after the fall of Richmond in 1865, departing just two days before Union pursuers captured the Confederate president on May 10 at Irwinville, Georgia. Several sketches show the group in flight, including one of Davis "signing acts of government by the roadside" and another of him "bidding farewell to his escort two days before his capture."[66]

For a fuller appreciation of Waud and Vizetelly, readers should consult Frederic E. Ray's *Alfred R. Waud: Civil War Artist* (1974) and W. Stanley Hoole's *Vizetelly Covers the Confederacy* (1957). Both offer an array of the artists' work, though the quality of the reproductions in Hoole's volume is less than ideal.

✇ VI ✇

PLACES AND PUBLIC CULTURE

Echoes of the Civil War show up consistently in American popular culture. The conflict's personalities and events periodically appear in feature films, miniseries and other television programs, and documentaries. Because concerns about race play a major role in modern American politics and life, issues and symbols tied to the war—most particularly the Confederate memorial landscape and the Saint Andrew's Cross battle flag—serve as flash points for heated debates. Even preserved historic ground at National Park Service sites and elsewhere provokes disagreements about what constitutes suitable interpretation. Some of the sharpest exchanges occur on Twitter and other social media, while at the same time easy web access to an incredible array of photographs, prints, and artworks enables far more people than ever before to appreciate the war's visual culture. The first three essays in this section, grounded in innumerable visits over a period of five decades, contemplate Gettysburg and other battlefields as interpretive sites and changing landscapes. The fourth moves to highly charged political issues relating to Virginia's official treatment of the state's Civil War history, while the final three, which round out the section and the volume, address the individual and cultural power of wartime photographs and Hollywood films.

GO TO GETTYSBURG!

There has never been a better time to visit Gettysburg. Both the historical landscape and the National Park Service's interpretation afford visitors a perfect opportunity to understand what brought the armies to Pennsylvania, how the battle unfolded, what Union victory meant in the broader sweep of the war, and how Americans have remembered what the soldiers—and Abraham Lincoln—did there in 1863.

I make this claim on the basis of more than a hundred visits to the battlefield. My first, as a fourteen-year-old from Colorado entranced with the Civil War, came in 1965; my most recent, with middle and high school teachers, was just a few weeks ago. The changes have been striking over the years. On my initial trip, Gouverneur K. Warren still reigned as the hero of Little Round Top. Joshua Lawrence Chamberlain was virtually invisible—a circumstance Michael Shaara's novel *The Killer Angels* (1974), Ken Burns's documentary *The Civil War* (1990), and Ron Maxwell's film *Gettysburg* (1993) would alter dramatically. The National Tower appeared in the mid-1970s, an affront to the battlefield that was mercifully demolished in 2000. A Ford dealership on the Carlisle Road mocked the landscape of the first day's fight until its recent removal. Trees obscured so many parts of the field from the 1960s through the 1990s—including, among many others, Devil's Den, Oak Hill, and the ground along Plum Run north of the Trostle house—that important elements of the tactical action made little sense.

Resolute leadership by Superintendent John Latschar over the past dozen years has yielded spectacular results. The park has cut trees (despite shrill opposition from people who don't understand the difference between a historic park and Yosemite), built miles of historically accurate fences, planted orchards, and otherwise labored to restore the battlefield to its 1863 appearance. Visitors can now stand where John Bell Hood's division formed for its assault on July 2, look toward Devil's Den and the Round Tops, and understand what those Texans, Georgians, Alabamians, and Arkansans saw. They can retrace the steps of the attackers in the largely open ground of July 1863—whereas just two years ago they would have had to fumble through confusing woods to find the Triangular Field where the First Texas and Third Arkansas collided with the 124th New York and two sections of Captain James E. Smith's New York battery. Before the tree cutting, when I led tours that included the walk from Hood's jump-off point to Devil's Den, I always breathed a private sigh of relief when we emerged from the woods in the right place. Anyone who has not been to the park recently will appreciate the revelatory impact of the scene restoration.

They also will benefit from a greatly improved visitor center. Generations of tourists crowded into two large buildings on Cemetery Ridge—one housing French artist Paul Philippoteaux's cyclorama, the other a nondescript brick structure offering cramped exhibits that lacked any real theme. Both structures stood on a crucial part of the battlefield, erected in eras before it became unacceptable to so violate historic ground. A new visitor center opened this past summer, with more exhibit space and state-of-the-art storage for the park's priceless collection of relics and research materials. Soon the buildings on Cemetery Ridge will be razed and the terrain restored to its wartime contours. That will be a tremendous victory for all who have lamented their jarring presence and huge parking lots.

The new visitor center and its exhibits have drawn extensive fire from a range of critics. In the spirit of full disclosure, I will say that I served as one of the historians who advised designers about the exhibits. I have been fascinated by the reaction—much of which has broken down along a line separating those who know a great deal about Gettysburg and those who might visit the battlefield just once or twice. It is the former who seem most upset. They lament the absence of long rows of shoulder arms that filled a wall in the old museum, insist that far more relics should be on display, wonder why there is not more explanation of different types of artillery rounds, and worry that visitors might be denied a full appreciation of the variety of Union and Confederate belt buckles and buttons. On a broader level, some critics believe the new exhibits devote far too much attention to framing the battle and not enough to its tactical ebb and flow. Why so much about slavery and the causes of the war? Why a section on how the conflict was remembered? Why so much material on civilians?

I believe the critics care deeply about Gettysburg but miss several key points. First, exhibits should convey just a general sense of the battle's tactical story. Walking the battlefield, where hundreds of interpretive markers assist visitors, is the only way to achieve real tactical understanding. Second, it is very important to explain why a battle mattered, how it fit into the greater sweep of the conflict. If a visitor leaves the park knowing where Company B of the Twentieth Maine fought on July 2 but ignorant about the volatile Northern political situation within which the campaign unfolded, I would reckon the visit a failure. Finally, I believe Gettysburg functions as the closest thing we have to a national Civil War museum. Most of the park's visitors are neither experts on the battle nor well informed about the war. The new exhibits may be their only significant opportunity to learn about the Civil War, and for most tourists the difference between a Schenkl shell and a Hotchkiss bolt is utterly beside the point. But if they gain some knowledge about the battle's tactics, why the armies were in Adams County, and how the site became a focus of reconciliation, I would judge their visit a success. Because of exemplary work at the park over the past few years, the chances of such success are far greater than ever before.[1]

BATTLEFIELDS AS TEACHING TOOLS

Civil War battlefields bring the past vividly to life. These sites permit us literally to touch our history, and in that moment to make a connection with earlier Americans that cannot be duplicated in a classroom or anywhere else. I have taken students to Antietam, Gettysburg, Chancellorsville, Bull Run, Petersburg, Cedar Creek, and other sites for more than thirty years, and the experience has proved singularly effective in helping to illuminate nineteenth-century attitudes and motivations.

I want to focus on Antietam to illustrate how battlefields resonate with students. Many undergraduates begin my classes without knowing that Antietam, fought on September 17, 1862, closed Robert E. Lee's first invasion of the United States and produced approximately twenty-three thousand casualties.

My students and I follow the battle chronologically during a six-hour walking tour. Traversing the field most obviously enables them to understand the tactical ebb and flow. I take them to the hill east of the National Park Service visitor center to set up the campaign, then proceed around the battlefield, with stops at the Dunker Church, the Joseph Poffenberger farm near the North Woods, the southern edge of D. R. Miller's cornfield, the West Woods, the Sunken Road, Burnside's Bridge, and the national cemetery. While examining the tactical action, I point out other landmarks, such as Nicodemus Heights and the ridge where the Pry House sits above Antietam Creek.

Because the battlefield offers a tangible link to a watershed event in our history, students easily move from specifics concerning leadership and combat to larger questions. Did the founding generation envision a true nation or a collection of semiautonomous states? Why was emancipation added to restoration of the Union as a goal for U.S. armies? How did events on the battlefield influence morale behind the lines? Were the soldiers in the two armies more alike than different? How did women such as Clara Barton, who made her first major appearance at Antietam (though not where her monument stands), overcome obstacles to play a significant role in a conflict too often seen as overwhelmingly the province of men?

Antietam is especially useful for exploring how the military and nonmilitary spheres intersected. For example, I talk about the battle's importance in giving Abraham Lincoln the opportunity to announce his preliminary proclamation of emancipation on September 22, 1862. I examine the nature of the proclamation, its relationship to congressional actions such as the Second Confiscation Act, and the shift in historical analysis regarding emancipation, from a preoccupation with political events in Washington to a more complex interpretation that considers actions by African Americans—both enslaved and free—as well as the essential role of Union military forces.

Antietam also provides a good place to discuss the diplomatic implications of military events—how England and France backed away from some type of mediation in the American war following Lee's retreat. I point out that as the armies maneuvered and fought in Maryland, British Prime Minister Palmerston and Foreign Secretary John Russell agreed to try to broker a cessation of hostilities if Lee added a third victory to those at the Seven Days and Second Bull Run.

Although no student has prodded me to talk at greater length about diplomacy, many have asked about burial practices. I address that question at the Fifteenth Massachusetts Infantry's monument at the western fringe of the West Woods. I show Henry W. Ainsworth's name on the monument, listed with eight others in Company H killed on September 17, and read what a comrade wrote to Henry's father. "I went down to the front of the wood, and here I found a burying party from the 15th under a Lieu[tenant] from Co. H. I asked him if he had got the body of Henry Ainsworth. . . . But I was too late, he was buried." Henry's body was in a trench "25 feet long, 6 feet wide and about 3 feet deep." The trench contained two layers of dead soldiers: "The bottom tier was laid in, then straw laid over the head and feet, then the top tier laid on them and covered with dirt about 18 inches deep. Henry is the 3rd corpse from the upper end on the top tier next to the woods." After this precise description, Henry's friend added, "Mr. Ainsworth, this is not the way we bury folks at home."[2] As I read this letter and point to Alfred Poffenberger's cabin, near where Union soldiers dug the trench, students invariably grow very quiet.

Other monuments also have great interpretive value. At the Maryland monument, near the junction of the Hagerstown Pike and Smoketown Road, I discuss factors that led four slaveholding states to remain in the Union while eleven others seceded. At the 132nd Pennsylvania's monument beside the Sunken Road, I talk about that outfit as typical of the green regiments, raised as nine-month units in the summer of 1862, that composed a significant percentage of the Army of the Potomac at Antietam. Students especially like William McKinley's monument, not far from Burnside's Bridge, where I discuss how memorial landscapes develop. Erected two years after the president's assassination, it features a bas-relief bronze sculpture showing Sergeant McKinley serving coffee to men of the Twenty-Third Ohio Infantry. The monument's inscription informs observers that the martyred president had come "under fire" on September 17 and acted "personally and without orders."

One last theme I develop is how the war affected civilians caught in its path. Major battles overwhelmed local people, who faced catastrophic loss of property, helped care for thousands of wounded men, and cleaned up dead animals and untold material wreckage. I emphasize that civilians in the vicinity of Sharpsburg were among the very few residents of the Union who experienced the war so directly. For most of the loyal citizenry, the conflict unfolded as for Jo March and her sisters in *Little Women*. Their father is gone and they miss him, but otherwise their days proceed very much as before the war. Few Confederates, white or black, could claim as much.

I thoroughly enjoy visiting Civil War battlefields with my students. I have seen hundreds of them benefit from walking historic fields and woods, and I believe it is our obligation to make certain that future generations will have this same opportunity.

FLUID LANDSCAPES

A recent examination of some old files turned up a trove of photographs I took with a Kodak Brownie camera on trips to battlefields in the summers of 1965 and 1967. On the most immediate level, these images summoned memories of my first visits to Civil War–related sites, of my excitement at seeing places I had been reading about since I was ten years old, and of the books, booklets, souvenirs, and relics I purchased on the trips (many of which I still have after more than half a century). I also found a diary my grandmother kept during June 1965, which includes information about the earlier of the two trips. She paid eighty cents for lunch in Gettysburg on June 26 and noted that we "spent about one hour and a half taking the tour" and "saw the battle map which was very good." The next day we drove to Chancellorsville "for Gary to pick up an Ames saber [he] had seen on our way to Gettysburg." Earlier, on June 21 at Vicksburg, she described my reaction to seeing a real battlefield: "It was very interesting going thru the Military Park. Gary was thrilled with the whole deal."[3]

As I looked at the photographs, my focus shifted from personal memories to how the slightly faded color prints, which now constitute historical evidence, document striking changes in many of the historical landscapes. Some of those changes reflect the inexorable toll development has taken since the mid-1960s. At Salem Church in 1965, for example, we parked my grandmother's 1963 Ford Fairlane on a gravel lane and walked around the brick structure that stood near the center of action on May 3, 1863, during the Chancellorsville campaign. Looking eastward, I could see monuments to the

Fifteenth and Twenty-Third New Jersey Infantry—the former situated north and the latter south of Virginia Route 3 (the wartime Orange Plank Road). The church stood well beyond the area of growth along the Route 3 corridor, with open fields, broken by scattered woods dotting the undulating ground, stretching off in every direction. It was easy to imagine the fighting on May 3, when William T. H. Brooks's Federal division assaulted Lafayette McLaws's defending Confederates. Anyone visiting Salem Church today would find it impossible to imagine what I could see in 1965. Isolated on a small green patch amid overwhelming development and buffeted by the sounds of heavy traffic, the church seems a forlorn historical relic devoid of topographical context.

A number of my photographs reveal that numerous sites have been improved since the mid-1960s. Three in the Fredericksburg area and one at Antietam will illustrate this phenomenon. The battles of Chancellorsville, the Wilderness, and Spotsylvania all featured, to a greater or lesser degree, the second- and third-growth scrub forest popularly known as the Wilderness of Spotsylvania. I visited all three battlefields in 1967 and at several crucial places could form no idea of what had happened in 1863 and 1864. I took pictures of Union cannons at Fairview Cemetery and Confederate cannons at Hazel Grove—all the muzzles of which pointed directly toward thick woods. How could batteries in these two positions have dueled with one another on the morning of May 3, 1863, I wondered? In the small visitor shelter along Route 3 in the Wilderness (at that point the old Orange Turnpike), I was hemmed in by trees on all sides as I sought to reconstruct what happened when units from Gouverneur K. Warren's Union Fifth Corps collided with elements of Richard S. Ewell's Second Corps in Saunders Field on the morning of May 5, 1864. And at Spotsylvania I trudged along the path behind the Confederate works in the Mule Shoe salient, again denied any grasp of the contours of the terrain, and by extension of the ebb and flow of action on May 10 and 12, 1864, due to encroaching trees.

Because of impressive scene restoration in the years after I took my pictures, the action at all three of these sites is now far more understandable. Robert K. Krick, the longtime chief historian at Fredericksburg and Spotsylvania National Military Park, pioneered the removal of trees from National Park Service battlefields. These efforts opened the wartime vista between Hazel Grove and Fairview, allowing visitors to see why artillery in the two positions figured prominently in the climax of heavy combat on May 3. Eventually, as

This view taken in the summer of 1967 looks down the Orange Turnpike (modern Virginia Route 20) from the Union perspective toward the position held by Richard S. Ewell's Confederate Second Corps on May 5, 1864. The main action took place to the viewer's left in Saunders Field, which in 1967, as the photograph shows, was completely wooded. The National Park Service cleared the field in the mid-1980s. (Collection of the author.)

Edward Porter Alexander wrote in his memoirs, Confederate artillerists won the duel: "I rode rapidly to the Hazel Grove position to bring forward all [guns] from there. . . . The enemy had abandoned his 25 gunpits [at Fairview], & we deployed on the plateau, & opened on the fugitives, infantry, artillery, wagons—everything—swarming about the Chancellorsville house, & down the broad road leading thence to the river."[4] In the Wilderness, Saunders Field is now open ground, which vastly increases the value of a stop at the NPS shelter. Equally impressive, cleared areas along the northern and western sections of the Confederate works in the Mule Shoe render intelligible Emory Upton's famous attack against George Doles's Georgians on May 10 and Winfield Scott Hancock's massive assaults that led to hideous fighting at the Bloody Angle two days later.

My last example of improved landscapes concerns the Dunker Church at Antietam. Surely one of the most iconic buildings on any Civil War battlefield, it captured Alexander Gardner's attention when he took his celebrated photographs on September 19, 1862, several of which featured the detritus—hu-

Another photograph from the summer of 1967, this one shot across the old Hagerstown Pike toward the Dunker Church at Antietam. The trailer house is visible to the left of the tall trees, and the property's mailbox sits by the fence opposite the driveway. (Collection of the author.)

man, equine, and material—of Stephen D. Lee's artillery battalion just across the Hagerstown Pike from the church. As I framed my picture in June 1967, I was disappointed to see a red and white house trailer, complete with lawn furniture and a mailbox by the side of the road, less than fifty yards from the southern entrance to the church. I tried to keep the trailer out of my shot but later discovered that part of it lurked at the left-center edge of the image. Today, thankfully, the Dunker Church suffers no such intrusive indignity.

Overall, the discovery of these photographs reminded me that no historical landscape is immutable. Natural and built features change regularly, sometimes for the better and sometimes not. The omnipresence of camera phones guarantees that a few decades hence there will be a profusion of opportunities to chart how historic places change.

REEVALUATING VIRGINIA'S "SHARED HISTORY"

It is difficult to imagine what prompted Virginia's governor Robert F. McDonnell to ignore the institution of slavery and the process of emancipation in a proclamation announcing Confederate History Month. The "people of Virginia joined the Confederate States of America in a four year war between the states for independence," observed the proclamation, which was issued in April 2010 and encouraged Virginians "to reflect upon our Commonwealth's shared history, to understand the sacrifices of the Confederate leaders, soldiers and citizens during the period of the Civil War." The proclamation mentioned historical sites such as the White House of the Confederacy and welcomed visitors from the United States and around the world to visit Virginia during the sesquicentennial anniversary of the Civil War.[5]

An avalanche of negative reaction in newspapers, on television, and on the internet prompted McDonnell to apologize for what he termed a "major omission" and to offer a revised version of the proclamation. "The institution of slavery," read the new language, "led to this war and was an evil and inhumane practice that deprived people of their God-given inalienable rights." All Virginians, added the governor, "are thankful for its permanent eradication from our borders." The changes inspired mixed responses: representatives of the Sons of Confederate Veterans denounced them, charging that the governor had sold out to the forces of political correctness, while some former critics expressed appreciation for McDonnell's about-face. Still others said the changes had come too late. Among the last group, an analyst for CNN avowed that, for him, Confederate soldiers "were, and forever will be, domestic terrorists."[6]

The whole controversy had a distinctly familiar quality. Comparable debates had arisen in the 1990s when then-governor George F. Allen proclaimed Confederate History Month without mentioning slavery, and again in 2001 when his successor, James S. Gilmore, included a denunciation of the peculiar institution as part of "A Proclamation in Remembrance of the Sacrifices and Honor of All Virginians Who Served in the Civil War." Gilmore's proclamation mentioned not only Robert E. Lee and Stonewall Jackson but also William H. Carney of the Fifty-Fourth Massachusetts Infantry, a Norfolk resident and Medal of Honor recipient, and William R. Terrill, a native of Covington who served as a Union general. Henry E. Kidd, commander of the Virginia Division of the Sons of Confederate Veterans, reacted angrily to Gilmore's inclusion of Union figures: "This may say that it's honoring Confederates but this is not what we asked for. . . . Apparently [Gilmore] has bowed to the wishes of the NAACP. This is nothing more than a political ploy to pander to minority votes, I don't doubt." L. Douglas Wilder, elected as the state's first African American governor in the early 1990s, deemed Gilmore's inclusion of Virginia's black people and white unionists a noteworthy step forward in a state that had long celebrated Lee–Jackson Day.[7]

The consensus among those who paid attention labeled McDonnell's first proclamation a major step backward from Gilmore's approach in 2001. (Gilmore's two successors—Mark R. Warner and Timothy M. Kaine—did not call for observance of Confederate History Month.) In explaining the original version, McDonnell said he had been focused on Civil War history rather than on slavery, which raises an obvious question. How can anyone discuss the Civil War era in Virginia without alluding to slavery? It is especially odd in light of the fact that the governor mentioned "the people of Virginia" and "our Commonwealth's shared history," suggesting, though not stating outright, that his proclamation applied to all Virginians during the period 1861 to 1865.

A few words about Virginia's population and "shared history" will shed light on how badly McDonnell went wrong. In 1860, Virginia ranked first among the fifteen slave states in population, with 1,105,453 white residents, 490,865 enslaved African Americans, and 58,042 free black people. Among these "people of Virginia," to use the governor's phrase, 376,688 became residents of the new state of West Virginia in 1863 (23 percent of the 1860 population, and a much higher percentage of the white portion, because western Virginia was home to relatively few slaves). This part of Virginia's wartime story powerfully underscores the extent of unionist—or anti-Confederate—sentiment in the state. The vast majority of the half million black residents similarly should not be considered Confederates.

Governor McDonnell's "shared history" thus included thousands of Virginians who fought in storied campaigns under Robert E. Lee, Stonewall Jackson, Jeb Stuart, A. P. Hill, and other Virginia-born officers—but also featured huge numbers of people who opposed both secession and the Confederacy. Of 126 West Point graduates in the army who were native Virginians or were appointed to the academy from the state, forty-four (35 percent) remained loyal to the United States in 1860. So also did non–West Pointer Winfield Scott, by far the nation's best soldier and architect of a broad strategic plan that eventually brought United States victory against the breakaway slaveholding republic. Southampton County's George Henry Thomas became the fourth-greatest Union military hero, ranking behind U. S. Grant, William Tecumseh Sherman, and Philip H. Sheridan. More than thirty thousand white men from the western regions of Virginia fought for the Union cause, as did black Virginians who served in United States Colored Troops units. Many thousands of black refugees, called "contrabands" during the war, assisted United States military forces as noncombatants. White unionists also supplied information and otherwise helped invading Federal forces.

Virginia's wartime experience offers a number of compelling story lines. The most written about relates to the Army of Northern Virginia's operations. Virginia witnessed battles and smaller actions that claimed more than 350,000 Union and Confederate casualties, nearly one-third of the war's total. More men fell within twenty miles of Fredericksburg than in all the battles combined in any other state. The level of sacrifice by Confederate Virginians in and out of uniform, as McDonnell's proclamation noted, was immense. Other stories are equally compelling—most obviously the transition from slavery to freedom for 30 percent of the state's population. Virginia's governors might well continue to issue proclamations that remind modern residents of the conflict's seismic impact. They can use Governor McDonnell's initial effort as a model of how *not* to do so.

THE POWER OF PHOTOGRAPHS

The Civil War beckons to modern Americans in many ways. Most important is the mass of information in letters, diaries, memoirs, and other literary sources that allows us to reconstruct the world and experiences of the wartime generation. Often just as compelling is the immense photographic record of the conflict, which preserves the likenesses of participants, takes us onto battlefields, into military camps, aboard naval vessels, through ruined cities, and behind the lines in both the United States and the Confederacy. Many people have described to me how certain images made a profound impression on them. Some iconic examples come up again and again in such conversations: U. S. Grant leaning against a spindly tree outside his tent during the Overland campaign, three Confederate prisoners assuming casually defiant poses on Seminary Ridge just after Gettysburg, Alexander Gardner's staged dead "sharpshooter" in Devil's Den, black refugees crossing the Rappahannock River into Union lines in August 1862, and George Barnard's view of ruins in Columbia, South Carolina, are five such images. Despite repeated close viewings, these kinds of photographs never lose their descriptive power and analytical potential.[8]

I first glimpsed the most important photograph in my long relationship with the war when I purchased a copy of *The American Heritage Picture History of the Civil War* shortly after its publication in 1960. I found the illustrations in the book captivating—none more so than the full-page reproduction, situated at the beginning of the section on the 1862 Peninsula campaign, of a portrait of James Ewell Brown "Jeb" Stuart. I never had seen anything quite like this. The youthful general, seated with his legs crossed, gazes directly out from the page with eyes that have a startling clarity. Polished boots reach above his knees, the tasseled ends of a sash hang under his left elbow, a gauntleted left hand grips the hilt of his saber, and a plume adorns his hat at the far left of the photograph. I could imagine many of the figures represented in the book in modern dress, but Stuart seemed incontrovertibly anchored in another time and place.

The image prompted me to look him up in my family's copy of *The Columbia Encyclopedia*. That bulky one-volume reference work included suggested

Brigadier General James Ewell Brown "Jeb" Stuart, from *The American Heritage Picture History of the Civil War*. Accompanying text observes that "Stuart delighted in gaudy trappings—yellow sash, scarlet-lined cape, plumed hat, jack boots, gauntlets—but not without reason: 'We must substitute *esprit* for numbers,' he said. 'Therefore I strive to inculcate in my men the spirit of the chase.'" (Library of Congress, Prints and Photographs Division, LC-DIG-cwpb-07546.)

readings at the end of articles, which led me to Douglas Southall Freeman's *Lee's Lieutenants: A Study in Command.* My grandmother purchased the three-volume set for my next birthday, and I was delighted to find that Stuart, as painted by the French muralist Charles Hoffbauer, adorned the dust jacket of volume 3. Freeman's initial description of Stuart seemed perfectly compatible with the photograph, noting that the cavalryman possessed an "exhibitionist manner, a fondness for spectacular uniforms and theatrical appearance and a vast love of praise"—while also demonstrating attributes that soon would make him one of the Confederacy's military idols.[9]

Freeman's footnotes opened up the world of literature on Stuart, as it existed in the early 1960s, and I quickly collected a small shelf of books. Within a year, I worked my way through John W. Thomason's *Jeb Stuart,* Henry B. McClellan's *The Life and Campaigns of Major-General J. E. B. Stuart* (in a retitled reprint from Indiana University Press), William Willis Blackford's *War Years with Jeb Stuart,* Burke Davis's *Jeb Stuart: The Last Cavalier,* John Esten Cooke's *Wearing of the Gray,* and George Cary Eggleston's *A Rebel's Recollections* (the last two also in Indiana University Press reprints).

The compelling photograph often came to mind as I read about Stuart. Thomason seemingly cataloged elements of the image as I first observed it: Stuart "wore gauntlets of white buckskin, and rode in a gray shell jacket, double-breasted, buttoned back to show a close gray vest. His sword . . . was belted over a cavalry sash of golden silk with tasselled ends. . . . His soft, fawn-colored hat was looped up on the right with a gold star, and adorned with a curling ostrich feather." A combination of showman and gifted soldier, concluded Thomason, Stuart's "type, the general, charging with his sword out, in the front of battle, is gone from the world. His kind of war has given over to a drab affair of chemistry, propaganda, and mathematics. Never, anywhere, will there be his like again."[10]

Many passages in the books by former Confederates buttressed this view. Blackford, Cooke, and McClellan all served on Stuart's staff, and while their books left no doubt that Stuart excelled at the hard work of commanding cavalry, they also evoked the cavalier trappings so apparent in the photograph. A novelist, Cooke directly tied Stuart to a chivalric past. "There was about the man a flavor of chivalry and adventure," wrote Cooke in his book, first published in 1867, "which made him more like a knight of the middle ages than a soldier of the prosaic nineteenth century." I had thought no one who looked like Stuart's photograph belonged in the twentieth century; Cooke thought him an anachronism even in the nineteenth. More subdued in his prose than Cooke, Blackford wrote, "General Stuart always dressed well and was well mounted, and he liked his staff to do the same. In our gray uniforms, cocked felt hats, long black plumes, top boots and polished accoutrements, mounted on superb horses, the General and his staff certainly presented a dashing appearance."[11]

I soon expanded my range of interests beyond Stuart, and over time I realized that much of what I had read about him in my youth fit snugly within the Lost Cause tradition. But I never think of Stuart without having that photograph come instantly to mind. It brings back, however fleetingly, the sense of discovery and satisfaction that fueled my early explorations of the Civil War. That single arresting image served as a point of departure that led me to books, to historic sites, and, eventually, to a career as a historian of the conflict that created Stuart's fame and, just more than three months after his thirty-first birthday, took his life.

GLORY
Reflections on a Civil War Classic

Nearly twenty years have elapsed since *Glory*, director Edward Zwick's treatment of the Fifty-Fourth Massachusetts Infantry and Colonel Robert Gould Shaw, made its debut in late 1989. There had not been a true Civil War film for almost a quarter century—since *Shenandoah* in 1965—though westerns with Civil War connections such as *The Good, the Bad, and the Ugly* (1967), *The Undefeated* (1969), and *The Outlaw Josey Wales* (1976) had appeared at regular intervals. Because theaters in State College, Pennsylvania, did not book *Glory*, I drove with friends to see it in Altoona and shortly thereafter arranged a screening for students at Penn State University. I subsequently watched it for a third time at a large theater in New York City. As a result of those three viewings, *Glory* became, and has since remained, my favorite Civil War film.

I find it to be very satisfying on three levels. First, the principal actors do a fine job. Denzel Washington's Private Trip, Morgan Freeman's Sergeant John Rawlins, Jihmi Kennedy's Private Jupiter Sharts, and Andre Braugher's Private Thomas Searles compose a memorable quartet, who, as enlistees in the Fifty-Fourth, follow Hollywood's venerable tradition of placing men of divergent backgrounds together in military service. I initially doubted whether someone best known as the teenage Ferris Bueller should play Colonel Shaw, but Matthew Broderick proved a very pleasant surprise. Cliff De Young as Colonel James Montgomery, who memorably ordered the burning of Darien, Georgia, in June 1863, and John Finn as the unyielding Sergeant Major Mulcahy also contribute riveting supporting performances. A screenplay that draws heavily on Shaw's wartime letters and other historical materials gives the actors first-rate material with which to work.

I also believe that *Glory*'s staging of a Union attack at Antietam represents the best combat sequence in Civil War cinema. A junior officer in the Second Massachusetts infantry at Antietam, Shaw wrote about his experience shortly after the action: "Every battle makes me wish more and more that the war was over. It seems almost as if nothing could justify a battle like that of the 17th, and the horrors inseparable from it."[12] Those horrors stand out in *Glory*, as viewers move forward with Shaw's regiment. Artillery rounds burst in trees, Rebel defenders behind a rail fence send a shower of musketry into the blue ranks, and an officer's head bursts into red spray when hit by a shell. Unable to stand the fire, the Federals retreat, including one soldier, his right leg reduced to a bloody stump, who drags himself toward the relative safety of Union lines as a slightly wounded Shaw hugs the ground.

I consider *Glory* to be most important as the first film to present black soldiers as significant military actors in the Civil War. Prior to its release, African Americans in the Union army had been largely absent from modern American conceptions of the conflict. Sixteen students at Ohio State University played members of the Fifty-Fourth in the film, one of whom spoke to this point: "This information wasn't in the history books. It's like an unquenchable thirst. The history is so rich—you want to jump right in with both feet." Denzel Washington, whose performance as the embittered Trip earned him an Oscar for best supporting actor, reacted similarly. "I knew absolutely nothing," he confessed. "I didn't even know that blacks fought in the Civil War."[13] Theatergoers across the United States left screenings with a similar realization that the military struggle between 1861 and 1865 had not been an all-white affair. In that respect, *Glory* worked a sea change in popular perceptions about the conflict.

Greater attention to the United States Colored Troops—as the black regiments were denominated—reached a high point with the dedication, on September 12, 1996, of the African American Civil War Memorial in the historic Shaw neighborhood of Washington, D.C. The monument features a sculpture by Ed Hamilton titled *The Spirit of Freedom,* around which a series of stainless steel plaques list the names of approximately two hundred thousand black soldiers and seven thousand white officers who served in USCT units. In January 1999, a facility that offered exhibits and research materials, operated by the African American Civil War Memorial Freedom Foundation and Museum, opened a short distance from the monument. *Glory* surely deserves considerable credit for spurring interest in creation of the monument.

Zwick's film gets most important aspects of the Fifty-Fourth's story right. These include the second-class treatment of black soldiers in terms of pay and duty, open hostility to their recruitment by many white Union soldiers, and the importance of military service to the black men's sense of manhood. The film often aligns perfectly with historical evidence. For example, deployment of the Fifty-Fourth to Beaufort, South Carolina, brings the men, and the viewer, face-to-face with slavery. The soldiers encounter a number of local black children, and Rawlins urges them to tell their parents that the appearance of the Fifty-Fourth means the year of jubilee has come. On June 8, 1863, Corporal James Henry Gooding of the Fifty-Fourth wrote about recently liberated black residents in Beaufort: "The contrabands did not believe we were coming; one of them said, 'I nebber bleeve black Yankee comee here help culer men.' They think now the kingdom is coming sure enough."[14]

This is not to say that no errors or distortions mar the film. The Fifty-Fourth's climactic assault along the beach toward Fort Wagner goes in the wrong direction, too many members of the regiment are former slaves (most were free black men from the North), Broderick's Shaw lacks some of the real man's ambivalence about abolition, and Trip's character betrays anachronistically modern attitudes, to name four instances.

Yet such lapses detract only slightly from a film that combines a compelling story, memorable characters, fine acting, strong direction, beautiful cinematography, and a haunting musical score. *Glory* holds up remarkably

well after twenty years, evoking a powerful range of emotions in viewers—
including many, such as I, who have seen it multiple times and certainly will
watch it again.

HOLLYWOOD'S
TWENTY-FIRST-CENTURY LINCOLN

Glory marked a significant turning point in Hollywood's long relationship with
the Civil War. Edward Zwick's treatment of the Fifty-Fourth Massachusetts
Infantry introduced millions of viewers to black Union soldiers and, beyond
that, anticipated a strong cinematic turn toward emancipationist narratives.
Steven Spielberg's *Lincoln* and Timur Bekmambetov's *Abraham Lincoln: Vampire Hunter,* both released in 2012, interpret the sixteenth president in ways
that reflect and reinforce the current ascendancy of the Emancipation Cause
memory of the conflict. Daniel Day-Lewis's transcendent performance in *Lincoln,* which earned him an Oscar for best actor, virtually assures the film's
continuing impact on Civil War memory.

Lincoln signals its focus on emancipation in the first scenes. It opens with
black soldiers fighting Confederates and then moves into a conversation between Lincoln and one of the African American combatants. The soldier mentions Rebel atrocities against USCT men, after which one of his comrades
joins the conversation to lecture Lincoln about discrimination in the army
and the need to grant black men the vote. The scene ends, in stunningly improbable fashion, with the second man quoting the "new birth of freedom"
passage from the Gettysburg Address to the president. (My essay "Revisiting
the Gettysburg Address," in part 1, addresses the implausibility of anyone's
quoting from the speech at the time.)

The film's central narrative concerns Lincoln's determination, in January 1865, to secure passage of the Thirteenth Amendment in the House of
Representatives. Along the way, Spielberg repeatedly reminds viewers about
emancipation's centrality. Tad Lincoln examines photographs of slaves and
asks a White House butler and Elizabeth Keckley if they were beaten while

in bondage, Mary Todd Lincoln urges her husband not to squander political capital by pushing for emancipation, and Radical Republicans debate whether to support Lincoln or to punish him for dragging his feet on their proposals relating to black people and ending slavery. Spielberg does an excellent job with the give-and-take on the floor of the House and, through a Missouri couple named Jolly, conveys a common white attitude that emancipation made sense only if connected directly to saving the Union.

Daniel Day-Lewis's Lincoln performs the heavy lifting about emancipation and leaves no doubt that, for him at least, the war was preeminently about ending slavery. The key moment comes in a cabinet meeting, when Lincoln grows agitated at the absence of clear support to push hard for immediate passage in the House. He slams his hand on the table and, with voice rising, says, "I can't listen to this anymore. I can't accomplish a god damned thing of any human meaning or worth until we cure ourselves of slavery and end this pestilential war." Looking at his advisers and pounding the table again, he presses for the amendment: "And whether any of you or anyone else knows it, I know I need *this*. This amendment *is that cure.*" The United States occupied the world stage "with the fate of human dignity in our hands. Blood's been spilt to afford us this moment." Lincoln wants House action "Now! *Now! Now!*" "Abolishing slavery by constitutional provision," he asserts in closing, would settle the fate "not only of the millions now in bondage but of unborn millions to come."

The final vote in the House supplies the film's emotional climax, and Spielberg ably portrays the historic moment of unrestrained celebration among Republicans and the mixed gallery of white and black spectators. Very near the film's end, Lincoln speaks the passages from his second inaugural address dealing with slavery, to reinforce the message of a war waged for emancipation.

Abraham Lincoln: Vampire Hunter, although radically different in tone, matches *Lincoln's* emancipationist theme. Indeed, it presents the sixteenth president as a lifelong abolitionist. During his boyhood in Indiana, young Abe sees his black friend, Will—the best friend of his life, viewers later learn—being whipped, tries to help him, and receives blows himself. Thomas Lincoln intervenes to protect the boys, and Nancy Hanks Lincoln intones, "Till every man is free, we are all slaves." A slave-catching vampire, it turns out, had ventured into nonslaveholding Indiana and administered the beating. That villain later kills Lincoln's mother, leading Abe to become a vampire hunter and avenge her death.

The mature Lincoln enters politics and delivers a speech that does the work Spielberg assigned to the presidential outburst with the cabinet. "The demon of slavery is tearing our country apart," Lincoln tells the packed venue. "We must stand up. We must stand strong and fight, fight for the very soul of our nation." Summoning his mother's words from Indiana, he insists, "Until every man is free, we are all slaves." Lincoln knows all friends of freedom must take on the slaveholders, prominent among them vampires who have benefited from trafficking in human beings, and eventually pursues the presidency to follow this path.

Improbable but entertaining events ensue, as Abe wields a wicked silver-clad ax against innumerable proslavery vampires. Union victory at Gettysburg finally vanquishes the vampires/Rebels, and Lincoln travels to the battle site with Will for a vignette featuring the "new birth of freedom" portion of the Gettysburg Address, thereby assuring viewers that slavery is dead. In a voice-over just before the credits, Lincoln observes that triumph over the vampires guarantees "America shall forever be a nation of living men, a nation of free men."

An emancipationist Lincoln presiding over a war waged to end slavery resonates with twenty-first-century audiences. Other recent films and television projects, among them *Mercy Street* (PBS, 2016–2017) and director Gary Ross's *Free State of Jones* (2016), further illuminate the degree to which the Emancipation Cause narrative has taken hold in Hollywood. Films focused on slavery, among them *12 Years a Slave* (2013) and *The Birth of a Nation* (2016), link well with those dealing more specifically with the Civil War. This development affords wonderful teaching opportunities regarding historical memory when juxtaposed against the dominant influence of the Lost Cause for more than half of the twentieth century in *The Birth of a Nation* (1915), *Gone with the Wind* (1939), and innumerable other films.

Yet the new emphasis carries dangers of misrepresentation as well as welcome attention to foundational aspects of the war. First to last, Lincoln, who understood attitudes among the loyal white citizenry, framed the war as one for Union. As late as his annual message to Congress in December 1864, he cast the Thirteenth Amendment as one of the tools to achieve the greater goal of Union. But Hollywood seldom traffics in historical subtlety. An uncomplicated and powerful story line, something *Lincoln* and *Vampire Hunter* deliver, attracts filmgoers most effectively.

APPENDIX: ROSTER OF ESSAYS

This chronological listing contains seventy-two essays published in *Civil War Times* (one in a joint issue with *America's Civil War*) as well as two from the *Civil War Monitor*. The three from *Civil War Times* preceded by an asterisk are not included in this book—one because I substituted a longer version and two because their topics are dated. Thirty-four of the essays have been retitled for this collection.

CIVIL WAR TIMES, "GARY W. GALLAGHER'S BLUE & GRAY"

"Go to Gettysburg!" (February 2009), 21–23.
"Let the Chips Fall Where They Will" (April 2009), 19–21.
"*Glory*: Reflections on a Civil War Classic" (June 2009), 18, 20–21.

CIVIL WAR TIMES, "BLUE & GRAY"

"Two Ways to Approach One War" (August 2009), 18, 20.
"Masters of Their Medium" (October 2009), 20–21. Retitled "Two Gifted Writers."
"Why Doesn't Grant Get the Love?" (December 2009), 20–21. Retitled "Tracking U. S. Grant's Reputation."
"Do the Numbers Add Up for 'Marse Robert'?" (February 2010), 19–20. Retitled "R. E. Lee as a General."
"Will Biographers Ever Get Out of a Rut? (April 2010), 19–20. Retitled "Biographers and Generals."
"The Chorus of the Union'" (June 2010), 22, 24. Much expanded and retitled "The Union in Memory."
"Reevaluating Virginia's 'Shared History'" (August 2010), 21–22.

"The Union Army Brought Emancipation to Thousands" (October 2010), 22–25. Retitled "The Union Army and Emancipation."

"Union Vets Claimed They Fought for a 'Higher' Cause" (December 2010), 19, 21–22. Retitled "Union Veterans Claimed They Fought for a Higher Cause."

"The War Was Won in the East" (February 2011), 19–21.

"The War's Overlooked Turning Points" (April 2011), 21–23.

"How Lee's 'Old War-Horse' Gained a New Following" (June 2011), 21–23.

"Did the Fall of Vicksburg Really Matter?" (August 2011), 23–25.

"Robert E. Lee's Conflicted Loyalties" (October 2011), 23–25. Retitled "Robert E. Lee's Multiple Loyalties."

"Seeing the War Through Soldiers' Letters" (December 2011), 22, 26–27.

"Death and Wounds Plagued Lee's Command" (February 2012), 18, 20, 23. Retitled "Attrition in Lee's High Command."

"To Love or Loathe McClellan?" (April 2012), 18, 20, 22. Retitled "Little Mac."

*"Tramp, Tramp, Tramp, the Bloggers March" (June 2012), 18, 20.

"'The Plain Folk's Pioneer' Reframed History" (August 2012), 18, 22.

"What If?" (October 2012), 18, 20.

"Perfect Southern Soldier" (December 2012), 18, 20. Retitled "Stonewall Jackson and the Confederate People."

"Shelby Foote, Popular Historian" (February 2013), 18, 20.

"Revolutionary Ties to Civil Strife" (April 2013), 18, 20. Retitled "Linking America's Two Most Important Wars."

"Photography's Power" (June 2013), 18, 20. Retitled "The Power of Photographs."

"Admirers Across the Big Pond" (August 2013), 18, 20. Retitled "British Writers View the Confederacy."

"Deciding What to Read" (October 2013), 18, 20.

"Poor George Gordon Meade" (December 2013), 18, 20.

"The Supreme Partnership" (February 2014), 18, 20.

"Bold Rebel Venture in the Desert" (April 2014), 20, 22, 24. Retitled "Toward Santa Fe and Beyond: Confederates in New Mexico."

"John B. Jones' Confederate War" (June 2014), 18, 20. Retitled "John B. Jones's War."

"A One-Sided Friendship" (August 2014), 18, 20, 22.

"Forgotten Master" (October 2014), 18, 20. Retitled "Recovering Allan Nevins."

"'Stonewall' and 'Old Jube' in the Valley" (December 2014), 18, 20.

"Unconventional Warfare" (February 2015), 18, 20, 22.

*"'Flaggers' on the Fringe" (April 2015), 19–21.

"Every Sketch Tells a Story" (October 2018), 18–19.

"Fluid Landscapes" (December 2018), 18, 20.

"The Desperate Gamble" (February 2019), 18, 20–21.

"Language Misconception" (April 2019), 22, 24. Retitled "Antebellum."

"Fighting on Multiple Fronts" (April 2019), 46–53. Retitled "One War or Two?: The United States Versus Confederates and Indians, 1861–1865."

"Off the Tracks" (June 2019), 22, 24.

"Abner Doubleday's Revenge" (August 2019), 22–23.

"Collateral Damage" (October 2019), 22, 24. Retitled "Environmental Shocks."

"Sheridan Makes His Name" (December 2019), 22–23. Retitled "Sheridan Makes His Name in the Valley."

"A Master's Lessons" (February 2020), 20, 22. Retitled "Lessons from David M. Potter."

"Bang Up Job" (April 2020), 16, 18. Retitled "An Indispensable Confederate and His Diary."

"Behind the Lines" (June 2020), 16, 18. Retitled "Occupation and the Union Military Effort."

"Hollywood's Twenty-First-Century Lincoln" (August 2020), 16, 18.

GETTYSBURG: THREE DAYS OF COURAGE AND SACRIFICE, JOINT ISSUE OF CIVIL WAR TIMES AND AMERICA'S CIVIL WAR (SUMMER 2013)

"Lee's Great Gamble," 14–19 [expanded version of pp. 18–19]. Retitled "Gettysburg in Perspective."

CIVIL WAR MONITOR

"Voices from the Army of the Potomac" (Fall 2013), 69–71.

"Voices from the Army of the Potomac, Part 5" (Summer 2015), 65–69. Retitled "Harvard Men at War."

NOTES

INTRODUCTION

1. The essays have run under three titles: "Gary W. Gallagher's Blue & Gray" (February, April, and June 2009); "Blue & Gray" (August 2009 through April 2015); and "Insight" (June 2015 to the present). The magazine's name changed from *Civil War Times Illustrated* to *Civil War Times* in April 2003. A forerunner, also titled *Civil War Times,* ran from 1959 to 1962. For my first article, see "The A'Vache Tragedy," *Civil War Times Illustrated* 18 (February 1980): 4–10.

2. Walt Whitman, *Specimen Days & Collect* (Glasgow: Wilson & McCormick, 1883), 80–81.

3. On the developing literature through the mid-twentieth century, see Thomas J. Pressly, *Americans Interpret Their Civil War* (Princeton, N.J.: Princeton University Press, 1954), and the two revised paperback editions (New York: Collier, 1962; New York: Free Press, 1965). For works published after Pressly's survey, see James M. McPherson and William J. Cooper, eds., *Writing the Civil War: The Quest to Understand* (Columbia: University of South Carolina Press, 1998); Lacy J. Ford, ed., *A Companion to the Civil War and Reconstruction* (Malden, Mass.: Blackwell, 2005); Aaron Sheehan-Dean, ed., *A Companion to the U.S. Civil War,* 2 vols. (Malden, Mass.: Wiley-Blackwell, 2014).

4. For discussions of some of the changes in the field, see Paul A. Cimbala and Randall M. Miller, eds., *The Great Task Remaining Before Us: Reconstruction as America's Continuing Civil War* (New York: Fordham University Press, 2010); Yael A. Sternhell, "Revisionism Reinvented?: The Antiwar Turn in Civil War Scholarship," *Journal of the Civil War Era* 3 (June 2013): 239–56; Patrick J. Kelly, "The European Revolutions of 1848 and the Transnational Turn in Civil War History," *Journal of the Civil War Era* 4 (September 2014): 431–43; David M. Prior et al., "Teaching the Civil War in Global Context: A Discussion," *Journal of the Civil War Era* 5 (March 2015): 126–53; Stacy L. Smith, "Beyond North and South: Putting the West in the Civil War and Reconstruction," *Journal of the Civil War Era* 6 (December 2016): 566–91.

5. For an example of linking scholarship to recent events, see Michael Fellman, *In the Name of God and Country: Reconsidering Terrorism in American History* (New Haven, Conn.: Yale University Press, 2010), which devotes three of its five chapters to John Brown's Raid, the Civil War, and Reconstruction. "As I am a subjective human being living in the early twenty-first century," Fellman explains, "it is inevitable that my lens on history will have been constructed during my lifetime and reconstructed in the post–September 11, 2001, world" (232). See also Guy R. Hasegawa, *Mending Broken Soldiers: The Union and Confederate Programs to Supply Arti-*

ficial Limbs (Carbondale: Southern Illinois University Press, 2012), which connects "history to current events" because "the conflicts in Afghanistan and Iraq are producing grim casualties among service members, many of whom can be assisted by artificial limbs" (xiii).

6. Abraham Lincoln, *The Collected Works of Abraham Lincoln,* ed. Roy P. Basler, 9 vols. (New Brunswick, N.J.: Rutgers University Press, 1953), 8:332. On the importance of military history within the larger framework of Civil War studies, see Gary W. Gallagher and Kathryn Shively Meier, "Coming to Terms with Civil War Military History," *Journal of the Civil War Era* 4 (December 2014): 487–508.

7. For coverage and discussion of the visitor center's opening, see Kurt Repanshek, "Gettysburg National Military Park: Of Cycloramas, Museums and Visitor Centers," National Parks Traveler, April 13, 2008, https://www.nationalparktraveler.org/2008/04/gettysburg-national-military-park-cycloramas-museums-and-visitor-centers; and Eric J. Wittenberg, "Gettysburg's New Visitor Center," Rantings of a Civil War Historian, August 5, 2008, http://civilwarcavalry.com/?p=817.

8. On differing views among academic historians about preserving battlefields, see Gary W. Gallagher, *Lee and His Generals in War and Memory* (Baton Rouge: Louisiana State University Press, 1998), 271–79. During testimony given before Congress in September 1990, the deputy executive director of the American Historical Association made the case against battlefields: "Historians today have redefined the study of the Civil War," he stated, "shifting attention from military action to the diverse experiences of individual groups, the impact of emancipation," and the ways in which the war exacerbated old social divisions and created new ones. Acknowledging the "emotional appeal of 'hallowed ground,'" the AHA's spokesman deplored the "assumption of the special historical significance of Civil War battlefields." See *Testimony of James B. Gardner, Deputy Executive Director American Historical Association, Before the Subcommittee on National Parks and Public Lands, Committee on Interior and Insular Affairs of the U.S. House of Representatives, H.R. 3513 and S. 1770, September 4, 1990* (Washington, D.C.: American Historical Association, 1990), 2–3.

9. For a protracted discussion about black Confederates, overseen by Kevin Levin, see the back-and-forth postings on his blog "Civil War Memory," at http://cwmemory.com. For Levin's own take on the subject, see his *Searching for Black Confederates: The Civil War's Most Persistent Myth* (Chapel Hill: University of North Carolina Press, 2019).

10. For Hollywood and the four memory traditions through the early twenty-first century, see Gary W. Gallagher, *Causes Won, Lost, and Forgotten: How Hollywood and Popular Art Shape What We Know About the Civil War* (Chapel Hill: University of North Carolina Press, 2008), especially chapters 1 through 3. On the larger topic of memory, see David W. Bight, *Race and Reunion: The Civil War in American Memory* (Cambridge, Mass.: Harvard University Press, 2001); and Caroline E. Janney, *Remembering the Civil War: Reunion and the Limits of Reconciliation* (Chapel Hill: University of North Carolina Press, 2013).

11. The two quoted readers' reactions appeared in the June 2009 issue of *Civil War Times.* For some of the reaction to the essays on the West, see Megan Kate Nelson, "Why the Civil War West Mattered (and Still Does)," Historista, June 29, 2017, http://www.megankatenelson.com/why-the-civil-war-west-mattered-and-still-does.

12. For a roundtable discussion among four senior scholars about a range of contemporary controversies, see Catherine Clinton, ed., *Confederate Statues and Memorialization* (Athens: University of Georgia Press, 2019).

13. Few figures have become more controversial than Robert E. Lee, a longtime cultural presence in the form of his national memorial at Arlington, Virginia; statues; schools named after him; postage stamps featuring his visage; and state holidays devoted to his memory. For analysis of the debates at Washington and Lee University about how best to handle Lee's legacy, see Scott Jaschik, "Race, History and Robert E. Lee," *Inside Higher Ed,* May 29, 2018, https://www.insidehighered.com/news/2018/05/29/washington-and-lee-faces-unusual-challenges-confronting-its-history, as well as reader comments on this article. See also Adam Serwer, "The Myth of the Kindly General Lee," *The Atlantic,* June 4, 2017, https://www.theatlantic.com/politics/archive/2017/06/the-myth-of-the-kindly-general-lee/529038. Serwer's essay typifies the search for uncomplicated heroes or villains in the past.

14. For Shelby Foote's quotation, see John Griffin Jones, ed., *Mississippi Writers Talking: Interviews with Eudora Welty, Shelby Foote, Elizabeth Spencer, Barry Hannah* (Jackson: University Press of Mississippi, 1982), 64. In Ken Burns's series *The Civil War* and the picture book that accompanied it, Foote stated of Nathan Bedford Forrest, "Well, you're asking about the most man in the world in some ways. Forrest was a natural genius." Geoffrey C. Ward, *The Civil War: An Illustrated History* (New York: Knopf, 1990), 270. I can only speculate about what "the most man in the world" might mean.

15. Barnes F. Lathrop published relatively little during his career but directed more than forty dissertations at the University of Texas. For a sketch of him, see Gary W. Gallagher, ed., *Essays on Southern History: Written in Honor of Barnes F. Lathrop* (Austin: General Libraries of the University of Texas, 1980), 9–13.

PART I. FRAMING THE WAR

1. R. E. Lee, "General Orders, No. 7," January 22, 1864, in R. E. Lee, *The Wartime Papers of R. E. Lee,* ed. Clifford Dowdey and Louis H. Manarin (Boston: Little, Brown, 1961), 659.

2. Robert Gould Shaw, *Blue-Eyed Child of Fortune: The Civil War Letters of Colonel Robert Gould Shaw,* ed. Russell Duncan (Athens: University of Georgia Press, 1992), 73.

3. Abraham Lincoln, *The Collected Works of Abraham Lincoln,* ed. Roy P. Basler, 9 vols. (New Brunswick, N.J.: Rutgers University Press, 1953), 7:23.

4. For a brief comparative overview, see Benjamin L. Carp, "Nations of American Rebels: Understanding Nationalism in Revolutionary North America and the Civil War South," *Civil War History* 48 (March 2002): 5–33.

5. George Templeton Strong, *The Diary of George Templeton Strong,* ed. Allan Nevins and Milton Halsey Thomas, 4 vols. (New York: Macmillan, 1952), 3:358, 363–64, 366.

6. Stephen Dodson Ramseur, *The Bravest of the Brave: The Correspondence of Stephen Dodson Ramseur,* ed. George G. Kundahl (Chapel Hill: University of North Carolina Press, 2010), 43.

7. On Grant's changing reputation, see Joan Waugh, *U. S. Grant: American Hero, American Myth* (Chapel Hill: University of North Carolina Press, 2009).

8. Gary H. Rawlins, "Gettysburg, July 1–3, 1863," *USA Today,* special edition titled *Civil War* (April 2011): 43.

9. *American Heritage Picture History of the Civil War* (New York: American Heritage Publishing Company and Doubleday, 1960), 335; Frederick Tilberg, *Gettysburg National Military Park, Pennsylvania* (Washington, D.C.: National Park Service, 1962), 17–18.

10. On Chamberlain's presence in art of the period 1980 through the early twenty-first century, see Gary W. Gallagher, *Causes Won, Lost, and Forgotten: How Hollywood and Popular Art Shape What We Know About the Civil War* (Chapel Hill: University of North Carolina Press, 2008), 184–89, 197–99 (figures 70–74).

11. For a sample of directions scholarship has taken, see Adam Arenson and Andrew R. Graybill, eds., *Civil War Wests: Testing the Limits of the United States* (Oakland: University of California Press, 2015).

12. See "The War Was Won in the East" in part 3, "Controversies."

13. "One War or Two? The United States Versus Confederates and Indians, 1861–1865" is an expanded version of a shorter piece titled "A Conflict Apart," *Civil War Times* (April 2017):14, 16. The shorter version is not included in this book.

14. U.S. War Department, *The War of the Rebellion: The Official Records of the Union and Confederate Armies,* 127 vols., index, and atlas (Washington, D.C.: U.S. Government Printing Office, 1880–1901), ser. 1, vol. 13, 599. (*War of the Rebellion* is hereafter cited as *Official Records.*) See also Gideon Welles, *The Civil War Diary of Gideon Welles, Lincoln's Secretary of the Navy,* ed. William E. Gienapp and Erica L. Gienapp (Urbana: Knox College Lincoln Studies Center and University of Illinois Press, 2014), 28; Special Orders, No. 218, in *Official Records,* ser. 1, vol. 12, part 3, 807.

15. On the importance of West's work, see Stacy L. Smith, "Beyond North and South: Putting the West in the Civil War and Reconstruction," *Journal of the Civil War Era* 6 (December 2016): 566–91 (quotation is from 573).

16. Megan Kate Nelson, "The War from Apache Pass," *Journal of the Civil War Era* 6 (December 2016): 530; Durwood Ball, "Liberty, Empire, and the Civil War in the American West," in Virginia Scharff, ed., *Empire and Liberty: The Civil War and the West* (Oakland: Autry National Center for the American West and University of California Press, 2015), 66.

17. Ulysses S. Grant, *The Papers of Ulysses S. Grant,* ed. John Y. Simon et al., 32 vols. (Carbondale: Southern Illinois University Press, 1967–2012), 28:412–13; U.S. House of Representatives, Committee on Military Affairs, *Proposed Reduction of the Military Establishment, Sea-Coast Fortifications, and National Foundries and Arsenals. Notes of Consultation . . . with General W. T. Sherman, Adjutant-General Townsend, the Secretary of War, etc.* (Washington, D.C.: U.S. Government Printing Office, 1874), 12.

18. Clifford E. Trafzer, *The Kit Carson Campaign: The Last Great Navajo War* (Norman: University of Oklahoma Press, 1982), 89.

19. *Official Records,* ser. 1, vol. 4, part 2, 695; Thaddeus Stevens, *The Selected Papers of Thaddeus Stevens,* ed. Beverly Wilson Palmer and Holly Byers Ochoa, 2 vols. (Pittsburgh: University of Pittsburgh Press, 1997), 1:476–77.

20. *Official Records,* ser. 1, vol. 13, 599–600; John G. Nicolay, "The Sioux War," *Continental Monthly* 3 (February 1863): 195.

21. Lincoln, *Collected Works,* 5:519, 521, 525–26.

22. *Official Records,* ser. 2, vol. 4, 499; Lincoln, *Collected Works,* 5:432.

23. *Official Records,* ser. 2, vol. 4, 593, 598; Lincoln, *Collected Works,* 5:449.

24. Lincoln's reply to Ramsey is in Lincoln, *Collected Works,* 5:396.

25. Mildred Thorne, "Iowa Troops in Dakota Territory, 1861–1864," *Iowa Journal of History* 57 (April 1959): 108–9; Charles E. Flandrau et al., eds., *Minnesota in the Civil and Indian Wars, 1861–1865* (Saint Paul, Minn.: Pioneer Press, 1890), 198.

26. Jerry Don Thompson, ed., *New Mexico Territory During the Civil War: Wallen and Evans Inspection Reports* (Albuquerque: University of New Mexico Press, 2008), 41–42, 47.

27. George Forsyth, *The Story of the Soldier* (New York: D. Appleton, 1900), 168; George W. Baird, "A Winter Campaign in Montana and its Results," in *Personal Narratives of Events in the War of the Rebellion, Addresses Delivered Before the Commandery of the State of New York,* 4 vols. (Rhode Island Soldiers and Sailors Historical Society, 1891–1912), reprinted as part of the sixty-six-volume *Military Order of the Loyal Legion of the United States* (Wilmington, N.C.: Broadfoot, 1992), 22:422; George H. Holliday, *On the Plains in '65: Twelve Months in the Volunteer Cavalry Service, Among the Indians of Nebraska, Colorado, Dakota, Wyoming, and Montana* (Wheeling, W.Va., 1883), 3, 6–7.

28. U.S. Senate, 69th Congress, 2nd Session, Committee on Pensions, Report No. 1613, *Granting Pensions to Certain Soldiers Who Served in the Indian Wars from 1859 to 1898, and for Other Purposes* (Washington, D.C.: U.S. Government Printing Office, 1927), 2.

29. U.S. House of Representatives, Committee on Pensions, *Pensions—Indian Wars, Hearing before the Committee on Pensions House of Representatives Seventy-Fourth Congress, Second Session, on . . . Increase of Pensions to Indian War Soldiers Their Widows, and Minor Children, April 7, 1936* (Washington, D.C.: U.S. Government Printing Office, 1936), 2, 6, 4; William Henry Glasson, *Federal Military Pensions in the United States* (New York: Oxford University Press, 1918), 115.

30. Algernon Badger to Dear Father, September 8, 1865, box 1, Algernon Badger Family Papers, 1813–1900, Louisiana Research Collection, Howard-Tilton Library, Tulane University, New Orleans.

31. Francis Lieber's letter is reproduced in D. H. Dilbeck, *A More Civil War: How the Union Waged a Just War* (Chapel Hill: University of North Carolina Press, 2016), 81–82.

32. Jefferson Davis, *Jefferson Davis Constitutionalist: His Letters, Papers and Speeches,* ed. Dunbar Rowland, 10 vols. (Jackson: Mississippi Department of Archives and History, 1923), 5:51–52.

33. P. G. T. Beauregard to Col. A. Herman, September 4, 1861, quoted in Stan V. Henkels Auction House, *Catalogue 1148: The Beauregard Papers* (Philadelphia: Henkels, 1915), item 51.

34. Davis, *Jefferson Davis Constitutionalist,* 6:530.

35. Frank Wilkeson, *Recollections of a Private Soldier in the Army of the Potomac* (New York: G. P. Putnam's Sons, 1886), 3, 14. Wilkeson's book was reprinted in paperback as *Turned Inside*

Out: Recollections of a Private Soldier in the Army of the Potomac (Lincoln: University of Nebraska Press, 1997).

36. Wilkeson, *Recollections,* 202–3, 206.

37. Ibid., 232–33.

38. Ambrose Bierce, *Ambrose Bierce's Civil War,* ed. William McCann (1956; reprint, Avenal, N.J.: Wings Books, 1996), 46–47.

39. Ibid., 106.

40. Ibid., 69, 35.

41. Ibid., 37.

42. William Dickey to his wife, July 13, 1864, in Mills Lane, ed., *"Dear Mother: Don't grieve about me. If I am killed, I'll only be dead.": Letters from Georgia Soldiers in the Civil War* (Savannah, Ga.: Beehive Press, 1977), 315.

43. Jubal A. Early, *A Memoir of the Last Year of the War for Independence, in the Confederate States of America* (Toronto: Lovell & Gibson, 1866), 127–28.

44. David Williams, *Bitterly Divided: The South's Inner Civil War* (New York: New Press, 2008), 242.

45. This and the following paragraph are based on a fuller discussion of the issue of Confederate desertion in Gary W. Gallagher, "Disaffection, Persistence, and Nation: Some Directions in Recent Scholarship on the Confederacy," *Civil War History* 55 (September 2009): 348–51.

46. *Baltimore American,* May 27, 1865. For more detail on the Grand Review, see Gary W. Gallagher, *The Union War* (Cambridge, Mass.: Harvard University Press, 2011), 7–32.

47. *New York Times,* May 26, 1865; *Liberator,* June 2, 1865.

48. *New York Herald,* May 24, 1865.

49. *Daily National Intelligencer* [Washington, D.C.], May 23, 1865; Lois Bryan Adams, *Letter from Washington, 1863–1865,* ed. Evelyn Leasher (Detroit, Mich.: Wayne State University Press, 1999), 265–66; *Baltimore American and Commercial Advertiser,* May 27, 1865.

50. Garry Wills, *Lincoln at Gettysburg: The Words that Remade America* (New York: Simon and Schuster, 1992), 37–38, 145.

51. Welles, *Civil War Diary,* 316–17.

52. John Hay, *Inside Lincoln's White House: The Complete Civil War Diary of John Hay,* ed. Michael Burlingame and John R. Turner Ettlinger (Carbondale: Southern Illinois University Press, 1997), 113; Benjamin Brown French, *Witness to the Young Republic: A Yankee's Journal, 1828–1870,* ed. Donald B. Cole and John J. McDonough (Hanover, N.H.: University Press of New England, 1989), 435.

53. Herbert Mitgang, ed., *Abraham Lincoln: A Press Portrait* (1971; reprint, Athens: University of Georgia Press, 1989), 356–57; *Frank Leslie's Illustrated Newspaper,* December 5, 1863, 171.

54. Frank L. Byrne and Andrew T. Weaver, eds., *Haskell of Gettysburg: His Life and Civil War Papers* (1970; reprint, Kent, Ohio: Kent State University Press, 1989), 233–34. On the absence of soldiers' reaction to the speech, see Gabor S. Boritt, *The Gettysburg Gospel: The Lincoln Speech that Nobody Knows* (New York: Simon & Schuster, 2006), 136–38.

55. Charles Sumner, *Charles Sumner: His Complete Works,* 15 vols. (Boston: Lee and Shepard, 1900), 12:271–72.

56. *Official Records,* ser. 1, vol. 43, part 2, 308; William T. Sherman, *Sherman's Civil War: Selected Correspondence of William T. Sherman, 1860–1865,* ed. Brooks D. Simpson and Jean V. Berlin (Chapel Hill: University of North Carolina Press, 1999), 657.

57. Arthur James Lyon Fremantle, *Three Months in the Southern States: April–June, 1863* (1863; reprint, Lincoln: University of Nebraska Press, 1991), 223; Stephen V. Ash, *Middle Tennessee Society Transformed, 1860–1870: War and Peace in the Upper South* (Baton Rouge: Louisiana State University Press, 1988), 85–86.

58. Worthington Chauncey Ford, ed., *A Cycle of Adams Letters, 1861–1865,* 2 vols. (Boston: Houghton Mifflin, 1920), 2:5.

59. *Harper's Weekly,* August 20, 1864, 541–42.

60. William A. Blair, "Barbarians at Fredericksburg's Gate: The Impact of the Union Army on Civilians," in Gary W. Gallagher, ed., *The Fredericksburg Campaign: Decision on the Rappahannock* (Chapel Hill: University of North Carolina Press, 1995), 161.

PART II. GENERALS AND BATTLES

1. Jubal A. Early, *The Campaigns of Gen. Robert E. Lee. An Address by Lieut. General Jubal A. Early, Before Washington and Lee University, January 19th, 1872* (Baltimore: John Murphy, 1872), 50–51; Winston S. Churchill, *A History of the English-Speaking Peoples,* 4 vols. (New York: Dodd, Mead, 1956–1958), 4:253. Churchill's sections on the Civil War in volume 4 were reprinted separately as *The American Civil War* (New York: Dodd, Mead, 1961).

2. William S. McFeely, *Grant: A Biography* (New York: W. W. Norton, 1981), xii–xiii.

3. Michael Korda, *Ulysses S. Grant: The Unlikely Hero* (New York: HarperCollins, 2004), 2.

4. Since my essay on Grant appeared in the December 2009 issue of *Civil War Times,* two scholarly editions of the general's *Personal Memoirs* (Cambridge, Mass.: Belknap Press of Harvard University Press, 2017; New York: Liveright, 2019) have joined the ranks of earlier books. The film *Lincoln* (2012) also features Grant as a secondary character.

5. Abraham Lincoln, *The Collected Works of Abraham Lincoln,* ed. Roy P. Basler, 9 vols. (New Brunswick, N.J.: Rutgers University Press, 1953), 7:234; *New York Herald,* May 24, 1865.

6. William T. Sherman, *Sherman's Civil War: Selected Correspondence of William T. Sherman, 1860–1865,* ed. Brooks D. Simpson and Jean V. Berlin (Chapel Hill: University of North Carolina Press, 1999), 166; James Harrison Wilson, *Under the Old Flag: Recollections of Military Operations in the War for the Union, the Spanish War, the Boxer Rebellion, Etc.,* 2 vols. (New York: D. Appleton, 1912), 2:17.

7. Ulysses S. Grant, *The Papers of Ulysses S. Grant,* ed. John Y. Simon et al., 32 vols. (Carbondale: Southern Illinois University Press, 1967–2012), 13:203; 10:187–88 (note).

8. Ulysses S. Grant, *Memoirs and Selected Letters,* ed. William S. McFeely (New York: Library of America, 1990), 652; Sherman, *Sherman's Civil War,* 526.

9. Grant, *Memoirs and Selected Letters,* 69; Sherman, *Sherman's Civil War,* 466.

10. *The War of the Rebellion: The Official Records of the Union and Confederate Armies,* 127 vols., index, and atlas (Washington, D.C.: U.S. Government Printing Office, 1880–1901), ser. 1, vol. 39, part 3, 222; Sherman, *Sherman's Civil War,* 697.

11. *Dallas Morning News*, June 13, 1936. Roosevelt made these comments in Dallas, at the dedication of an equestrian statue of Lee, which was removed in 2017 during a nationwide debate over the Confederate memorial landscape. Much of that debate centered on statues of Lee in New Orleans; Baltimore; Charlottesville, Virginia; and elsewhere. By the middle of the second decade of the twenty-first century, just a few years after my essay was published in *Civil War Times*, Lee's reputation had suffered considerable erosion across much of the nation. His position in the slaveholding class and his centrality to Lost Cause memorialization, rather than his military actions and attributes, took center stage in innumerable assessments of his life and character.

12. Thomas Conolly, *An Irishman in Dixie: Thomas Conolly's Diary of the Fall of the Confederacy*, ed. Nelson D. Lankford (Columbia: University of South Carolina Press, 1988), 52.

13. R to Editor of *The Daily South Carolinian*, May 1, 1864 (published in the May 10, 1864, issue of this Columbia newspaper).

14. R. E. Lee, *The Wartime Papers of R. E. Lee*, ed. Clifford Dowdey and Louis H. Manarin (Boston: Little, Brown, 1961), 9–10; William M. E. Rachal, ed., "'Secession Is Nothing But Revolution': A Letter of R. E. Lee to His Son 'Rooney,'" *Virginia Magazine of History and Biography* 69 (January 1961): 6; J. William Jones, *Life and Letters of Robert Edward Lee: Soldier and Man* (New York: Neale, 1906), 124.

15. Rachal, "Secession Is Nothing But Revolution," 5.

16. Robert E. Lee, *"To Markie": The Letters of Robert E. Lee to Martha Custis Williams*, ed. Avery Craven (Cambridge, Mass.: Harvard University Press, 1933), 71–72; Rachal, "Secession Is Nothing But Revolution," 6.

17. *The Columbia* [S.C.] *Daily Phoenix*, May 26, 1865 (reprinting Lee's interview with Thomas M. Cook from the *New York Herald*, April 29, 1865).

18. Lee, *Wartime Papers*, 94.

19. Craig L. Symonds, *Joseph E. Johnston: A Civil War Biography* (New York: W. W. Norton, 1992), 51.

20. Gary W. Gallagher, "'We Are Our Own Trumpeters': Robert E. Lee Describes Winfield Scott's Campaign to Mexico City," *Virginia Magazine of History and Biography* 95 (July 1987): 373.

21. Lee to Johnston, July 24, 1861, "Letters of Confederate Generals Robert E. Lee/Stonewall Jackson," MS 11576, Albert and Shirley Small Special Collections Library, University of Virginia, Charlottesville.

22. Robert Garlick Hill Kean, *Inside the Confederate Government: The Diary of Robert Garlick Hill Kean, Head of the Bureau of War*, ed. Edward Younger (New York: Oxford University Press, 1957), 50.

23. Joseph E. Johnston, *Narrative of Military Operations, Directed, During the Late War Between the States* (New York: D. Appleton, 1874), 355–56.

24. Robert M. Hughes, *General Johnston* (New York: D. Appleton, 1893), 290.

25. Emma LeConte, *When the World Ended: The Diary of Emma LeConte*, ed. Early Schenck Miers (New York: Oxford University Press, 1957), 83.

26. Lee, *Wartime Papers*, 484; Robert K. Krick, *The Smoothbore Volley That Doomed the Confederacy: The Death of Stonewall Jackson and Other Chapters on the Army of Northern Virginia* (Baton Rouge: Louisiana State University Press, 2002), 1–41.

27. Francis W. Dawson, *Reminiscences of Confederate Service, 1861–1865*, ed. Bell I. Wiley (1882; reprint, Baton Rouge: Louisiana State University Press, 1980), 116.

28. Warren W. Hassler, *George B. McClellan: Shield of the Union* (Baton Rouge: Louisiana State University Press, 1957), xvi; Edward H. Bonekemper III, *McClellan and Failure: A Study of Civil War Fear, Incompetence and Worse* (Jefferson, N.C.: McFarland, 2007), 3.

29. George B. McClellan, *The Civil War Papers of George B. McClellan: Selected Correspondence, 1860–1865*, ed. Stephen W. Sears (New York: Ticknor & Fields, 1989), 473.

30. Ibid., 345.

31. Ibid., 521.

32. Thomas Jewett Goree, *Longstreet's Aide: The Civil War Letters of Major Thomas J. Goree*, ed. Thomas W. Cutrer (Charlottesville: University Press of Virginia, 1995), 98; William Miller Owen, *In Camp and Battle with the Washington Artillery of New Orleans: A Narrative* (Boston: Ticknor, 1885), 157.

33. Edward Porter Alexander, *Fighting for the Confederacy: The Personal Recollections of General Edward Porter Alexander*, ed. Gary W. Gallagher (Chapel Hill: University of North Carolina Press, 1989), 261.

34. Lee, *Wartime Papers*, 722.

35. Judith W. McGuire, *Diary of a Southern Refugee During the War* (1867; reprint, Lincoln: University of Nebraska Press, 1995), 120–21.

36. Catherine Ann Devereux Edmondston, *"Journal of a Secesh Lady": The Diary of Catherine Ann Devereux Edmondston, 1860–1866*, ed. Beth Gilbert Crabtree and James W. Patton (Raleigh: North Carolina Division of Archives and History, 1979), 191–92.

37. Betty Herndon Maury, *The Civil War Diary of Betty Herndon Maury (June 3, 1861–February 18, 1863)*, ed. Robert A. Hodge (Fredericksburg, Va.: by the editor, 1985), 69–70; McGuire, *Diary of a Southern Refugee*, 157.

38. Letter of Union surgeon C. H. Parry, quoted in Bruce Catton, *Never Call Retreat* (Garden City, N.Y.: Doubleday, 1965), 393.

39. Lincoln, *Collected Works*, 8:58, 73–74; Sherman, *Sherman's Civil War*, 743.

40. Grant, *Papers*, 12.313 (note), 327.

41. Phillip H. Sheridan, *Personal Memoirs of P. H. Sheridan*, 2 vols. (1888; reprint, Wilmington, N.C.: Broadfoot, 1992), 1:471, 474–75; Grant, *Memoirs and Selected Letters*, 617.

42. Alexander Neil, *Alexander Neil and the Last Shenandoah Valley Campaign: Letters of an Army Surgeon to His Family, 1864*, ed. Richard R. Duncan (Shippensburg, Pa.: White Mane, 1996), 74; Beverly Hayes Kallgren and James L. Crowthamel, eds., *"Dear Friend Anna": The Civil War Letters of a Common Soldier from Maine* (Orono: University of Maine Press, 1992), 106–7.

43. Lincoln, *Collected Works*, 6:327–28, 328 note 1.

44. Charles S. Wainwright, *A Diary of Battle: The Personal Journals of Colonel Charles S. Wainwright, 1861–1865*, ed. Allan Nevins (New York: Harcourt, Brace, and World, 1962), 227.

45. George Gordon Meade, *The Life and Letters of George Gordon Meade, Major-General United States Army,* 2 vols. (New York: Charles Scribner's Sons, 1913), 2:205–6, 271.

46. Harry W. Pfanz, *Gettysburg—The First Day* (Chapel Hill: University of North Carolina Press, 2001), 77, 393–94 note 26; Gordon C. Rhea, *The Battles for Spotsylvania Court House and the Road to Yellow Tavern, May 7–12, 1864* (Baton Rouge: Louisiana State University Press, 1997), 94.

47. William Swinton, *Campaigns of the Army of the Potomac: A Critical History of Operations in Virginia, Maryland, and Pennsylvania from the Commencement to the Close of the War, 1861–5* (New York: Charles B. Richardson, 1866), 330, 447; Richard Winslow Elliott III, *General John Sedgwick: The Story of a Union Corps Commander* (Novato, Calif.: Presidio, 1982), xi.

48. Francis Augustin O'Reilly, *The Fredericksburg Campaign: Winter War on the Rappahannock* (Baton Rouge: Louisiana State University Press, 2003), 501.

49. Alexander, *Fighting for the Confederacy,* 212.

50. Theodore Lyman, "Addenda to the Paper by Brevet Lieutenant-Colonel Swan on the Battle of the Wilderness," *The Wilderness Campaign, May–June 1864* (Boston: Military Historical Society of Massachusetts, 1905), 170–71; Lyman, *Meade's Army: The Private Notebooks of Lt. Col. Theodore Lyman,* ed. David W. Lowe (Kent, Ohio: Kent State University Press, 2007), 139.

51. Stephen Minot Weld, *War Diary and Letters of Stephen Minot Weld, 1861–1865* (Boston: Riverside, 1912), 230; Thomas W. Hyde, *Following the Greek Cross, or, Memories of the Sixth Army Corps* (Boston: Houghton, Mifflin, 1894), 193.

52. Edward J. Nichols, *Toward Gettysburg: A Biography of General John F. Reynolds* (State College: Pennsylvania State University Press, 1958), 215.

53. *Official Records,* ser. 1, vol. 4, 89.

54. Martin Hardwick Hall, *Sibley's New Mexico Campaign* (Austin: University of Texas Press, 1960), 226; Jerry Thompson, *Henry Hopkins Sibley: Confederate General of the West* (Natchitoches, La.: Northwestern State University Press, 1987), xix, 301.

55. Donald S. Frazier, *Blood & Treasure: Confederate Empire in the Southwest* (College Station: Texas A&M University Press, 1995), 22, 260–61.

56. Don E. Alberts, *The Battle of Glorieta: Union Victory in the West* (College Station: Texas A&M University Press, 1998), 165.

57. Ovando J. Hollister, *Colorado Volunteers in New Mexico, 1862,* ed. Richard B. Harwell (1863; reprint, Chicago: Lakeside, 1962), xvii; Flint Whitlock, *Distant Bugles, Distant Drums: The Union Response to the Confederate Invasion of New Mexico* (Boulder: University Press of Colorado, 2006), xix.

58. Theophilus Noel, *A Campaign from Santa Fe to the Mississippi; Being a History of the Old Sibley Brigade* (1865; reprint, Raleigh, N.C.: Charles R. Sanders, Jr., 1961), 38–39.

59. Rob Attar, ed., *The American Civil War Story* (Bristol: Immediate Media, 2013), 56; *The Civil War: The Conflict that Changed America, National Geographic,* special edition, 2013: 48–49; Kelly Knauer, ed., *Gettysburg: A Day-by-Day Account of the Greatest Battle of the Civil War* (New York: Time Books, 2013).

60. George Templeton Strong, *The Diary of George Templeton Strong,* ed. Allan Nevins and Milton Halsey Thomas, 4 vols. (New York: Macmillan, 1952), 3:330, 346–47.

61. Lincoln, *Collected Works,* 6:328.

62. Emma Holmes, *The Diary of Miss Emma Holmes, 1861–1866,* ed. John F. Marszalek (Baton Rouge: Louisiana State University Press, 1979), 278, 281–83; William Alexander Thom to Pembroke Thom, August 31, 1863, quoted in Catherine Thom Bartlett, ed., *"My Dear Brother": A Confederate Chronicle* (Richmond, Va.: Dietz Press, 1952), 106.

63. Josiah Gorgas, *The Civil War Diary of General Josiah Gorgas,* ed. Frank E. Vandiver (University: University of Alabama Press, 1947), 55, 59, 61.

PART III. CONTROVERSIES

1. Joseph Warren Keifer, *Slavery and Four Years of War: A Political History of Slavery in the United States,* 2 vols. (New York: G. P. Putnam's Sons, 1900), 1:133–35.

2. Alexander H. Stephens, *A Constitutional View of the Late War Between the States: Its Causes, Character, Conduct, and Results,* 2 vols. (Philadelphia: National Publishing, 1868, 1870), 1:10.

3. *Kirkus Reviews,* July 15, 1997.

4. James M. McPherson, *Battle Cry of Freedom: The Civil War Era* (New York: Oxford University Press, 1988), x.

5. George Templeton Strong, *The Diary of George Templeton Strong,* ed. Allan Nevins and Milton Halsey Thomas, 4 vols. (New York: Macmillan, 1952), 3:127.

6. Walt Whitman, *Memoranda During the War* (1875; reprint, Boston: Applewood, 1990), 49.

7. John Hay, *Inside Lincoln's White House: The Complete Civil War Diary of John Hay,* ed. Michael Burlingame and John R. Turner Ettlinger (Carbondale: Southern Illinois University Press, 1997), 211. Hay heard Seward make this comment on June 24, 1864.

8. James M. McPherson, *For Cause and Comrades: Why Men Fought in the Civil War* (New York: Oxford University Press, 1997), 113.

9. Abraham Lincoln, *The Collected Works of Abraham Lincoln,* ed. Roy P. Basler, 9 vols. (New Brunswick, N.J.: Rutgers University Press, 1953), 8:149; Special Field Orders No. 76, May 30, 1865, in William Tecumseh Sherman, *Memoirs of General W. T. Sherman,* ed. Charles Royster (New York: Library of America, 1990), 865–66.

10. Lincoln, *Collected Works,* 8:332–33.

11. Ira Berlin et al., *Slaves No More: Three Essays on Emancipation and the Civil War* (New York: Cambridge University Press, 1992), 5–6

12. Robert Gould Shaw, *Blue-Eyed Child of Fortune: The Civil War Letters of Colonel Robert Gould Shaw,* ed. Russell Duncan (Athens: University of Georgia Press, 1992), 245.

13. Executive Committee of the Maine Commissioners, *Maine at Gettysburg* (1898; reprint, Gettysburg, Pa.: Stan Clarke Military Books, 1994), 546–47, 551, 555.

14. [L. S. Trowbridge and Fred. E. Farnsworth, eds.], *Michigan at Gettysburg, July 1st, 2nd, 3rd, 1863: Proceedings Incident to the Dedication of the Michigan Monuments upon the Battlefield at Gettysburg, June 12th, 1889. . . .* (Detroit: Winn & Hammond, 1889), 53–54; New York Monuments Commission for the Battlefields of Gettysburg and Chattanooga, *Final Report for the Battlefield of Gettysburg,* 3 vols. (Albany: J. B. Lyon, 1902), 2:807–8.

15. [Ohio Gettysburg Memorial Commission], *Report of the Gettysburg Memorial Commission* (1889; reprint, Baltimore: Butternut and Blue, 1998), 79, 88.

16. *Final Report of the Gettysburg Battle-field Commission of New Jersey* (Trenton: John L. Murphy, 1891), 84; *Michigan at Gettysburg*, 54, 66; John Page Nicholson, ed., *Pennsylvania at Gettysburg: Ceremonies at the Dedication of the Monuments Erected by the Commonwealth of Pennsylvania* [. . .] *to Mark the Positions of the Pennsylvania Commands Engaged in the Battle,* 2 vols. (Harrisburg: E. K. Meyers, 1893), 1:167.

17. *Final Report,* 48; *Maine at Gettysburg,* 220–21.

18. Thomas L. Connelly, *The Marble Man: Robert E. Lee and His Image in American Society* (New York: Alfred A. Knopf, 1977), xi.

19. Herman Hattaway and Archer Jones, *How the North Won: A Military History of the Civil War* (Urbana: University of Illinois Press, 1983), 690.

20. Richard M. McMurry, *The Fourth Battle of Winchester: Toward a New Civil War Paradigm* (Kent, Ohio: Kent State University Press, 2002), 140.

21. Mary Greenhow Lee, *The Civil War Journal of Mary Greenhow Lee (Mrs. Hugh Holmes Lee) of Winchester, Virginia,* ed. Eloise C. Strader (Winchester, Va.: Winchester-Frederick County Historical Society, 2011), 514; Eliza Francis Andrews, *The War-Time Journal of a Georgia Girl 1864–1865,* ed. Spencer Birdwell King Jr. (1908; reprint, Atlanta: Cherokee, 1976), 154–55.

22. *Frank Leslie's Illustrated Newspaper,* June 10, 1865, 177–78; Lincoln, *Collected Works,* 5:355–56.

23. Arthur James Lyon Fremantle, *Three Months in the Southern States: April–June, 1863* (1863; reprint, Lincoln: University of Nebraska Press, 1991), 269.

24. Edward Porter Alexander, *Fighting for the Confederacy: The Personal Recollections of General Edward Porter Alexander,* ed. Gary W. Gallagher (Chapel Hill: University of North Carolina Press, 1989), 92; Wade Hampton, quoted in Hattaway and Jones, *How the North Won,* 414.

25. Charles Marshall, *An Aide-de-Camp of Lee; Being the Papers of Colonel Charles Marshall, Sometime Aide-de-Camp, Military Secretary, and Assistant Adjutant General on the Staff of Robert E. Lee 1862–1865,* ed. Sir Frederick Maurice (Boston: Little, Brown, 1927), 173.

26. Fremantle, *Three Months,* 256; Justus Scheibert, *Seven Months in the Rebel States During the North American War, 1863,* ed. William Stanley Hoole (Tuscaloosa, Ala.: Confederate, 1958), 118.

27. R. E. Lee, *The Wartime Papers of R. E. Lee,* ed. Clifford Dowdey and Louis H. Manarin (Boston: Little, Brown, 1961), 560, 565.

28. Henry Heth, "Letter from Major-General Henry Heth, of A. P Hill's Corps, A.N.V.," in J. William Jones et al., eds., *Southern Historical Society Papers,* 52 vols. (1876–1959; reprint, with three-volume index, Wilmington, N.C.: Broadfoot, 1990–1992), 4:160.

29. Heth, "Letter from Major-General Henry Heth," 155; Lincoln, *Collected Works,* 6:327–28.

30. Michael B. Ballard, *Vicksburg: The Campaign That Opened the Mississippi* (Chapel Hill: University of North Carolina Press, 2004). Ballard posits that "the Vicksburg campaign's significance demands that we pay attention to it" as the crucial episode of the "war in the Western Theater, the decisive theater I would argue" (xiii).

31. Lincoln, *Collected Works*, 6:409; Brooks D. Simpson, *Ulysses S. Grant: Triumph over Adversity, 1822–1865* (Boston: Houghton Mifflin, 2000), 215.

32. U.S. War Department, *The War of the Rebellion: The Official Records of the Union and Confederate Armies*, 127 vols., index, and atlas (Washington, D.C.: U.S. Government Printing Office, 1880–1901), ser. 1, vol. 51, part 1, 369.

33. McPherson, *Battle Cry of Freedom*, 638; Terry L. Jones, *The American Civil War* (Boston: McGraw-Hill, 2010), 384; David Goldfield, *America Aflame: How the Civil War Created a Nation* (New York: Bloomsbury, 2011), 290.

34. Catherine Ann Devereux Edmondston, *"Journal of a Secesh Lady": The Diary of Catherine Ann Devereux Edmondston, 1860–1866*, ed. Beth Gilbert Crabtree and James W. Patton (Raleigh: North Carolina Division of Archives and History, 1979), 167; Varina Davis, *Jefferson Davis, Ex-President of the Confederate States of America: A Memoir*, 2 vols. (New York: Bedford, 1890), 2:250.

35. For an excellent description of the bond between McLellan and soldiers in the Army of the Potomac, see Bruce Catton, *Mr. Lincoln's Army* (Garden City, N.Y: Doubleday and Company, 1951), 51–53. One soldier, searching for a way to explain the bond, stated, "The love borne by soldiers to a favorite chief, if it does not surpass, is more unreasoning than the love of a woman" (53).

36. Gideon Welles, *The Civil War Diary of Gideon Welles, Lincoln's Secretary of the Navy*, ed. William E. Gienapp and Erica L. Gienapp (Urbana: Knox College Lincoln Studies Center and University of Illinois Press, 2014), 621; Strong, *Diary*, 3:581; E. A. Pollard, *Southern History of the Late War* (New York: Charles B. Richardson, 1866), 516.

37. Ulysses S. Grant, *Memoirs and Selected Letters*, ed. William S. McFeely (New York: Library of America, 1990), 741.

38. Eric T. Dean Jr., *Shook Over Hell: Post-Traumatic Stress, Vietnam, and the Civil War* (Cambridge, Mass.: Harvard University Press, 1997), 53; Brian Matthew Jordan, *Marching Home: Union Veterans and Their Unending Civil War* (New York: Liveright, 2015), 3.

39. William F. Fox, *Regimental Losses in the American Civil War, 1861–1865* (1889; reprint, Dayton, Ohio: Morningside Bookshop, 1985), 67, 555.

40. Charles O. Musser, *Soldier Boy: The Civil War Letters of Charles O. Musser, 29th Iowa*, ed. Barry Popchock (Iowa City: University of Iowa Press, 1995), 135–36.

41. Benjamin F. McIntyre, *Federals on the Frontier: The Diary of Benjamin F. McIntyre, 1862–1864*, ed. Nannie M. Tilley (Austin: University of Texas Press, 1963), 326–27.

42. Robert E. Bonner, ed., *The Soldier's Pen: Firsthand Impressions of the Civil War* (New York: Hill and Wang, 2006), 192.

PART IV. HISTORIANS AND BOOKS

1. David M. Potter, *Lincoln and His Party in the Secession Crisis* (New Haven, Conn.: Yale University Press, 1942), 13. Yale published a slightly revised edition of the book in 1962, which Louisiana State University Press reprinted, with an introduction by Daniel E. Crofts, in 1995.

2. Ibid., 12–13.

3. Ibid., 13–14.

4. Ibid., 374–75.

5. David M. Potter, "The Historian's Use of Nationalism and Vice Versa," in *The South and the Sectional Conflict* (Baton Rouge: Louisiana State University Press, 1968), 54, 56.

6. David M. Potter, *The Impending Crisis, 1848–1861,* ed. Don E. Fehrenbacher (New York: Harper & Row, 1976), 16–17.

7. Ibid., 528–29, 583.

8. Bruce Catton, *Glory Road: The Bloody Route from Fredericksburg to Gettysburg* (Garden City, N.Y.: Doubleday, 1952), 292.

9. Bruce Catton, *A Stillness at Appomattox* (Garden City, N.Y.: Doubleday, 1954), 242–43.

10. Douglas Southall Freeman, *R. E. Lee: A Biography,* 4 vols. (New York: Charles Scribner's Sons, 1934–1935), 4:494.

11. Douglas Southall Freeman, *Lee's Lieutenants: A Study in Command,* 3 vols. (New York: Charles Scribner's Sons, 1942–1944), 2:592.

12. Bell Irvin Wiley, *The Life of Billy Yank: The Common Soldier of the Union* (Indianapolis, Ind.: Bobbs-Merrill, 1952), 361.

13. Bell Irvin Wiley, *The Plain People of the Confederacy* (Baton Rouge: Louisiana State University Press, 1943), 69.

14. Ibid., 92.

15. Henry T. Malone, "Bell Irvin Wiley: Uncommon Soldier," in James I. Robertson Jr. and Richard M. McMurry, eds., *Rank and File: Civil War Essays in Honor of Bell Irvin Wiley* (San Rafael, Calif.: Presidio, 1976), 18.

16. Allan Nevins, *The War for the Union: The Organized War, 1863–1864* (New York: Charles Scribner's Sons, 1971), 272–73.

17. Ibid., 1.

18. Allan Nevins, *The War for the Union: The Organized War to Victory, 1864–1865* (New York: Charles Scribner's Sons, 1971), 252–53.

19. Ibid., 392–93.

20. Review by John A. Carpenter in *Civil War History* 18 (December 1972): 347.

21. David J. Eicher, *The Civil War in Books: An Analytical Bibliography* (Urbana: University of Illinois Press, 1997), 263–64.

22. Louise B. Hill, *State Socialism in the Confederate States of America* (Charlottesville, Va.: Historical Publishing, 1936), 3.

23. Ella Lonn, *Reconstruction in Louisiana After 1868* (New York: G. P. Putnam's Sons, 1918), 11.

24. Ella Lonn, *Desertion During the Civil War* (New York: Century, 1928), v. The University of Nebraska Press published a paperback reprint, with an introduction by William Blair, in 1998.

25. Ibid., 124, 230.

26. Ella Lonn, *Salt as a Factor in the Confederacy* (New York: Walter Neale, 1933), 230. The University of Alabama Press reprinted the book in 1965.

27. Ella Lonn, *Foreigners in the Union Army and Navy* (Baton Rouge: Louisiana State University Press, 1950), vii, 662.

28. Shelby Foote, *The Civil War: A Narrative*, 3 vols. (New York: Random House, 1958–1974), 1:3.

29. Ibid., 3:221.

30. Ibid., 3:1064–65.

31. Ibid., 1:816.

32. All quotations in this essay among Harry W. Pfanz, Matthew Hodgson, and me come from personal correspondence.

33. For excerpts from a number of reviews, see University of North Carolina Press, "Gettysburg—The Second Day," https://www.uncpress.org/book/9780807847305/gettysburg-the-second-day.

34. Robert K. Krick, dust jacket of Harry W. Pfanz, *Gettysburg—The First Day* (Chapel Hill: University of North Carolina Press, 2001).

35. R. E. Lee to Jubal A. Early, November 22, 1865, George H. and Katherine Davis Collection, Howard-Tilton Memorial Library, Tulane University, New Orleans; Jubal A. Early, "The Relative Strength of the Armies of Generals Lee and Grant," in J. William Jones et al., eds., *Southern Historical Society Papers*, 52 vols. (1876–1959; reprint, with three-volume index, Wilmington, N.C.: Broadfoot, 1990–1992), 2:7.

36. Arthur James Lyon Fremantle, *Three Months in the Southern States: April–June, 1863* (1863; reprint, Lincoln: University of Nebraska Press, 1991), 268.

37. Garnet Wolseley, *The American Civil War: An English View*, ed. James A. Rawley (Charlottesville: University Press of Virginia, 1964), 48, 53.

38. Douglas Southall Freeman, *The South to Posterity: An Introduction to the Writing of Confederate History* (1939; reprint, Baton Rouge: Louisiana State University Press, 1998), 160.

39. B. H. Liddell Hart, *Sherman: Soldier, Realist, American* (New York: Dodd, Mead, 1929), 430; Alfred H. Burne, *Lee, Grant and Sherman: A Study in Leadership in the 1864–65 Campaign* (1938; reprint, Lawrence: University Press of Kansas, 2000), 201, 198.

40. J. F. C. Fuller, *Grant and Lee: A Study in Personality and Generalship* (1933; reprint, Bloomington: Indiana University Press, 1957), 254; Fuller, *The Generalship of Ulysses S. Grant* (1929; reprint, Bloomington: Indiana University Press, 1958), 375–77.

41. Winston S. Churchill, *A History of the English-Speaking Peoples*, 4 vols. (New York: Dodd, Mead, 1956–1958), 4:169, 171, 251, 253–54, 249.

42. John W. Thomason, *Jeb Stuart* (New York: Charles Scribner's Sons, 1929), 14.

43. Lee, and especially Grant, also have attracted continuing attention from biographers.

44. Walter H. Hebert, *Fighting Joe Hooker* (Indianapolis, Ind.: Bobbs-Merrill, 1944), 294.

45. Salmon P. Chase, *The Salmon P. Chase Papers*, ed. John Niven, 5 vols. (Kent, Ohio: Kent State University Press, 1993–1998), 3:259–60.

46. John Bigelow Jr., *The Campaign of Chancellorsville: A Strategic and Tactical Study* (New Haven, Conn.: Yale University Press, 1910), xi. Quotations in the next two paragraphs, ibid.

47. Ibid., xiii.

48. Ibid., 477, 482.

49. Ibid., 477.

50. Ibid., 482, 488.

51. R. E. Lee, *The Wartime Papers of R. E. Lee,* ed. Clifford Dowdey and Louis H. Manarin (Boston: Little, Brown, 1961), 696.

52. Charles W. Ramsdell, "The Confederate Government and the Railroads," *American Historical Review* 22 (July 1917): 810; Freeman, *The South to Posterity,* 200.

53. Robert C. Black III, *The Railroads of the Confederacy* (1952; reprint, Chapel Hill: University of North Carolina Press, 1998), 294, xix.

54. Ibid., xii, 294.

55. Ibid., xii, 295.

56. Allan Nevins, James I. Robertson, Jr., and Bell I. Wiley, eds., *Civil War Books: A Critical Bibliography,* 2 vols. (Baton Rouge: Louisiana State University Press, 1967, 1969), 1:5; Richard B. Harwell, *In Tall Cotton: The 200 Most Important Confederate Books for the Reader, Researcher, and Collector* (Austin, Tex.: Jenkins, 1976), 3; "Behind the Lines," *Civil War Times Illustrated* 20 (August 1981): 47; Eicher, *Civil War in Books,* 289.

57. Edward Porter Alexander, *Fighting for the Confederacy: The Personal Recollections of General Edward Porter Alexander,* ed. Gary W. Gallagher (Chapel Hill: University of North Carolina Press, 1989), 286–87; Black, *Railroads of the Confederacy,* 282.

58. Stanley F. Horn, *The Army of Tennessee* (1941; paperback reprint, Norman: University of Oklahoma Press, 1993), xi.

59. Ibid., xii, 398, 428.

60. *Catalogue of Library of Brevet Lieutenant-Colonel John Page Nicholson . . . Relating to the War of the Rebellion 1861–1866* (Philadelphia, 1914), 4.

61. Eicher, *Civil War in Books,* 77–78.

62. Nevins, Robertson, and Wiley, eds., *Civil War Books,* 1:22–23.

63. Harwell, *In Tall Cotton,* x.

64. Gary W. Gallagher, Nathaniel Cheairs Hughes Jr., and Robert K. Krick, *In Taller Cotton: 200 More Important Confederate Books for the Reader, Researcher, and Collector* (Wilmington, N.C.: Broadfoot and First Corps, 2006), xix.

65. Michael Mullins and Rowena Reed, *The Union Bookshelf: A Selected Civil War Bibliography* (Wendell, N.C.: Broadfoot's Bookmark, 1982), iv–v, 17.

66. Garold L. Cole, *Civil War Eyewitnesses: An Annotated Bibliography of Books and Articles, 1955–1986* (Columbia: University of South Carolina Press, 1988), 3.

PART V. TESTIMONY FROM PARTICIPANTS

1. Clement Anselm Evans, *Intrepid Warrior: Clement Anselm Evans, Confederate General from Georgia—Life, Letters and Diaries of the War Years,* ed. Robert Grier Stephens Jr. (Dayton, Ohio: Morningside, 1992), 231, 235.

2. Ibid., 483.

3. Alpheus S. Williams, *From the Cannon's Mouth: The Civil War Letters of General Alpheus S. Williams,* ed. Milo M. Quaife (1959; reprint, Lincoln: University of Nebraska Press, 1995), 125.

4. Ibid., 387.

5. Edwin H. Fay, *This Infernal War: The Confederate Letters of Sgt. Edwin H. Fay,* ed. Bell I. Wiley (Austin: University of Texas Press, 1958), 56, 292, 290.

6. Abraham Lincoln, *The Collected Works of Abraham Lincoln,* ed. Roy P. Basler, 9 vols. (New Brunswick, N.J.: Rutgers University Press, 1953), 6:409–10.

7. My original essay focused on a forthcoming edition of Gideon Welles's wartime diary edited by John Rhodehamel and titled *Lincoln's Civil War Cabinet: The Diary of Gideon Welles.* I served as one of the referees for the manuscript, which was nearing the final stage of publication at Yale University Press when word came that the edition prepared by William E. Gienapp and Erica L. Gienapp soon would be published. Yale had no option but to drop Rhodehamel's project. I have left my essay essentially as written, merely changing the editors' names and the title of the book.

8. Gideon Welles, *The Civil War Diary of Gideon Welles, Lincoln's Secretary of the Navy,* ed. William E. Gienapp and Erica L. Gienapp (Urbana: Knox College Lincoln Studies Center and University of Illinois Press, 2014), 55.

9. Ibid., 247.

10. Ibid., 421.

11. Ibid., 621, 623.

12. U.S. War Department, *The War of the Rebellion: The Official Records of the Union and Confederate Armies,* 127 vols., index, and atlas (Washington, D.C.: U.S. Government Printing Office, 1880–1901), ser. 1, vol. 27, part 1, 366.

13. Abner Doubleday, *Chancellorsville and Gettysburg* (1882; reprint, New York: Da Capo, 1994), 135.

14. Ibid., 184–85, 202.

15. Oliver Otis Howard, *Autobiography of Oliver Otis Howard, Major General United States Army,* 2 vols. (New York: Baker & Taylor, 1907), 1:417.

16. George Gordon Meade, *The Life and Letters of George Gordon Meade, Major-General United States Army,* 2 vols. (New York: Charles Scribner's Sons, 1913), 2:173, 401.

17. John Hay, *Inside Lincoln's White House: The Complete Civil War Diary of John Hay,* ed. Michael Burlingame and John R. Turner Ettlinger (Carbondale: Southern Illinois University Press, 1997), 28; John G. Nicolay and John Hay, *Abraham Lincoln: A History,* 10 vols. (New York: Century, 1890), 5:150–51

18. George B. McClellan, *The Civil War Papers of George B. McClellan: Selected Correspondence, 1860–1865,* ed. Stephen W. Sears (New York: Ticknor & Fields, 1989), 540; Meade, *Life and Letters,* 2:176.

19. Charles S. Wainwright, *A Diary of Battle: The Personal Journals of Colonel Charles S. Wainwright, 1861–1865,* ed. Allan Nevins (New York: Harcourt, Brace and World, 1962), 329.

20. Ibid., 213, 261.

21. Theodore Lyman, *Meade's Headquarters, 1863–1865: Letters of Colonel Theodore Lyman from the Wilderness to Appomattox,* ed. George R. Agassiz (Boston: Atlantic Monthly Press, 1922); quotations are from a reprint titled *With Grant and Meade from the Wilderness to Appomattox* (Lincoln: University of Nebraska Press, 1994), 81, 126.

22. Lyman, *With Grant and Meade,* 102.

23. Robert McAllister, *The Civil War Letters of General Robert McAllister,* ed. James I. Robertson Jr. (New Brunswick, N.J.: Rutgers University Press, 1965), 219, 486.

24. Ibid., 459.

25. Edward Waldo Emerson, *Life and Letters of Charles Russell Lowell* (1907; reprint, Columbia: University of South Carolina Press, 2005), 224–25.

26. Bliss Perry, ed., *Life and Letters of Henry Lee Higginson* (Boston: Atlantic Monthly Press, 1921), 223.

27. Francis C. Barlow, *"Fear Was Not in Him": The Civil War Letters of Major General Francis C. Barlow, U.S.A.,* ed. Christian C. Samito (New York: Fordham University Press, 2004), 39, 105, 130.

28. Ibid., 209, 211.

29. Stephen Minot Weld, *War Diary and Letters of Stephen Minot Weld, 1861–1865* (Boston: Riverside, 1912), 318.

30. Ibid., 147, 368.

31. Henry Livermore Abbott, *Fallen Leaves: The Civil War Letters of Major Henry Livermore Abbott,* ed. Robert Garth Scott (Kent, Ohio: Kent State University Press, 1991), 161, 149.

32. Ibid., 243, 239.

33. Thomas Wentworth Higginson, *Harvard Memorial Biographies,* 2 vols. (Cambridge, Mass.: Sever and Francis, 1866), 1:iv–v.

34. J. B. Jones, *A Rebel War Clerk's Diary at the Confederate States Capital,* ed. James I. Robertson Jr., 2 vols. (1866; reprint, Lawrence: University Press of Kansas, 2015), 1:119, 125.

35. Ibid., 1:253, 255.

36. Ibid., 1:247; 2:360, 337.

37. Ibid., 2:434.

38. Terry L. Jones, ed., *Campbell Brown's Civil War: With Ewell and the Army of Northern Virginia* (Baton Rouge: Louisiana State University Press, 2001), 261.

39. Francis W. Dawson, *Reminiscences of Confederate Service, 1861–1865,* ed. Bell I. Wiley (1882; reprint, Baton Rouge: Louisiana State University Press, 1980), 129.

40. Ibid., 115–16.

41. Joseph Lancaster Brent, *Memoirs of the War Between the States* (New Orleans: Fontana, 1940), 192.

42. Catherine Ann Devereux Edmondston, *"Journal of a Secesh Lady": The Diary of Catherine Ann Devereux Edmondston, 1860–1866,* ed. Beth Gilbert Crabtree and James W. Patton (Raleigh: North Carolina Division of Archives and History, 1979), 189.

43. Ibid., 651, 713.

44. Mary Greenhow Lee, *The Civil War Journal of Mary Greenhow Lee (Mrs. Hugh Holmes Lee) of Winchester, Virginia,* ed. Eloise C. Strader (Winchester, Va.: Winchester-Frederick County Historical Society, 2011), 514–15.

45. Ibid., 563.

46. Edward A. Pollard, *Southern History of the War,* 4 vols. (New York: Charles B. Richardson, 1863–1866), vol. 1, unnumbered first page of preface. The Richmond firm of West & Johnston published Confederate editions of the first two volumes in 1862 and 1863.

47. Ibid., 1:168.

48. Ibid., 1:265.

49. Ibid., 2:142.

50. Ibid., 3:81.

51. Ibid., 4:176–77.

52. Ibid., 3:297.

53. Ibid., 4:229.

54. *Bivouac* 1 (September 1882): 80.

55. J. William Jones noting the inaugural issues of the *Bivouac* is from *Southern Historical Society Papers,* 52 vols. (1876–1959; reprint, with three-volume index, Wilmington, N.C.: Broadfoot, 1990–1992), 10:528; *Southern Bivouac* 1 (August 1883): 494.

56. *Southern Bivouac* 1 (August 1883): 485; *Southern Bivouac* 3 (January 1885): 239.

57. *Southern Bivouac,* new series 1 (August 1885): 187.

58. Basil W. Duke to Jubal A. Early, September 7, 1886, item 2695, Jubal A. Early Papers, Library of Congress, Washington, D.C.

59. Jefferson Davis, *The Rise and Fall of the Confederate Government,* 2 vols. (New York: D. Appleton, 1881), 1:310, 481.

60. Josiah Gorgas, *The Civil War Diary of General Josiah Gorgas,* ed. Frank E. Vandiver (University: University of Alabama Press, 1947), 1, 90–91; Joseph E. Johnston, *Narrative of Military Operations, Directed, During the Late War Between the States* (New York: D. Appleton, 1874), 297. For Gorgas's full journals, see Gorgas, *The Journals of Josiah Gorgas, 1857–1878,* ed. Sarah Woolfolk Wiggins (Tuscaloosa: University of Alabama Press, 1995).

61. Gorgas, *Civil War Diary,* 158.

62. Ibid., 150, 166.

63. Ibid., 16, 142.

64. Ibid., 183–84.

65. Philip Van Doren Stern, *They Were There: The Civil War as Seen by Its Combat Artists* (New York: Crown, 1961), 20–21; *Illustrated London News,* March 18, 1865, 262; September 26, 1863, 318.

66. *Illustrated London News,* August 29, 1863, 215; July 22, 1865, 65.

PART VI. PLACES AND PUBLIC CULTURE

1. Since I wrote this essay, the first of the series for *Civil War Times,* the National Park Service and preservation groups have continued to address the historic landscape at Gettysburg. The two large buildings with their parking lots on Cemetery Ridge are long gone, and, more recently, the Civil War Trust removed a motel and restored Lee's headquarters and adjacent areas along the wartime Chambersburg Pike, on the first day's battlefield.

2. Roland E. Bowen, *From Ball's Bluff to Gettysburg . . . and Beyond: The Civil War Letters of Private Roland E. Bowen, 15th Massachusetts Infantry, 1861–1864,* ed. Gregory A. Coco (Gettysburg, Pa.: Thomas, 1994), 124–28.

3. My grandmother, Rose Pearl Gray, did not really care about the Civil War but was the first in my family to purchase books on the topic for my birthdays and for Christmas. She gave me Douglas Southall Freeman's *Lee's Lieutenants* on my twelfth birthday and persuaded my mother to start buying books as gifts for me as well.

4. Edward Porter Alexander, *Fighting for the Confederacy: The Personal Recollections of General Edward Porter Alexander,* ed. Gary W. Gallagher (Chapel Hill: University of North Carolina Press, 1989), 210.

5. For the text of the proclamation, see "Virginia Gov. Robert F. McDonnell's Original Confederate History Month Proclamation," *Washington Post*, April 7, 2010, http://www.washington-post.com/wp-dyn/content/article/2010/04/07/AR2010040704411.html.

6. For Robert McDonnell's apology, see "Gov. McDonnell Apologizes for Omitting Slavery in Confederacy Proclamation," CNN, April 9, 2010, http://www.cnn.com/2010/POLITICS/04/07 /virginia.confederate.history/index.html. On reactions to the proclamation and the apology, see Anita Kumar and Rosalind S. Helderman, "McDonnell's Confederate History Month Proclamation irks Civil Rights Leaders," *Washington Post*, April 7, 2010, http://www.washingtonpost .com/wp-dyn/content/article/2010/04/06/AR2010040604416.html?sid=ST2010103105260; and Roland S. Martin, "Were Confederate Soldiers Terrorists?," CNN, April 12, 2010, http://www .cnn.com/2010/OPINION/04/11/martin.confederate.extremist/index.html.

7. On reaction to James Gilmore's proclamation, see Richard Foster, "Governor Dodges Confederate History Month," *Richmond Times-Dispatch,* March 20, 2001, https://www.richmond .com/city-life/article_ba2277c7-41a5-511a-925b-716d2ba7d1fd.html.

8. For a collection of short essays by leading historians devoted to individual images taken during the war, see J. Matthew Gallman and Gary W. Gallagher, eds., *Lens of War: Exploring Iconic Photographs of the Civil War* (Athens: University of Georgia Press, 2015). For a comparable set of essays by senior scholars that feature twenty-five modern black-and-white images of Civil War–related places, taken by Will Gallagher, see Gary W. Gallagher and J. Matthew Gallman, eds., *Civil War Places: Seeing the Conflict Through the Eyes of Its Leading Historians* (Chapel Hill: University of North Carolina Press, 2019).

9. Douglas Southall Freeman, *Lee's Lieutenants: A Study in Command,* 3 vols. (New York: Charles Scribner's Sons, 1942–1944), 1:xlviii.

10. John W. Thomason, *Jeb Stuart* (New York: Charles Scribner's Sons, 1929), 2, 15.

11. John Esten Cooke, *Wearing of the Gray* (1867; reprint, Bloomington: Indiana University Press, 1959), 7; William Willis Blackford, *War Years with Jeb Stuart* (New York: Scribner's, 1945), 93.

12. Robert Gould Shaw, *Blue-Eyed Child of Fortune: The Civil War Letters of Colonel Robert Gould Shaw,* ed. Russell Duncan (Athens: University of Georgia Press, 1992), 242.

13. Lynne M. Bonenberger, "Bound for Glory," in *Ohio State* (December 1989): 7–8; "For Washington, 'Glory' Was a Lesson," undated clipping (circa December 1989) from the West Chester *Daily Local News,* supplied to me by John Haas.

14. James Henry Gooding, *On the Altar of Freedom: A Black Soldier's Civil War Letters from the Front,* ed. Virginia M. Adams (Amherst: University of Massachusetts Press, 1991), 26–27.

INDEX